Donated by
John Kenneth Galbraith

S0-ABN-256

DISCARD

Property of
Townshend Public
Library

DISCARD

With deepest
appreciation

John E. Hill

Revolutionary Values for a New Millennium

Revolutionary Values for a New Millennium

John Adams, Adam Smith, and Social Virtue

John E. Hill

LEXINGTON BOOKS

LEXINGTON BOOKS

Published in the United States of America
by Lexington Books
4720 Boston Way, Lanham, Maryland 20706

12 Hid's Copse Road
Cumnor Hill, Oxford OX2 9JJ, England

Copyright © 2000 by Lexington Books

All rights reserved. No part of this publication may be reproduced,
stored in a retrieval system, or transmitted in any form or by any
means, electronic, mechanical, photocopying, recording, or otherwise,
without the prior permission of the publisher.

British Library Cataloguing in Publication Information Available

Library of Congress Cataloging-in-Publication Data

Hill, John E., 1942-
    Revolutionary values for a new millennium : John Adams, Adam Smith, and social
virtue / John E. Hill.
        p. cm.
    Includes bibliographical references and index.
    ISBN 0-7391-0102-1 (alk. paper)
    1. Social values—United States. 2. Adams, John, 1735-1826—Political and social
views. 3. Smith, Adam, 1723-1790—Political and social views. 4. Political culture—
United States. 5. Self-interest—United States. I. Title.

HM681 .H55 1999
303.3'72'0973—dc21   99-053664

Printed in the United States of America

♾™ The paper used in this publication meets the minimum requirements of American
National Standard for Information Sciences—Permanence of Paper for Printed Library
Materials, ANSI/NISO Z39.48–1992.

For Jeannette

Contents

Preface

Individualistic excess undermines the American dream of a just, democratic society. Misinterpretation and ignorance of the ideas of John Adams, "the Atlas of American independence," and Adam Smith, the founder of modern capitalism, are major factors which vitiate public spirit, democracy, and the egalitarian pursuit of life, liberty, and happiness. A strong ethical base was crucial to the establishment of the United States. Our founders were convinced that democracy would be impossible, unless the citizens were virtuous. But the virtues they desired were social virtues, not the moralisms so often paraded today.

Much of the founders' thought has been forgotten or misinterpreted. Adam Smith has had a similar fate. To correct the misinterpretations, I rely heavily throughout this work on what John Adams and Adam Smith wrote. Chapter 1, "John Adams?," explains why I compare the relatively unknown Adams with the still famous Smith. John Adams made major contributions to the revolutionary effort, as a politician, diplomat, and political thinker equal to, or, according to some authors, superior to, Thomas Jefferson. While I argue in much of this chapter for the inclusion of Adams and explain why he has virtually disappeared from the consciousness of most Americans, I also point out important connections between Smith and Adams, such as the concept of political balance among economic classes and their criticisms of excessive individualism.

In chapter 2, "Republican Values," I examine the broader assumptions the founders shared: "Nature's God," the pursuit of happiness, equality, and the interconnections of liberty and limited government. These values were the foundation for the civic virtues. Our political system requires virtuous citizens; human beings have both virtues and vices, but the virtues are now relatively underemphasized in both politics and society.

Moderation, public spirit, universalism (as opposed to factionalism), and justice are emphasized in chapter 3, "Virtues for Democratic Citizens." Contemporary Americans can scarcely comprehend one of the most important virtues, which John Adams and his generation called "public spirit." Adams thought it was imperative that individual interests be subordinated to the welfare of society as a whole; this required disinterested public service. Also, I look at various misuses of both values and virtues. For instance, Adams was well aware that politicians could cynically manipulate the citizens' desire for a virtuous government.

The founders' views of disinterested public service are related to their concern for the common (or public) good, the central concept developed in chapter 4, "Individuality within Communities." The public good should take precedence over local, factional, party interests. This was necessary to have a just society, a concern shared by Adams and Smith. The common good and extreme individualism are antonyms. Thus, I counterpose individuality (public spirited individuals) and individualism (anomic individuals oblivious to communities). The most important issue I address in this chapter is the necessity to balance individuality within communities so that both are strengthened. Adam Smith is often seen as an advocate of individualism; however, because community was also very important to him, I see him as an advocate of individuality within communities. I also look at why public spirit, so important to the founders, has atrophied over the centuries.

In chapter 5, "Government and Self-Interest," I consider the views of Smith and the founders on the proper balance between sufficient energy in government (to maintain a just society) and sufficient restrictions on government power (so that it could not threaten liberty). In particular, the founders and Smith believed strong government to be a necessary aspect of healthy, just communities. Ironically, the founders attempt to craft a strong, democratic but limited government, through the checks and balances system, resulted in encouragement of the vice of faction, which, in turn, weakened justice and strengthened anomic individualism.

Individual self-interest helps explain the economic development of the United States. Many people believe that actions based on individual self-interest support the common good. Chapter 6, "Self-Interest and the Economy," analyzes this interpretation of the American political economy. Individuality and free markets are both valuable concepts; but that is a *yin-yang* statement. When one moves away from *yin-yang* to a dialectical interpretation, these otherwise valuable concepts cause political problems. Americans have often misinterpreted the thought of Adam Smith on these points. Implications of individual self-interest for government's role in the economy are considered in the final section. Both Smith and Adams supported economically activist government, which was indeed the policy of the early American republic, in contrast to the radically limited government advocated by extreme individualists.

Adams's and other founders' arguments about the relationship of economics and American democracy are analyzed in chapter 7, "Property and Democracy." Our founders established a government with responsibility for all the people. John Adams understood that selfish individualism could destroy the necessary political balance among economic classes. Economic statistics indicate that the gap between rich and poor has been growing since the 1980s; the very imbalance which Adams feared in the eighteenth century seems to exist now in our political-economic system. Adams was concerned about more than separation of executive, legislative, and judicial power. He wanted a balanced system in which no economic class would be able to dominate another politically. He believed that the rich had rights and the poor had rights, but that no group should be able to use the government to exploit another.

Finally, I present some solutions to problems discussed throughout the book in chapter 8, "Democracy: Political Equality and Justice for All." Adams and Smith both argued that education is crucial for advancing the common good. Also, contemporary analysts have made suggestions, such as campaign finance reform and full federal funding of congressional and presidential elections. Diffusion of property ownership through cooperatives and worker-owned enterprises could also help to rebalance the economic system and thus restore some political balance. Finally, mandatory community service might be very good for individuals, polity, and society. All of these are presented to stimulate thinking about changes which might be considered if we want to move in the direction of the principles advocated by Adams and Smith.

A word about the author's perspective is in order. While I would characterize myself as a moderate liberal, some people might assume from the topic that I am from the religious right. One reason I write this book is that values, virtues, and morality are the property of all Americans, not just the religious right; liberals also must lay claim to morality. On this point, I am in agreement with Sinopoli, who argues that "there is a forceful voice in the liberal tradition contending that debates about [the 'value issue'] are the essence of liberal politics. Indeed, not to engage in such debates . . . is to be guilty of a kind of moral indifference."[1] Similarly, Holmes states that "liberalism has a robust normative basis and is not founded, as some have claimed, on radical moral skepticism."[2]

In addition, note that this work, like the works of Adams and Smith, is unabashedly didactic, but I would hope not too didactic. I am concerned that Americans are not well prepared either as individuals or as a nation for the challenges of the new millennium, and I believe that clearer understanding of the values of Adams and Smith could help us meet those challenges.

Throughout this work, I have tried to allow John Adams and Adam Smith to speak for themselves. Thus, direct quotations maintain their spelling, capitalization, and punctuation; the quotations are exactly as they appear in the sources. I believe this will not cause the reader any great difficulty in understanding; moreover, maintaining their forms has the potential benefit of emphasizing that they wrote 200 years ago.

I owe a debt of thanks to many people for their assistance with this project. Colleagues who encouraged me during this project and/or read parts or all of various drafts include Peter Hainer, Norma Morgan, Barbara Fournier, Nancy

Burrell, and Joseph A. Hunter. Others who provided valuable support include Tim Lee, Wally Monestime, Robert Weiss, and the dozens of students who, in my senior seminars, suffered through earlier drafts. President Kenneth Quigley and Dean David Fedo of Curry College encouraged and supported this project in numerous ways, not the least of which was the provision of sabbaticals. Without those sabbaticals plus three course reductions, provided by the joint Faculty-Administration Committee on Release Time, the manuscript would never have been completed. The Faculty Welfare Committee provided financial assistance for research expenses. I could always count on quick, efficient assistance from Eileen Hunter and Paula Cabral, administrative assistants, and from the librarians at Curry College, including Cathy King, David Miller, Kathy Russell, Gail Shank, and Charlene James. The technical wizardry of the staff in the Curry Macintosh laboratory, Maryann Gallant, Joan Manchester, and Bill Wellington, resolved numerous computer problems. Special thanks go to Larry Hartenian, Russell Pregeant, and James G. Salvucci for detailed comments on the penultimate draft. And, especially important, my family supported this project in innumerable ways. Most valuable to me were the non-specialist readings done by my mother, Anna E. Hill, my sister, Elizabeth H. Cutting, and my wife, Jeannette DeJong. Jeannette has my eternal gratitude not only for reading consecutive drafts but also for virtually living with Adams and Smith for more years than she and I care to remember. I alone am responsible, of course, for any errors which may remain despite all the fine efforts of family, friends, and colleagues.

Several editors of the *Adams Papers* provided much appreciated assistance. Richard A. Ryerson, editor-in-chief, kindly allowed me to quote from an unpublished lecture he gave at the Adams National Historical Site in Quincy. Gregg L. Lint agreed to my use of information he provided in a private conversation. And Celeste Walker facilitated permission for the extensive quotations from three series of *Adams Papers*: from *The Adams Papers: Diary and Autobiography of John Adams*: 4 volumes, edited by L. H. Butterfield, copyright © 1961 by The Massachusetts Historical Society, reprinted by permission of Harvard University Press; from *Adams Family Correspondence*: volumes 1 and 2, edited by L. H. Butterfield, copyright © 1963, volumes 3 and 4, edited by L. H. Butterfield and Marc Friedlaender, copyright © 1973, and volumes 5 and 6, edited by Richard Alan Ryerson, et al., copyright ©1993 by The Massachusetts Historical Society, reprinted by permission of The Belknap Press of Harvard University Press; and from *The Papers of John Adams*: volumes 1-6, edited by Robert J. Taylor, copyright © 1977-1983, and volumes 7-10, edited by Gregg L. Lint, et al., copyright © 1989-1996 by The Massachusetts Historical Society, reprinted by permission of The Belknap Press of Harvard University Press. The University of Chicago Press agreed to quotations from Herbert J. Storing, ed., *The Anti-Federalist, An Abridgment, by Murray Dry, of the Complete Anti-Federalist*, copyright © 1981, 1985 by The University of Chicago. Quotations from *Adam Smith, The Theory of Moral Sentiments* [Sixth Edition], edited by D. D. Raphael and A. L. Macfie, copyright © 1976, reprinted by permission of Oxford University Press. Quotations from *Adam Smith: An Inquiry into the Nature and Causes of the Wealth of*

Nations, edited by R. H. Campbell and A. S. Skinner, copyright © 1976, reprinted by permission of Oxford University Press.

The strength of the United States is a result of high ideals. Adams was well aware that politicians could cynically manipulate the citizens' desire for a virtuous and ethical government. It is also obvious that, as a nation, we have often fallen short of our ideals. Whenever we manipulate or ignore our values, we fundamentally weaken our country. So, let us look at the values and virtues our founders advocated, after first explaining why John Adams merits inclusion as an equal of Adam Smith.

Notes

1. Richard C. Sinopoli, "Thick-skinned Liberalism: Redefining Civility," *American Political Science Review* 89 (September 1995): 618.

2. Stephen Holmes, *Passions and Constraints: On the Theory of Liberal Democracy* (Chicago: University of Chicago Press, 1995), 16.

Chapter One

John Adams?

Adam Smith and John Adams? What could possibly connect the two? Both men were alive during the same historical era, but John Adams was twelve years younger and lived another thirty-six years after Adam Smith's death. One was a scholarly teacher who occasionally consulted with the British government and who served as a Commissioner of Customs in Scotland toward the end of his life; the other was a well-educated, well-read lawyer (the only member of the revolutionary generation better-read than Thomas Jefferson) who spent decades of his life in high political office. Both Adams and Smith struggled with the problem of how to organize society to provide justice for all. Each saw himself in the classic tradition of the great lawgiver, a modern-day Solon providing a constitution for his people.[1] Both wrote extensively. John Adams wrote prolifically, but, while his "Thoughts on Government" was influential with many of the craftsmen of early state constitutions, none of his writing is famous today. Adams's fame was won as a statesman, as one of the leaders of the American Revolution. Smith wrote painstakingly and became famous for writing *Wealth of Nations*, which is ironic since he thought his first book, *The Theory of Moral Sentiments,* was his better work. Both saw the importance of moral ideas in society. Both have been either fundamentally misinterpreted or ignored.[2]

Adams and Smith both lived in a revolutionary era of world history and both advocated revolutionary ideas. However, neither advocated revolution as the means of implementing his ideas—far from it! No one would question the radical implications of Adam Smith's *Wealth of Nations*; that book's analysis of free markets and prescriptions for improved economic performance, though often misunderstood or grossly oversimplified, has changed the political economies of most of the nations of the world. But some might question the appellation "radical" for John Adams, so often miscast as a conservative. The truth

1

is that twentieth-century ideological labels simply do not apply to John Adams, who was a congenital contrarian. His actions in the independence era, in Massachusetts politics, at the Continental Congress, and as a diplomat in Europe during the War for Independence supported the revolutionary concept of a sovereign people. His concept of checks and balances became the standard of American constitutionalism. But even more radical was his concern for political balance among the economic classes of American society. The implications of this idea were completely unacceptable in his own era and are probably still unacceptable today. Nonetheless, Smith and Adams are quite comparable on precisely this idea of balance. Smith prescribed wealth for his nation while Adams prescribed the political health of nations. Both abhorred the ability of the moneyed elite to obtain special governmental privileges.

Still unconvinced? Consider this: Smith was well informed about the American revolutionary crisis. Ross, a major Smith biographer, argues that America was "the major case study" for Smith's free market theory and "the most urgent point" for applying his theory "to end the cycle of violence caused by attempts to maintain the old colonial system."[3] In short, both Smith and Adams were deeply involved in the American Revolution. Still, some readers might wonder if I am examining two thinkers of quite different rank. Adam Smith is, after all, widely recognized as the father of capitalism. Why compare John Adams with such a master? History has not been kind to Adams, relegating him to the status of a minor figure. Many of his contemporaries also were not kind to him; for example, they did not reelect him to the presidency. He, himself, felt that his efforts were not appreciated.

Adams remains relatively unappreciated (although recently some historians have been trying to restore his reputation). Most Americans, if they think of him at all, still perceive John Adams to be unimportant. (Try a little experiment in bookstores: count books by or about Thomas Jefferson and compare to the number of books by or about John Adams. On one recent trip to a major bookstore, I counted twenty-four Jefferson works and none about John Adams.) The common underestimation of the importance of John Adams is seriously wrong. According to Ellis, "Adams remains the most misconstrued and unappreciated 'great man' in American history."[4] Thus, I emphasize Adams in this work because, in contrast to the low rank assigned him both historically and by contemporary Americans, his contributions to the American Revolution and founding fundamentally shaped our nation:

- Seen by delegates to the Continental Congress as "the first man in the House," "Our Colossus on the floor," "the Atlas of American Independence;"
- Chaired the committee responsible for writing the Declaration of Independence;

- Advocated that constitutions be drafted and ratified by representative conventions (possibly the first American to do so);[5]
- Served as virtual one-man Secretary of Defense during early Continental Congresses; pivotal in the creation of the American Navy;
- Wrote "Thoughts on Government," which contains one of the earliest statements of the classic American system of separation of powers,[6] was crucial to the establishment of the principle of an independent judiciary,[7] and had greater influence on the formation of the new state governments than any other document;
- Drafted the longest extant constitution in the English-speaking world (Massachusetts, 1780), which originated checks and balances and included a Bill of Rights;
- Wrote *Defence of the Constitutions of Government of the United States of America*, which was influential at the Constitutional Convention, so much so that he was called "the soul of the Philadelphia Convention";[8] combined with the two preceding items, this probably made him the grandfather of the United States Constitution;
- Negotiated official recognition by, and a loan from, Holland at the end of the Revolutionary War;
- Negotiated (along with the other American peace commissioners) the treaty ending the Revolutionary War with Great Britain;
- Prevented war with France while serving as president in the late 1790s, even though many in his own party were scheming for war;
- Expressed and implemented (as an American diplomat serving in Europe from 1776 on) the principles which guided American foreign policy until at least World War II, even though Washington, who enunciated the ideas in his Farewell Address, is given the credit;[9]
- Turned the presidency over to Thomas Jefferson, after he lost the rancorous presidential election campaign of 1800; he thus established the model of peaceful transitions from one party to another (today we expect such transitions, but in 1801, given the virulent animosities between the two parties, this was no small feat; in fact, it was quite revolutionary).[10]

A member of the Continental Congress said of Adams: "In a word I deliver to you the opinion of every man in the house when I add, that he possesses the clearest head and firmest heart of any man in the congress."[11] His record was characterized by Conkin as follows: "In the scope of his contributions, in length of service and degree of personal sacrifice, and in the sophistication of his political advice, John Adams outranked all the other architects of American independence."[12] If all these contributions to the founding and early development of the new republic seem like overstatement, note Rossiter's statement that without

Adams's help, "the founding might have miscarried." Further, "he has as much to teach us as any American who ever lived."[13]

In addition to his major contributions, he left a voluminous record of his thoughts on the political process. And those documents place him in the first rank of American thinkers. Ellis writes: "if Adams should not be seen, indeed did not wish to be seen as a political theorist or philosopher, he does merit recognition as one of America's most notable political thinkers."[14] Chinard called him "one of the most original and penetrating writers of his generation."[15] Some scholars rank him above Jefferson as the premier American political theorist of the revolutionary era. For instance, Rossiter writes: "In the realm of political ideas, however, he had no master—and I would think no peer—among the founding fathers."[16] Gebhardt states that *Defence of the Constitutions* "was the only attempt at a far-ranging *political theory* produced by the American Revolution."[17]

Finally, I focus on Adams because he was a real person. He was not a personality manufactured by a spin doctor to win elections. He was a politician who was not afraid to allow his fundamental humanity to show. Yet, we Americans have such a fixation on great leaders that we often forget that we share a common humanity with them. That forgetfulness sometimes leads to an assumption that the individual has no political power; Adams was harshly critical of such apathy. As usually written, history emphasizes the leaders; however, ordinary people, men and women, played central roles in our freedom struggle. In a May 22, 1779, letter to Edmund Jenings, Adams wrote: "As to your Idea of the *great Men,* there is not much in it. It is a great people, that does great Things. They will always find Instrument[s] to employ that will answer their Ends. I am more and more convinced that every great Character in the World is a Bubble, and an Imposture."[18] In short, each of us must remember that we are individuals with our own power.[19] Nevertheless, this book deals with the ideas of leaders, but with full awareness that none of their ideas would have been implemented without massive popular support.

If not absolutely equivalent to Smith, John Adams is certainly close to an equal in the importance of his ideas; thus, he merits consideration in the same work as Adam Smith. Much of the beginning of this book develops the case for the importance of his ideas. What requires investigation now is the cause of the virtual disappearance of John Adams. He was among the first rank of revolutionary leaders. Why has he been excluded from the pantheon?

The Strange Case of the Disappearance of John Adams

It would be too facile to argue that political losers do not get to write history, but that is part of the answer. Even though Thomas Jefferson had only eight more electoral votes than John Adams in the 1800 presidential election, ultimately this defeat led to the disappearance of the Federalists. But John Adams had the additional disadvantage of being the presidential candidate of a split party (notice that one even debates calling him the head of his own party). The machinations of the Hamiltonian faction of Adams's own political party contributed mightily to his defeat. This had happened before; Tench Coxe, a Hamilton aide, published a series of articles in favor of Thomas Jefferson(!) in the *Gazette of the United States,* a Federalist Party paper, during the 1796 election campaign.[20] The 1800 election pamphlet war against John Adams, supported again by Hamilton, contributed grist for the propaganda mills of those who wished to destroy Adams's reputation. History is not only unkind to losers, but even more so to losers with weak organizational support. That Adams saw himself as being above party politics did not help; the result of this approach to the presidency was that few people would be his foot soldiers in the propaganda wars, only the Adams faction in his own party.

In spite of the great significance of his multiple roles, Adams did not have high profile positions during the Continental Congress and the Revolutionary War. His positions were important demonstrations of his colleagues' trust, but they were not significant in the public eye. His rhetorical skills and unmatched legal acumen were central to the effort to unite all thirteen colonies in a desire for independence. The significance of this contribution is easy to overlook today because we know the end of the story, but independence was by no means a foregone conclusion. Many delegates to the first Continental Congress thought that Samuel and John Adams were much too radical. Convincing these delegates that independence was the best solution took months of astute politicking.

John Adams eventually chaired the committee to write the Declaration of Independence, but Thomas Jefferson was the wordsmith who actually wrote it. Adams was a virtual one-man department of defense and a prime supporter of the infant American navy, but these contributions to the cause were not known by those outside the Continental Congress. Securing an important loan from Holland and participating in the negotiation of the peace with Great Britain pale in comparison to the military legends of war heroes. Further, he remained in Europe as the first United States Ambassador to the Court of St. James (Great Britain), a difficult and relatively invisible position, to say the least, given George III's pique at losing the colonies. In short, many of his accomplishments were very important, but well known only to the cognoscenti, in contrast to ordinary citizens.

One reason his accomplishments were not well known was his unwillingness to publicize his own accomplishments. When a French historian told
Adams that he was going to write about Adams as one of the central figures in
the American Revolution, Adams argued that only 1/3,000,000th of the credit
belonged to him.[21] Yet he commented caustically about the difficulty of thriving
in public life while remaining modest. He was aware that other public figures believed it was necessary to increase their own reputations but that was not
Adams's style, as is seen in a letter to a Massachusetts friend, James Warren.

> You and I have had an ugly Modesty about Us, which has despoyled Us of,
> almost all our Importance. We have taken even Pains to conceal our Names,
> We have delighted in the shade, We have made few Friends, no Tools, and
> what is worse when the Cause of Truth, Justice, and Liberty have demanded
> it We have even Sacrificed Those who called themselves our Friends and
> have made Ennemies.
>
> No Man ever made a great Fortune in the World, by pursuing these
> Maxims, We therefore do not expect it, and for my own Part I declare, that
> the Moment, I can get into Life perfectly private, will be the happiest of my
> Life. [22]

He was caustic in what he wrote about politicians who blew their own trumpets.
In an August 18, 1776, letter to his wife, John Adams stated that there was
much "Ostentation and Affectation" of patriotism, but too few people who were
disinterested.

> A Man must be selfish, even to acquire great Popularity. He must grasp for
> himself, under specious Pretences for the public Good, and he must attach
> himself to his Relations, Connections and Friends, by becoming a
> Champion for their Interests, in order to form a Phalanx, about him for his
> own defence; to make them Trumpeters of his Praise, and sticklers for his
> Fame, Fortune, and Honour.[23]

Part of this is Adams's distaste for the easy political success of some of his
peers, a popularity Adams never had. But even discounting for Adams's
wounded pride, his is a telling critique.

A related factor was Adams's habit of intense introspection, a habit with
remarkable similarity to Adam Smith's concept of the "impartial spectator"[24] in
The Theory of Moral Sentiments:

> More than any other prominent American of the revolutionary generation,
> Adams brought the private energies generated by a truly searching self-
> scrutiny into the public arena. Unlike Benjamin Franklin's similar-sound-
> ing injunctions—work hard, conquer pride, rise early, resist temptations—

Adams's introspections remained true to the original intent of reformed Christianity. That is, Adams was obsessed with interior integrity, not with the external rewards that mastery of appearances could bring. Humility, piety, self-denial, and other habits of the heart were not just means to an end for him, but the ends themselves.[25]

Such introspection is quite distant from modern American politics. Politicians today seem to be guided by the rapidly shifting partialities of opinion pollsters, not by an "impartial spectator." But this habit also indicates a contradiction between Adams's character and his political life—he craved fame and assumed that it would be gained by serving the public good. Rare is the case when government action is seen by a united people as being in the common good; ordinarily some significant group of the people will see the action as partisan.

When there were partisan attacks or when the public did not recognize his contributions, Adams fretted over the lack of appreciation for his work. Such fretting is usually interpreted as indicative of Adams's vanity. There is no denying Adams's streak of vanity, but note Rossiter's statement: "no one labored more devotedly for freedom through all the years from 1765 to 1801, and no one had reaped less public acclaim."[26] Adams also admitted, in a July 23, 1806, letter to Benjamin Rush (the Pennsylvania doctor, patriot, fellow signer of the Declaration of Independence, and a friend since their days serving together in the Continental Congress) that his emotional "words, actions, and even writings" were counterproductive to his quest for fame.[27] Adams was a curious mixture of the inner- and other-directed person and thus, for contemporary Americans, he is difficult to understand, just as he was something of a mystery to his own contemporaries. Being guided by one's own inner compass, not being willing to trim one's sails for the sake of popularity, is not our usual experience of politicians.

On his return from Europe, Adams became the nation's first vice president, which meant that he was in the shadow of the immortal George Washington. He further exposed himself to ridicule by suggesting aristocratic-sounding titles for the officials of the new government. Had the "Atlas of American Independence" changed his political principles during his years in Europe? Howe's *The Changing Political Thought of John Adams* (1966) is one example of the argument that he returned from Europe a different person from the revolutionary founder. Did Adams change? Other than normal maturation in his thought over the span of his 91 years, I think not. I agree with Rossiter who states that Adams's purpose "remained steadfast from the 'Dissertation on the Canon and Feudal Law' in 1765 to his last letter to Jefferson sixty years later."[28] There are several reasons for agreeing with Rossiter that Adams did not change:

First, at the beginning of the revolutionary era, his republican credentials could not be questioned. But there were conservative elements in his political thought, elements which were a product of the times. Adams had grown up in a

British colony, a fairly egalitarian colony to be sure, but one where the governor was still the King's representative and therefore was due some deference. For some individuals, such as Governor Hutchinson, deference was destroyed by revolutionary ferment, but John Adams still thought that legitimate leaders deserved respect. For example, he wrote to his friend, James Warren, on April 22, 1776:

> There is one Thing, my dear sir, that must be attempted and most Sacredly observed or We are all undone. There must be a Decency, and Respect, and Veneration introduced for Persons in Authority, of every Rank, or We are undone. In a popular Government, this is the only Way of Supporting order.[29]

His diplomatic service in Europe would reinforce this idea. Adams found that he got much better service from various merchants in France after he started to use his full ambassadorial title, but he made it very clear, in a letter to a merchant friend in Bordeaux, that he did not like having to do so. "There is not a Being upon Earth who has a greater Contempt for all kind of Titles than I have."[30] In this light, Adams made a political mistake when he suggested fancy titles for high government officials; others used this mistake to embarrass him politically, but it was not a sign of change on his part. Legitimate democratic leaders deserved deference which the political system also required in order to avoid anarchy.

Second, Miroff argues persuasively that the suggestion of titles was consistent with Adams's vision of a republican America.[31] He feared that, without titles of office, which would be different from aristocratic titles because they would not be hereditary, people would seek distinction in the economic rather than the political realm and merit would not count in society. Those who were economically successful were not necessarily virtuous. "Political symbols focused a people on who public actors really were and what merits they could claim; economic symbols shifted the people's gaze to the impressive possessions that private persons owned and displayed."[32]

Third, Adams did not change, but America did, partly before he left for Europe, but definitely while he was abroad on diplomatic duty. The young lawyer in the 1760s lived in a British colony. The vice president, in 1790, lived in a land of egalitarian ferment he clearly did not appreciate. This did not make him any the less republican; his consistent concern for balance of the one, the few, and the many demonstrate his democratic credentials.

Finally, the combination of his argument that America needed to control the power of the "aristocrats" (an argument that is inherently democratic but which many Jeffersonian-Republicans misconstrued as advocating aristocracy), and his association with Hamilton and the Federalist Party, strained as that relationship was, fueled attacks on Adams as a crypto-monarchist. The fight, unfortunately for Adams, was not evenly matched. Despite all of his diplomatic skills, which he used effectively for the American cause while in Europe, he was no match for Republican propagandists, especially when Federalists were also sniping at him from within his "own" party.[33]

Criticisms of Adams as a monarchist and as an advocate of aristocratic titles are examples of what I noted previously: his ideas have been deliberately misconstrued and grossly misunderstood. In other words, his disappearance can be explained, but he still deserves consideration in the same book with Smith. So, in looking at these two men, what does this book attempt to do?

Hypothesis

A strong moral-ethical-religious base with a focus on justice was central to the thought of Adam Smith, John Adams, and many of the founders of the new American republic, and was crucial to the establishment and early development of the United States. In that era, the United States was a society based on the interplay of individual drive, energy, creativity, *and* mutual support within values-based communities. Several implications are inherent in this argument: (1) Respect for the individual, a major factor contributing to development of this country, requires that government not be absolute. Therefore, we have had limited government, but government with a very important role in economic development. A relatively unquestioned part of limited government is providing for national defense, but our government once had a larger role in other areas as well and could again have a larger role, consistent with the thought of both John Adams and Adam Smith. (2) The community aspect of this relationship includes cooperation of neighbors, acting through various associations (clubs, churches, Chambers of Commerce, unions) and through various levels of government. In short, Americans have been and still are conformist members of communities, while being at the same time strong believers in individual rights. (3) Individualistic excess has undermined public spirit, weakened democracy, and vitiated the egalitarian pursuit of life, liberty, and happiness. Failure to attain the American dream of a just, democratic society can be attributed to misinterpretation and/or ignorance of the ideas of Adams and Smith.

Adams exemplifies a moral-ethical-religious concern that was widely shared by the revolutionary generation. Indeed, this is another point of contact between Adams and Smith. Adams found much of Smith's moral thought congenial, as presented in *The Theory of Moral Sentiments,* a work which Adams read and clearly appreciated.[34] Some of these shared values seem almost foreign to contemporary Americans. For instance, while the founding fathers[35] fought for individual liberty, they assumed that liberty would be within a community context. We are individuals but exist within communities, communities which have many aspects: political, religious, economic, social, cultural. How does one balance individual liberty, that American icon, with existence within communities? Ultimately, one has to decide that for oneself.

The issue of individuals in communities is one of many political-economic-ethical issues to be considered herein. However, a word of warning is needed from the start. Especially when dealing with ethical issues, one must be very cautious. Our founders were aware that individuals convinced they were right had, throughout history, committed gross atrocities against fellow human beings; thus our founders were concerned about the dangers of enthusiasm when applied to politics. They were especially worried about the religious variety of enthusiasm but also abhorred political factionalism. (In this century we have faced an analogous danger of true believers.) In short, they feared intolerance. They knew that many evils had been committed in the name of various absolute truths. When anyone who believes he has an absolute truth also holds power, the danger is immense. John Adams was very much aware that power was seductive in the sense that anyone holding power could easily delude himself to believe in the rightness of virtually any action. Note what he wrote to Thomas Jefferson on February 2, 1816:

> You ask, how it has happened that all Europe, has acted on the Principle "that Power was Right." I know not what Answer to give you, but this, that Power always sincerely, conscientiously . . . believes itself Right. Power always thinks it has a great Soul, and vast Views, beyond the Comprehension of the Weak; and that it is doing God Service, when it is violating all his Laws. Our Passions, Ambition, Avarice, Love, Resentment etc possess so much metaphysi[c]al Subtilty and so much overpowering Eloquence, that they insinuate themselves into the Understanding and the Conscience and convert both to their Party. And I may be deceived as much as any of them, when I say, that Power must never be trusted without a Check.[36]

There is a huge irony in this quotation. Little more than fifteen years before Adams wrote this letter, Jeffersonian true believers (aided and abetted by Hamiltonian Federalist true believers) destroyed John Adams's reputation and denied him reelection to the presidency. If even such a great patriot can have his reputation shredded by factional enthusiasts, egged on by jealous and ambitious rivals, who is safe? (Was it truly ironic? Or was John Adams slyly criticizing Thomas Jefferson for his less than forthright role in the propagandistic destruction of Adams's reputation in the 1800 presidential campaign? I doubt it, but I also doubt that we can ever know.)

Assumptions

One must have a critical perspective about power (whenever a person or a group has any degree of control over another, whether in a governmental or corporate office, or in a church, or a school—anywhere); but one must also have a critical perspective on one's own motives. It is very easy to assume that your personal motives are pure and therefore whatever you are doing is just and right. This is especially true of anyone who believes s/he is an ethical person. In short, Adams argues for a critical humility about personal motivations when one has power. I argue that his concern applies to contemporary ethical dilemmas, that this is not just an historical problem. No matter what your political persuasion, you can deceive yourself into that dangerous trap of enthusiasm.

The above should not be taken to mean that I believe in ethical relativism. In fact, I personally believe in ethical absolutes. This is not a position which I take lightly; nor is it unique. Political philosophy has been struggling with this issue for centuries. Note, for instance, Sabia's comments about one of the leading twentieth-century American political philosophers, Leo Strauss, who argues

> that "political philosophers from Plato to Hegel" all wrestled with the problem of "natural right"—i.e., with the proposition that the discovery and justification of transhistorical standards of right or justice are possible. Premodern, especially Greek, political philosophers defended this proposition; modern theorists (after Aquinas) rejected it. On both philosophical and political grounds, Strauss favored the Greek position and therefore characterized the tradition of political theory as degenerative; it culminates in the rise of ethical relativism and the death of political theory as traditionally practiced.[37]

To those who believe in absolutes, a word of warning is imperative: when dealing with other human beings, one must be very careful about absolutes. Assuming one has the whole truth about anything assumes perfect knowledge. A French scholar who has resided in the United States wrote about this type of hubris, about an intellectual America which "held its truths to be absolutes, forgetting that no one truth is ever complete and that a partial truth embraced for too long becomes an insane idea."[38] He was referring to the Vietnam War era, and was criticizing both the right and the left on that issue. I believe that the dangers of such absolutist thinking are always present. To some extent, this problem is traceable to a misunderstanding of science; many people assume that if some idea is scientific, it must be true. But my understanding of modern science and the scientific pretensions of the social sciences indicates that one rarely has the whole truth. If one's "truth" were distorted in any way and one were to act on such distorted "truth," one could cause great harm.

So, one might say that this book deals in absolutes, relatively, or that this author wants to be a tolerant universalist, a skeptical absolutist. (That last statement pertains to values, not to political power; absolute political power is contrary to all that I believe). In spite of all these caveats, one must continue to strive for the truth; and one cannot allow one's uncertainty about the truth to prevent action. But, one has to balance thought and action.[39] Here Americans could learn from Mohandas Gandhi, whose constant struggle for truth, understanding that the other may very well have part of the truth, resulted in the peaceful independence of the Indian subcontinent. I am well aware that the aftermath has been anything but peaceful. But there are two important points here: Britain gave up the prime jewel in its imperial crown without rancor for the newly independent states; and Gandhi did not allow his openness to the truth held by the other side to prevent his action. So, I believe one must act on one's beliefs, but thoughtfully, perhaps with Adam Smith's impartial spectator peering over the shoulder. And because many human beings are self-interested and prideful, and thus often short-sighted and unaware of gaps in their own knowledge, I also believe one must be tolerant of all others, be open-minded to those others who may have part or all of the truth, and, like Adams, maintain critical humility about one's own motives.

Earlier, I wrote that I believe in absolutes; I have just made an argument for acting with tolerance. Let me try to use the issue of slavery in the United States to illustrate the need for tolerance when acting on one's moral absolutes. President Lincoln insisted on a principled fight against slavery.[40] He realized that liberty and slavery were incompatible principles, but he also would not condemn the South because he was not certain he understood God's will.[41] One acts on one's sense of the good and just and right, but one must always act with the consciousness, the humility, that one might not know what the divinity would have us do. Such comments on religion and divinity are probably grating to many rationalists. But this type of thinking is very close to the approach of many of our founders. While the founders feared enthusiasm, they also appreciated the contributions of religion to civil society (see chapter 2 for more detail). The danger of religious enthusiasm is still real. People of religion, as well as rationalists, must practice tolerance, not only for people of other religions, but also for people who do not believe in religion or divinity.

That leads to another assumption. Western thought, going back at least to ancient Greece, has been dialectical. I recognize that life is full of conflict, and thus gives much evidence of a dialectic. But pitting a thesis against its opposite (antithesis) with the eventual result of some new idea (synthesis), places too much emphasis, I believe, on the conflict in life. From some reading in Asian history, I am convinced that a *yin-yang* approach is closer to reality than a dialectical approach. I think that life is often an interrelationship of opposites. When I wrote earlier that I wanted to be a "tolerant universalist, a skeptical absolutist," that was *yin-yang*, not dialectical thinking. In other words, I take a "both/and" approach to life, rather than an "either/or" approach. In contrast, Ellis wrote the following about John Adams:

> What many commentators on his life diagnosed as sheer irascibility was less a mood than a habit of mind. It was related to his urge toward alienation and an isolated version of independence—the kind of tendency best illustrated in his behavior as president. But what we might call his dialectical style had a separate set of causes and consequences most closely associated with his almost instinctive need to establish balance in conversations and political arguments.[42]

Such a concern for balance is not dialectical, but *yin-yang*. Indeed I believe that Adam Smith and John Adams are better understood when viewed from a "both/and" perspective.

Ratification of the United States Constitution, for another example, is often portrayed as dialectical conflict between Federalist supporters and Anti-Federalist opponents. These two groups certainly argued in conventions and campaigned in the media of the day. As a result, we have extensive documentation of their disagreements. But one expert on this conflict has observed that moderate Federalists and Anti-Federalists often held similar views. Also, "There were in fact diverse and contradictory opinions among the Federalists just as there were among their opponents."[43] Storing goes on to say that the Federalists and Anti-Federalists were in agreement on such fundamentals as the nature of man and the purposes of politics. So the apparent conflict masks some basic agreement. And, even more important for my argument, Storing describes what he calls a tension at the heart of the Anti-Federalist positions, but what I would call the *yin-yang* of Anti-Federalism:

> The Anti-Federalists were committed to both union and the states; to both the great American republic and the small, self-governing community; to both commerce and civic virtue; to both private gain and public good. At its best, Anti-Federal thought explores these tensions and points to the need for any significant American political thought to confront them; for they were not resolved by the Constitution but are inherent in the principles and traditions of American political life.[44]

I argue that such tensions, such *yin-yang* situations, permeate not only American politics today, as in the past, but also many other areas of life.

Finally, I assume that we can learn from history. John Adams certainly would have argued that we should learn from history, but feared that instead we were corrupting tradition.[45] Indeed, it is quintessentially American to learn from history. Our Founding Fathers certainly thought long and hard about the lessons of history for their new republic. For instance, Commager argues that Americans "were the creatures of history, but not the prisoners. They were indebted to history, but they triumphed over it."[46] In a similar vein, Novak writes: "The liberal tradition seeks progress, but is also respectful of the wisdom of the past and constantly revitalized by the study of experience. It values habits and institutions, as well as new ideas."[47] (Note that when Novak writes about the "liberal tradition," he refers to the American belief in individual liberty, in economic, social, and political terms. This is the philosophic use of "liberal." Throughout this work, "liberal" is used with this philosophic meaning, not the common political meaning of someone who advocates leftist policies.) Modern writers of various ideological persuasions, as well as our founders, have argued that our nation would be strengthened by learning from history.[48]

Our forefathers' use of history may be illustrated by looking at the issue of the size of the new republic. Some founders were concerned that no republic had ever existed over such a vast territory as the thirteen colonies (and note that the thirteen colonies were much smaller than the current United States, even without Alaska). In contrast, James Madison argued that the extended republic should not be rejected simply because of its novelty. Americans, he stated, respected traditions but did not allow "a blind veneration for antiquity, for custom, or for names, to overrule the suggestions of their own good sense."[49] That this American republic has survived for over 200 years owes much to our founding fathers' foresight in learning from history while applying a critical perspective to that history.

We can learn, and I hope this book will help people learn, from history. One of the first lessons we can learn is that the problems we face today are not necessarily intractable. As Commager shows, contemporary problems might be complex, but our founders also faced complex, seemingly unresolvable problems. He lists the many problems our forefathers faced, such as lack of unity among the thirteen colonies, the immensity of the territory, and lack of common loyalties.[50] The founders dealt with difficult problems in the revolutionary era; so contemporary Americans should not be defeatist in the face of modern difficulties.

Adams and Smith both learned from history. They based their theories on what they saw as the actual facts of history, which they contrasted with baseless theorizing. A central problem of contemporary America is just such dogmatism. Too often we assume the foundational principles of life, liberty, and the pursuit of happiness within an egalitarian framework but fail to analyze the reality of conflict between liberty and equality,[51] which in turn causes truncated lives and significant unhappiness, instead of the "private rights and public happiness" Madison touted. So, we must now examine these fundamental values of the revolutionary era.

Notes

1. On Adams as such a lawgiver, see C. Bradley Thompson, *John Adams and the Spirit of Liberty* (Lawrence: University Press of Kansas, 1998), 43; on Smith, see Charles L. Griswold, Jr., *Adam Smith and the Virtues of Enlightenment* (New York: Cambridge University Press, 1999), 367.

2. That Adams has been misinterpreted and/or ignored is not a surprise. But some might question this characterization for Smith. While he certainly has not been ignored, he definitely has been misinterpreted; that thought is developed throughout this book, but note also Athol Fitzgibbons, *Adam Smith's System of Liberty, Wealth and Virtue* (Oxford: Clarendon Press, 1995), 170-71, on the large number of economists unfamiliar with Smith's philosophic ideas. Similarly, see Heinz Lubasz, "Adam Smith and the 'free market,'" in *Adam Smith's Wealth of Nations: New Interdisciplinary Essays,* Stephen Copley and Kathryn Sutherland, eds. (Manchester: Manchester University Press, 1995), 63; Griswold, *Smith and Enlightenment*, 8-9; and Jerry Z. Muller, *Adam Smith: In His Time and Ours* (Princeton: Princeton University Press, 1993), 6-7.

3. Ian Simpson Ross, *The Life of Adam Smith* (Oxford: Oxford University Press, 1995), 250.

4. Joseph J. Ellis, *Passionate Sage: The Character and Legacy of John Adams* (New York: W. W. Norton & Company, 1993), 12.

5. Thompson, *Adams and the Spirit of Liberty,* 40, states that this idea has been called "America's greatest contribution to Western constitutionalism."

6. Unpublished address delivered at the Adams National Historic Site in Quincy by Richard Alan Ryerson, editor-in-chief of the *Adams Papers*, June 24, 1997.

7. Gregg L. Lint, et al., eds., *Papers of John Adams,* 8 (Cambridge: Belknap Press of Harvard University Press, 1989), 229.

8. Thompson, *Adams and the Spirit of Liberty,* 251-54.

9. This might seem to be an outrageous claim, but note what the editors of the *Papers of John Adams* say about his 1776 Continental Congress work developing instructions for American diplomats:

> The Plan of Treaties was the work of John Adams, and of all the documents composed by him during his career in the congress, it was perhaps the most important and certainly had the most lasting effect. It was the first major state paper dealing with the conduct of the United States toward other sovereign states. It would guide the makers of American foreign policy far beyond the exigencies of the Revolution. Indeed, its tone and the principles on which it was based lie at the core of almost all major pronouncements on foreign policy by American statesmen from that time until at least the beginning of World War II (Robert J. Taylor, ed., *The Papers of John Adams,* 4 [Cambridge: Belknap Press of Harvard University Press, 1979], 260).

10. See Lynne Withey, *Dearest Friend: A Life of Abigail Adams* (New York: Free Press, 1981), 257, for the deep suspicions some Federalists had of the Jeffersonian-Republicans. Henry F. May, *The Enlightenment in America* (New York: Oxford University Press, 1976), 244-75, also deals with this turbulent time and the strong fears of some Federalists that the young republic could fall to the French and to irreligious, radical, licentious democrats. On the other hand, Joyce Appleby, *Capitalism and a New Social Order: The Republican Vision of the 1790s* (New York: New York University Press, 1984), 104, states that the Republicans were convinced that advocates of aristocracy had been defeated; she notes Jefferson's evaluation that the Republican principle had been to cherish the people while the Federalists feared and distrusted them. This point emphasizes the tragedy of the 1800 election for John Adams. He always was democratic, but lost reelection because he was in a party perceived to be aristocratic and because his own writings were willfully misinterpreted as advocating aristocracy. Still, no one can doubt that the country gained, in the long run, by learning to make a peaceful transition of power between two harshly antagonistic parties.

11. Taylor, ed., *Papers*, 5, 133.

12. Paul K. Conkin, *Puritans and Pragmatists: Eight Eminent American Thinkers* (New York: Dodd, Mead and Company, 1968), 123.

13. Clinton Rossiter, "The Legacy of John Adams," *Yale Review* 46 (1957): 529.

14. Ellis, *Passionate Sage*, 172-73.

15. Gilbert Chinard, *Honest John Adams* (Gloucester, Mass.: Peter Smith, 1976), ix.

16. Rossiter, "Legacy of John Adams," 548.

17. Jurgen Gebhardt, *Americanism: Revolutionary Order and Societal Self-Interpretation in the American Republic,* Ruth Hein, trans. (Baton Rouge: Louisiana State University Press, 1993), 20.

18. Lint, ed., *Papers*, 8, 68.

19. Howard Zinn makes this same point as follows:

All those histories of this country centered on the Founding Fathers and the Presidents weigh oppressively on the capacity of the ordinary citizen to act. They suggest that in times of crisis we must look to someone to save us . . . .

The idea of saviors has been built into the entire culture, beyond politics. We have learned to look to stars, leaders, experts in every field, thus surrendering our own strength, demeaning our own ability, obliterating our own selves (Howard Zinn, *A People's History of the United States* [New York: Harper and Row, 1980], 570).

John Adams would have agreed with Zinn.

20. Manning J. Dauer, "The Political Economy of John Adams," *Political Science Quarterly* 56 (1941): 567. Ralph Adams Brown, *The Presidency of John*

Adams (Lawrence: University Press of Kansas, 1975), 15, states that the campaign of 1796 "has been termed one of the most violent and scurrilous in American history."

21. John Adams, letter to James Warren, December 9, 1780, in Lint, ed., *Papers*, 10, 405.

22. John Adams, letter to James Warren, December 2, 1778, in Lint, ed., *Papers*, 7, 244-45.

23. John Adams, letter to Abigail Adams, August 18, 1776, in L. H. Butterfield, ed., *Adams Family Correspondence*, 2 (Cambridge: Belknap Press of Harvard University Press, 1963), 99.

24. The "impartial spectator" is central to Smith's arguments in *The Theory of Moral Sentiments*. The following passage explains the concept as a means of determining whether or not the motives for one's own conduct are acceptable:

We can never survey our own sentiments and motives, we can never form any judgment concerning them; unless we remove ourselves, as it were, from our own natural station, and endeavour to view them as at a certain distance from us. But we can do this in no other way than by endeavouring to view them with the eyes of other people, or as other people are likely to view them. Whatever judgment we can form concerning them, accordingly, must always bear some secret reference, either to what are, or to what, upon a certain condition, would be, or to what, we imagine, ought to be the judgment of others. We endeavour to examine our own conduct as we imagine any other fair and impartial spectator would examine it (Adam Smith, *The Theory of Moral Sentiments*, 6th ed., D. D. Raphael and A. L. Macfie, eds. [Oxford: Oxford University Press, 1976], III.i.2, 109-10).

25. Ellis, *Passionate Sage*, 52-53.

26. Rossiter, "Legacy of John Adams," 529.

27. John A. Schutz and Douglass Adair, eds., *The Spur of Fame: Dialogues of John Adams and Benjamin Rush, 1805-1813* (San Marino, Cal.: Huntington Library, 1966), 61.

28. Rossiter, "Legacy of John Adams," 534.

29. John Adams, letter to James Warren, in Taylor, ed., *Papers*, 4, 137.

30. John Adams, letter to John Bondfield, May 25, 1780, in L. H. Butterfield and Marc Friedlaender, eds., *Adams Family Correspondence*, 3 (Cambridge: Belknap Press of Harvard University Press, 1973), 300.

31. Bruce Miroff, *Icons of Democracy: American Leaders as Heroes, Aristocrats, Dissenters, and Democrats* (New York: Basic Books, 1993), 58-61.

32. Miroff, *Icons of Democracy*, 61. Thompson, *Adams and the Spirit of Liberty*, 224 and 266-68, largely agrees with Miroff. Adams wanted talented, ambitious, virtuous citizens to have some incentive to serve the public. While Adams committed a grievous political error in suggesting titles, the problem he attacked is still a real problem, just as it was in 1949 when Walter Lippmann argued: "Somehow or other we must find ways to recognize distinction, to use experience and not to discard it." Otherwise we shall "waste good public servants, when they

are most fit to serve," and "we shall never recruit great talents that are so desperately needed"; in Clinton Rossiter and James Lare, eds., *The Essential Lippmann: A Political Philosophy for Liberal Democracy* (Cambridge: Harvard University Press, 1982), 312.

33. Thompson, *Adams and the Spirit of Liberty,* 269-75, blames Jefferson for smearing Adams's reputation; he spread the charges behind Adams's back many times and did not respond to Adams's request that Jefferson document the charges by specifying the "'Chapter and Verse'" where Adams advocated monarchy and aristocracy.

Ironically, Chinard (*Honest John Adams,* 239) argues that Jefferson as well as Adams was victimized by "the blind and irresponsible passions" of public opinion and partisan editors "fond of simplifications and generalizations."

34. George A. Peek, Jr., ed., *The Political Writings of John Adams: Representative Selections* (Indianapolis: Bobbs-Merrill Co., Inc., 1954), 175; also Frank Donovan, ed., *The John Adams Papers* (New York: Dodd, Mead and Co., 1965), 201.

35. The term "founding fathers" is a precise term. Women had a distinct role in our revolution, which will be discussed below; however, given the patriarchal nature of eighteenth-century America, that the founders were not gender balanced should not be surprising.

36. Lester J. Cappon, ed., *The Adams-Jefferson Letters: The Complete Correspondence between Thomas Jefferson and Abigail and John Adams,* 2 (Chapel Hill: University of North Carolina Press, 1959), 462-63.

37. Daniel R. Sabia, Jr., "Political Education and the History of Political Thought," *American Political Science Review* 78 (December 1984): 991.

38. Michael Crozier, *The Trouble with America: Why the System Is Breaking Down* (Berkeley: University of California Press, 1984), 37.

39. As Crozier writes: "More than any other people in the civilized world, Americans overemphasize action. Looking decisive for them remains the only way to be taken seriously. . . . In many circumstances, however, one is tempted to tell them: 'Act less, think more'" (Crozier, *Trouble with America,* 145).

40. There are, of course, less charitable interpretations of Lincoln and the end of slavery. For instance, see Zinn (*People's History,* 187):

Thus, when the Emancipation Proclamation was issued January 1, 1863, it declared slaves free in those areas still fighting against the Union (which it listed very carefully), and said nothing about slaves behind Union lines. As Hofstadter put it, the Emancipation Proclamation "had all the moral grandeur of a bill of lading." The *London Spectator* wrote concisely: "The principle is not that a human being cannot justly own another, but that he cannot own him unless he is loyal to the United States."

41. John P. Diggins, *The Lost Soul of American Politics: Virtue, Self-Interest, and the Foundations of Liberalism* (Chicago: University of Chicago Press, 1984), 315-16 and 346.

42. Ellis, *Passionate Sage*, 87. My interpretation of dialectics is a deliberate attempt to deemphasize conflict. Inherent in the dialectical thinking which I am criticizing is an assumption of conflict which becomes a self-fulfilling prophecy. The search for values for a diverse and inclusive society will involve enough conflict without artificially stimulating it through unexamined thought processes.

43. Herbert J. Storing, ed., *The Anti-Federalist: An Abridgment, by Murray Dry, of the Complete Anti-Federalist* (Chicago: University of Chicago Press, 1985), 3.

44. Storing, *Anti-Federalist*, 4.

45. See Schutz and Adair, eds., *Spur of Fame*, 186.

46. Henry Steele Commager, *Jefferson, Nationalism and the Enlightenment* (New York: George Braziller, 1975), 137-39.

47. Michael Novak, *Free Persons and the Common Good* (New York: Madison Books, 1989), 80.

48. So many authors could be cited here. I refer you to only two: Barry A. Shain, *The Myth of American Individualism: The Protestant Origins of American Political Thought* (Princeton: Princeton University Press, 1994), 4, on learning from the American revolution, and Fitzgibbons, *Smith's System*, 194, on Smith's insight into contemporary problems.

But note also two cautionary comments on the misuse of history: Stephen Holmes, *Passions and Constraint: On the Theory of Liberal Democracy* (Chicago: University of Chicago Press, 1995), 237, warns that debates on policy "cannot be sensibly conducted as legacy disputes"; and Rossiter, "Legacy of John Adams," 528, states that the appeal to our great men has for many Americans "become a substitute for thought," and that this appeal "is a weapon that is easy to wield and hard to parry, and therefore a weapon we wield at our peril."

49. *Federalist*, #14, Madison, 62.

50. Commager, *Jefferson, Nationalism and the Enlightenment*, xii-xiii.

51. Francis Fukuyama, *The End of History and the Last Man* (New York: Avon Books, 1992) is a prime example of such theorizing.

Chapter Two

Revolutionary Values

Most contemporary Americans are proud of the longevity of our system and take it for granted. But the founders knew there was no guarantee of the success of the new republic. Most Americans are unaware of the tenuous, experimental nature of our government, but our founders understood that they were sailing into uncharted seas. They were concerned about two issues: the sheer geographic size of the new country, and whether the citizens possessed the necessary virtue.[1] The founders were aware of many republican governments, including ancient Greece and Rome. These small city-states had existed for short periods of time. The founders, however, were establishing a continental republic; there simply were no examples of a republic covering such a vast territory. One measure of the size problem they faced is the time it took to travel the length of the thirteen colonies; by land or sea, our forebears needed weeks to travel from New England to Georgia.

Citizen virtue was the second issue of concern to our founders. They thought it was absolutely necessary for the success of their great experiment. In his Farewell Address (September 19, 1796), George Washington repeated what many believed when he wrote: "'Tis substantially true, that virtue or morality is a necessary spring of popular government. The rule indeed extends with more or less force to every species of free Government. Who that is a sincere friend to it, can look with indifference upon attempts to shake the foundation of the fabric.'"[2] John Adams agreed: "It may be said that Virtue, that is Morality, applied to the Public is the rule of Conduct in Republicks."[3] They feared that any type of democracy, not just the republican variant, could be destroyed if the moral support structure of government were undermined.

While Washington and Adams repeated accepted wisdom on the necessity of virtue in popular government, the founders still wondered if human beings were capable of the virtue required of republican citizens. John Adams hoped that the new republic's citizens would be virtuous enough to sustain the government. But he wrote voluminously about balanced government, by which he meant that each socioeconomic class should be able to check and control the excesses of the others. However, if the citizens were virtuous, why were such controls needed? Indeed, Diggins sees Adams's arguments for balance as undermining classical republicanism.[4] This view may be too dialectical; Adams can be appreciated as believing in the importance of virtue, while also agreeing with Washington that many people would talk of virtue but few would put their words into action. For instance, in 1790 he wrote to Sam Adams "that all projects of government founded in the supposition or expectation of extraordinary degrees of virtue are evidently chimerical." However, he thought men could improve if there were "assistance from the principles and system of government."[5]

Adams's thinking and writing were always based on an assumption of individual human imperfection. He wrote to Mercy Warren in 1776: "But there is So much Rascallity, so much Venality and Corruption, so much Avarice and Ambition such a Rage for Profit and Commerce among all Ranks and Degrees of men even in America, that I sometimes doubt whether there is public Virtue enough to support a Republic."[6] The family biographers wrote that "He finds the human race impelled by their passions as often as guided by their reason, sometimes led to good actions by scarcely corresponding motives, and sometimes to bad ones rather from inability to resist temptation than from natural propensity to evil."[7] On July 3, 1776, John wrote Abigail with some foreboding of the trials of war that lay ahead:

> The Furnace of Affliction produces Refinement, in States as well as Individuals. And the new Governments we are assuming, in every Part, will require Purification from our Vices, and an Augmentation of our Virtues or they will be no Blessings. The People will have unbounded Power. And the People are extreamly addicted to Corruption and Venality, as well as the Great.—I am not without Apprehensions from this Quarter. But I must submit all my Hopes and Fears, to an overruling Providence, in which, unfashionable as the Faith may be, I firmly believe.[8]

Perhaps Adams had a jaundiced view of human nature; however, such "social pessimism" was combined "with a curious belief in the reliability and soundness of judgment of the common people, at least the common people of New England, and more particularly of Braintree."[9] On February 9, 1811, he wrote the following to Josiah Quincy: "However lightly we may think of the voice of the people sometimes, they not unfrequently see farther than you or I, in many great fundamental questions."[10] In addition, note what he wrote in his diary on July 16, 1786:

It is an Observation of one of the profoundest Inquirers into human Affairs, that a Revolution of Government, successfully conducted and compleated, is the strongest Proof, that can be given, by a People of their Virtue and good Sense. An Interprize of so much difficulty can never be planned and carried on without Abilities, and a People without Principle cannot have confidence enough in each other.[11]

In short, Adams agreed with the concept of republican virtue, but was ambivalent about the human capability to live up to ideal levels of virtue.

Scholars who have criticized Adams for a pessimistic view of human nature need to explain why Adams's view was so widely shared by the revolutionary generation. "Were Americans capable of receiving a republican government? asked an anxious Virginian in June of 1776. 'Have we that Industry, Frugality, Economy, that Virtue which is necessary to constitute it?'" In addition, Robert R. Livingston of New York said that "'More virtue is expected from our People . . . than any People ever had.'"[12] Adams was within the mainstream of political and social thought of most Americans of that era; that mainstream was shaped by the belief in original sin, or the depravity of human nature.[13]

The concern Adams expressed so often in 1776 about the capacity of the people for virtue was prophetic. By the 1780s, many founders feared the revolution was failing. "'What astonishing changes a few years are capable of producing,' said Washington in a common exclamation of these years. 'Have we fought for this?'"[14] Within a very few years, the Federalists were crafting a system designed to control vice on the part of the people. Still, the authors of the *Federalist*, commenting on civic virtues, continued to insist that "Republican government presupposes the existence of these qualities in a higher degree than any other form" [of government].[15] Anti-Federalist writers agreed that republican government could exist only if the people were virtuous.[16] An Anti-Federalist made the following comment on the issue: "Corruption, he knew, was unfashionable amongst us, but he supposed that Americans were like other men; and tho' they had hitherto displayed great virtues, still they were men; and therefore such steps should be taken as to prevent the possibility of corruption."[17]

The opponents in the Constitutional debate realized the necessity of some degree of virtue, to supplement the new government's structural checks against vice. In fact, Storing argues that energetic government teaching the duties of citizenship was seen as necessary by the Federalists. Without that teaching (supplemented by preaching) of civic morality, the country would degenerate into licentiousness.[18] Throughout Sheehan and McDowell's *Friends of the Constitution; Writings of the "Other" Federalists* are multiple examples of supporters of the constitution advocating virtue in both leaders and citizens. James Madison also agreed on the necessity of virtue.[19] In addition, many religious people, ministers and parishioners, continued thinking that republicanism and virtue "remained essentially bound together."[20] For them, the Constitution did not eliminate the need for virtue.

However, the meaning of virtue was no longer the same as in the Revolutionary War, according to Pangle. Virtue was changing to more of an individual, and less of a community ideal: "It is moderation, frugality, and industry in the new sense, i.e., enlightened and sober individual self-interest, that the new Publius counts on as the root of the citizenry's respect for law and devotion to or sense of justice." While Publius did not disdain the public good, he usually meant this term to include, in addition to defense, "the commercial prosperity of America as a whole, and the protection of individual rights, especially rights to . . . property."[21]

Whatever the meaning of virtue, some skeptical contemporary Americans might question the excessive idealism of this emphasis on virtues. The founders, however, had a subtle approach. For instance, as he was preparing to go to the first Continental Congress, John Adams wrote in July 1774: "And indeed, It may well be expected, that many Men of Sound Judgment, will be of that Assembly. But, what avails Prudence, Wisdom, Policy, Fortitude, Integrity, without Power, without Legions?"[22] Much later in life, he wrote to Benjamin Rush: "My friend, the clergy have been in all ages and countries as dangerous to liberty as the army. Yet I love the clergy and the army. What can we do without them in this wicked world?"[23] Adams has been called "the supreme political realist of the revolutionary generation" and "the most astute analyst of political power's inherent intractability."[24] He, and the founders in general, did not allow their ideals to blind them to political realities; both in their struggle for independence and in crafting a new constitution, they understood the need for both virtue and power.

The founders' balanced approach was validated by success: American independence was secured, and the experimental republic survived. But, an underemphasized and misinterpreted element in their recipe for success, virtue, must be revived. For instance, Jencks, analyzing crime rates in contemporary America, finds the explanation for variation in those rates not solely in the realism of police, fines, and laws, but also in moral ideas. And he refers to Adam Smith's *Theory of Moral Sentiments* as an example of such moral ideas.[25] This is another similarity of the founders and Adam Smith, who also combined ideals and power; Smith saw virtue as the foundation for rules and law.[26]

Thus, in this and the next chapter, I argue that our revolutionary era political system required virtuous citizens whose civic virtues were based on a religious foundation and that citizens had (and still have) both virtues and vices. This argument is based on the values, virtues, and religious assumptions which were widely shared by the founders.

Founders' Assumptions

Several basic values were the foundation for the virtues needed for democratic citizenship. Before considering virtues in chapter 3, we must examine three broader assumptions of the founders' moral thought, which Pangle argues were based on Locke: "Nature or 'Nature's God'; property, or the 'pursuit of happiness'; and the dignity of the individual as rational human being, parent, and citizen."[27] I divide Locke's third value into equality and individual liberty, both of which are implied by "the dignity of the individual" and both of which were crucial values of the founders. In addition, individual liberty implies limited government. Before beginning with "Nature's God," it must be emphasized that all these values, as well as the virtues in the next chapter, had eighteenth-century meanings. We will misinterpret them if we see them through modern eyes; all came from a community orientation that we have difficulty comprehending today.[28]

"Nature's God"

"Nature's God" is often a shorthand expression for the deism of many of our founders. But shorthand can obscure part of the truth. While several revolutionary leaders were deists, other leaders were more traditional in their religious beliefs. Whatever their religious persuasion, the founders knew that religion could be and was an important support for republican virtue. Churches were seen by many of the revolutionary generation as "the most important institutions the country possessed."[29] George Washington is an example. Some historians question whether Washington personally was a believer in Christianity, but there can be no question that he was an important layman in the local Episcopal church, as indicated by his long service as a vestryman.[30] Regardless of his private religious beliefs, his church activism indicated an appreciation of the importance of religion for civil society. His Farewell Address (more famous for foreign policy advice) clearly shows his view of the connection; he warned his countrymen to be careful about assuming that morality could be maintained in the absence of religion. Washington continued: "Whatever may be conceded to the influence of refined education on minds of peculiar structure, reason and experience both forbid us to expect that National morality can prevail in exclusion of religious principle."[31] In short, he thought that rational individuals might indeed have very strong values, but was certain that this would not work for the entire nation.

Both George Washington and John Witherspoon, President of the College of New Jersey (now Princeton University) "expected churches to produce good citizens in grateful return for religious liberty."[32] The clergy delivered on this expectation, with multitudes of sermons extolling religious and political virtues as well as religious freedom.[33] For just one example, Samuel McClintock preached that it was God's "immutable law" that "we cannot be a happy, unless a virtuous people."[34] Throughout this period, religion, community, and family were the sources of moral education. Diggins states that Publius doubted "that politics could be the means of man's moral reformation. Government was not to be the agency of ethical education, the authority of the good, true, and just."[35] The founders continued to assume the importance of virtue but because of the religious grounding of society government did not have to be responsible for moral education; indeed, it should not have such responsibility.

John Adams had a life-long habit of church attendance and was thoroughly shaped in his character, thinking, and political ideals by his Puritan heritage.[36] Religion was so important to him that, as a young Harvard graduate, Adams seriously considered entering the ministry, but he eventually chose a career in law. Both John Adams and Adam Smith considered careers in the ministry and both rejected that choice, finding theological disputation distasteful. Adam Smith had a university scholarship that required preparation for the ministry. He eventually resigned the scholarship when he could no longer consider becoming a cleric. While there is some debate about this, it seems clear that he remained a religious person. The editors of his papers do, however, indicate that he moved away from orthodox Christianity "towards natural religion."[37] Both Adams and Smith have been labeled deistic, but theistic might be more accurate.[38] In addition, both Adams and Smith assumed that society was based on morality.[39]

Adams often wrote about the importance of religion for society: "I believe it will be found universally true, that no great enterprize, for the honour or happiness of mankind, was ever achieved, without a large mixture of that noble infirmity [religion]."[40] He even went so far as to write that: "Submission to the divine will is certainly one principle of the spirit of patriotism."[41] And he wrote the following to a cousin, a minister in Lunenberg, Massachusetts:

> Statesmen, my dear Sir, may plan and speculate for Liberty, but it is Religion and Morality alone, which can establish the Principles upon which Freedom can securely stand. . . . The only foundation of a free Constitution, is pure Virtue, and if this cannot be inspired into our People, in a greater Measure, than they have it now, They may change their Rulers, and the forms of Government, but they will not obtain a lasting Liberty.— They will only exchange Tyrants and Tyrannies.[42]

Not only republics, but any free government required religion and virtue.[43]

Even Jefferson "could never satisfy himself that morality or civic spirit in the population at large could dispense with religious faith, institutional religious guidance, and a belief in supernatural divine sanctions."[44] In addition, both Federalists and Anti-Federalists believed that religion was crucial to the survival of representative democracy.[45]

What was clear in the eighteenth century has recently become clear to scholars.[46] For many years, the revolution was seen in Lockean terms of individual liberty. Then the civic republicanism school, arguing the importance of values and civic virtues, challenged that interpretation. Now scholars are arguing that Protestant Christianity was a third strand of causation. For example, Bloch states that distrust of powerful hierarchies, the revolutionaries' moral asceticism, and patriot rituals all had Protestant roots.[47] Bloch also argues that the leaders of the American Revolution were able to mobilize a diverse population to support the new republican order because the American Protestant millennial tradition provided an ideological vision.[48] Sandoz quotes Perry Miller as making a similar argument.[49] Shain supports this point, arguing that between 75% and 90% of Americans at that time, even though many were formally unchurched, were steeped in a religious idiom that was foundational for all public events.[50] Vetterli and Bryner write that the Puritan ethic provided "the electricity that energized the republic."[51] Further, much of the revolutionary propaganda was written by ministers.[52] In short, many scholars assume that all three strands contributed to the founders' thinking,[53] and that is a basic assumption of this book.

Alexis de Tocqueville commented on the importance of religion for American democracy. He argued that "a healthy moral foundation" was more important for a democracy than for other forms of government. And he understood that religion was "an indispensable support of that moral foundation."[54] He also considered religion to be the first of our political institutions (even though he was well aware of the separation of church and state in this country); religion placed "limits on utilitarian individualism, hedging in self-interest with a proper concern for others. The 'main business' of religion, Tocqueville said, 'is to purify, control, and restrain that excessive and exclusive taste for well-being' so common among Americans."[55]

Restraining individual economic self-interest as a religious function may be traced back to New England Calvinist theologians. According to Diggins, they understood benevolence as a virtue involving "'disinterested affection to Being in general,' the soul's commitment to the whole of creation made possible by the one self-sufficient being, God."[56] The religious founders of Massachusetts Bay were very community oriented. However, the Puritan approach probably pushed the pendulum too far away from individual rights. Protecting individual rights while maintaining functioning communities is a problem which continues to bedevil the United States. (See chapter 4 for additional consideration of this problem.)

While the founders agreed on the civic value of religion, they were also very aware of the dangers of religious enthusiasm. Self-righteous zealots could imperil democracy.[57] Religious intolerance was (and still is) extremely dangerous for any political system. At least from his early twenties, Adams expressed his dislike for the doctrinaire types of religion which he had directly experienced as a resident of Protestant Massachusetts; note his negative opinion of "orthodoxy":

"I never thought of the frightful Ecclesiastical Apparatus, of Councils, Creeds &c. without extream Horror."[58] Like Smith, that was a major reason he decided not to become a minister.[59]

Note that Madison, who also wanted to control religious enthusiasm, believed the civic value of religion was limited; he argued that "neither moral nor religious motives can be relied on as an adequate control" of injustice and violence.[60] Madison intended to counterpose interest against interest, passion against passion, to check factions.[61] That applied to religious sects as well.[62] Note that Adam Smith made the same argument, stating that, in a society with religious freedom the multiplicity of different sects would force religious leaders to learn moderation in order to compete successfully for disciples.[63] While Madison might be right that religion, alone, is not a sufficient control of various enthusiasms, I argue that constitutional checks and balances, alone, also are insufficient. Both religious and governmental controls are needed.

Adams was well aware of the dangers of enthusiasm, the excesses committed in many times and places in the name of religion. In addition to Madison's solution of counterposing faction against faction, Adams emphasized tolerance as an antidote. Late in his life, in a letter to Dr. Benjamin Rush, he combined, in his quintessential style, a statement on the importance of Christianity with a comment on tolerance:

> The Christian religion, as I understand it, is the brightness of the glory and the express portrait of the character of the eternal, self-existent, independent, benevolent, all-powerful and all-merciful Creator, Preserver, and Father of the universe; the first good, first perfect, and first fair. It will last as long as the world. Neither savage nor civilized man, without a revelation, could ever have discovered or invented it. Ask me not, then, whether I am a Catholic or Protestant, Calvinist or Arminian. As far as they are Christians, I wish to be a fellow-disciple with them all.[64]

On this, Adams, Washington, and Franklin could agree. For George Washington, any religion that promoted civic virtue deserved governmental protection, and he repeated this belief to Protestant, Catholic, and Jewish religious groups.[65] Forde argues that tolerance, to combat the moralism characteristic of Puritan America, was a principal purpose of Benjamin Franklin's *Autobiography*.[66]

There was also a religious perspective on tolerance. Unfortunately, there was still too much intolerance, such as anti-Catholic sentiment in some circles.[67] But there were also Protestant leaders who saw tolerance as integral to their faith. Elisha Williams connected the protection of Christian liberty with practicing "that Christian charity towards such as are of different sentiments from us in religion that is so much recommended and inculcated in those sacred oracles, and which a just understanding of our Christian rights has a natural tendency to influence us to."[68] John Witherspoon argued that "the best friend to American liberty" promoted "true and undefiled religion" which required tolerance: "Perhaps there are few surer marks of the reality of religion, than when a man feels himself more joined in spirit to a true holy person of a different denomination, than to an irregular liver of his own."[69]

An individualistic, anti-hierarchical approach to religion was another of Adams's antidotes for enthusiasm: "I am not about to become a Leader or Follower in Theology. To my own Master I stand or fall."[70] In another letter to Benjamin Waterhouse seven months later (in December, 1815), Adams wrote: "The Christian is the Religion of the heart: but the heart is deceiptfull above all things and, unless controuled by the Dominion of the Head, will lead us into salt ponds."[71] Here Adams is part of a religious shift from the community-hierarchical religion of Winthrop and the early Puritans to a more community-individual religion. Adams combined "the predominant concerns of the Enlightenment" with "the attitudes and institutions of Puritan New England."[72] Religion was necessary (his Puritan heritage) but the danger of emotional, enthusiastic religion should be controlled by the rationality of individuals.[73] Political and religious freedom then went hand in hand.

Parenthetically, note that religious freedom would not only help reduce dangerous religious enthusiasm, but it would also provide an important side-benefit for the new nation, as is evident in this comment about the Massachusetts Constitution, in a letter Adams wrote from Paris in 1780:

> The Liberality on the Subject of Religion, does Us infinite Honor and is admired and applauded every where. It is considered not only as an honest and pious Attention to the unalienable Rights of Conscience, but as our best and most refined Policy, tending to conciliate the Good Will of all the World, preparing an Asylum, which will be a sure Remedy against persecution in Europe, and drawing over to our Country Numbers of excellent Citizens.[74]

Freedom of religion would attract skilled immigrants who would benefit the country.

Adam Smith agreed with the founders both on the importance of religion for society and on the dangers of enthusiasm.[75] Even though Smith was skeptical of religion, his writing assumed a values base stemming from religion and, like the founders, he thought that religion had an educative role to play in character formation.[76] But while Smith understood that many people "commonly regard basic moral principles as divinely sanctioned," he was very concerned about the corruption of such norms by human delusions, misinterpretations of divine principles, and the fanaticism that often resulted.[77] Smith argued that the state had two remedies to control fanatic sects. First was study of science and philosophy: "Science is the great antidote to the poison of enthusiasm and superstition; and where all the superior ranks of people were secured from it, the inferior ranks could not be much exposed to it."[78] The second remedy was state encouragement of public diversions "by giving entire liberty to all those who for their own interest would attempt, without scandal or indecency, to amuse and divert the people by painting, poetry, musick, dancing" and by dramatic presentations.[79] Smith also recognized, like the founders, that there were political fanatics as well as religious fanatics.[80]

Some, but certainly not all, religious Americans today would agree with Adams and Smith on the necessity of rationality to control the excesses of religion, but many Americans, some religious, some not, are very skeptical of any claims that religion has a crucial societal function. Why do so many reject Adams's balanced vision (religion is necessary for virtue; virtue is necessary for the republic; religion must be controlled by the "Dominion of the Head" so that "enthusiasm" does not destroy the republic)? Once again, the answer has several facets. Perhaps most important is the ascendance of the scientific spirit and the common collateral misperception that one cannot be both scientific and religious. (That this is too dialectical is another matter.) This scientific spirit is part of the historical period known as the Age of Reason. Adams criticized the rationalism of that age in a letter to Benjamin Rush (March 26, 1806):

> You ask also what will be the fate of our country? If the philosophers had not undermined the Christian religion and the morals of the people as much in America as they have in Europe, I should think civilization would take its flight over the Atlantic. But as it is, I see nothing but we must, or rather than we shall, follow the fate of Europe.[81]

Adams thought that various philosophers had "made all Europe so discontented with themselves, their government, and religion" that they exchanged the "whips of monarchy" for the "scorpions of despotism."[82] This does not mean that he was an opponent of science; he wrote on February 26, 1817: "My humble opinion is that Sciences and Arts have vastly and immensely ameliorated the condition of Man, and even improved his Morals. The progress however has been awfully slow." In addition, he feared that the Sciences and the Arts would be "prostituted to the Service of Superstition and despotism."[83] Adams wanted both religion and reason.

A second factor is the fear of the excesses of enthusiasm. The term, "puritanical," evokes American experiences with such excesses. Rationalists look at religion and see danger. Adams and Smith also saw danger in any religious excess; neither was blind to the dangers of theocratic power; neither liked theological hairsplitting. But perhaps Americans today have forgotten something they understood: the importance of internalized standards—character, virtue, whatever label one uses. Obviously, psychological repression or religious brainwashing absolutely will not do. But any society requires a degree of individual self-control for that society to avoid sliding toward anarchy. Those free market enthusiasts who argue that the market provides such discipline do not understand significant parts of Adams's arguments. He feared the corrupting influence of commerce and saw individual self-control, shaped by family, education, and religion, and further constrained by balanced government, as the answer. In addition, such free market enthusiasts cannot legitimately claim Adam Smith as authority for their views (as will be argued in chapters 5 and 6).

That self-control need not be repressive is indicated by the founders' agreement on a second value: the pursuit of happiness.

The Pursuit of Happiness

A common formulation before the American Revolution was that man had inalienable rights to life, liberty, and property. But the pursuit of happiness was sufficiently important to the founders that they substituted it for property in the Declaration of Independence.[84] According to Commager: "Happiness runs like a golden thread through the thinking and the writing of the revolutionary generation."[85] But for some of the founders, it was more important than we ordinarily think. Many of the state constitutions went beyond the pursuit of happiness and guaranteed the attainment of happiness.[86]

Happiness to John Adams was not what we would think today; in "Thoughts on Government" (1776), he wrote that happiness consisted in virtue:

> Upon this point all speculative politicians will agree, that the happiness of society is the end of Government, as all Divines and moral Philosophers will agree that the happiness of the individual is the end of man. From this principle it will follow, that the form of government, which communicates ease, comfort, security, or in one word, happiness to the greatest number of persons, and in the greatest degree, is the best.
>
> All sober inquirers after truth, ancient and modern, Pagan and Christian, have declared that the happiness of man, as well as his dignity consists in virtue. Confucius, Zoroaster, Socrates, Mahomet, not to mention authorities really sacred, have agreed in this.[87]

Like Adams, Adam Smith argued that, by acting consonant with our moral values, "we necessarily pursue the most effectual means for promoting the happiness of mankind, and may therefore be said, in some sense, to cooperate with the Deity."[88] Note the religious connection of virtuous behavior and the pursuit of happiness for all. Adams agreed with such universality. In 1765 he wrote that "The Happiness of a Million is in the sight of God, and in the Estimation of every honest and humane Mind, of more importance, than that of 20 or an

Hundred."[89] The pursuit of happiness was an egalitarian, and thus a radical concept. In America, all people, not just the rich, had a right to seek happiness.

Similarly, Jefferson also related virtue to happiness in an October 14, 1816, letter to Adams: "for virtue does not consist in the act we do, but in the end it is to effect. If it is to effect the happiness of him to whom it is directed, it is virtuous. . . . The essence of virtue is in doing good to others, while what is good may be one thing in one society, and its contrary in another."[90]

That connection of happiness and virtue leads to another relationship: happiness and liberty. Israel Evans, in a 1791 election sermon delivered in Concord, New Hampshire, argued that liberty without virtue would be licentious. "True liberty may be summed up in the declaration: that we have a right to do all the good we can; but have no right to injure our fellow man: we have a right to be as happy as we can; but no right to lessen the happiness of mankind."[91] Such individual happiness within community is obviously not the same as modern individualistic happiness. Happiness was the goal, but it was to be pursued within a community context.[92]

Anti-Federalists agreed on this right. Brutus, writing to the citizens of New York, criticized European governments for being too war-like and for not doing what governments should do: save lives, not destroy them. He felt that the United States should be a model: "We ought to furnish the world with an example of a great people, who in their civil institutions hold chiefly in view, the attainment of virtue, and happiness among ourselves."[93] Note the contrast with evil European governments; distrust of Europe was to be a staple of American political thought for much of the first 150 years of the United States.

In short, signers of the Declaration, plus Federalists and Anti-Federalists, agreed on the importance of the pursuit of a virtuous happiness.

Adam Smith also dealt with happiness in *Wealth of Nations*. He argued that we pursue wealth because we assume it brings happiness. But the nearly "universal toils of emulation" indicate a "deep misorientation about the true nature of the ends of human life (and especially happiness)."[94] So, what is true happiness? The founders would not have seen the acquisitiveness of the modern consumer society as virtuous. Ironically, because we are deluded on the nature of happiness, we are motivated to work hard in order to be able to afford to imitate those whom we see as better off than we are (keeping up with the Joneses); but this vicious acquisitiveness (from the founders' perspective) which is based, according to Smith, on a delusion as to the true nature of happiness, does have the beneficial effect (from Smith's perspective) of increasing the wealth of nations.[95]

Although the founders did not list property as an inalienable right in the Declaration of Independence, they knew that the right to property was an important component of the pursuit of happiness. According to John Dickinson, patriots objected to the Townshend Acts in 1767 (import duties on glass, white lead, paper, and tea) because they were an immediate threat to property. Property was a means to liberty. Americans fought the British to protect their property from governmental depredations; maintaining their property would in turn enable them to be free to act.[96] Dickinson's point is another formulation of the common revolutionary belief that propertyless people (landless laborers, women, children) could not act independently, a topic to which we shall return in chapter 7, "Property and Democracy."

Protecting property was central to the founders even though they encouraged some attacks on property during the Revolution. Samuel Adams is a good example of the distinction. He generally disapproved of mob action, but, when there was no other recourse, he supported destruction of property. He defended the Stamp Act uprising of August 14, 1765, as a legitimate defense of liberty because the people believed their rights had been denied by Parliament and legal means of redress had failed. "But he condemned the attack on the homes of Thomas Hutchinson and others on August 26, 1765, as a transaction of 'a truly *mobbish* Nature.'"[97] John Adams completely agreed with his cousin, as is evident in his discussion of a different incident:

> I am engaged in a famous Cause: The Cause of King of Scarborough vs. a Mob, that broke into his House, and rifled his Papers, and terrifyed him, his Wife, Children and Servants in the Night. The Terror, and Distress, the Distraction and Horror of this Family cannot be described by Words or painted upon Canvass. It is enough to move a Statue, to melt an Heart of Stone, to read the Story. A Mind susceptible of the Feelings of Humanity, an Heart which can be touch'd with Sensibi[li]ty for human Misery and Wretchedness, must reluct, must burn with Resentment and Indignation, at such outragious Injuries. These private Mobs, I do and will detest. If Popular Commotions can be justifyed, in Opposition to Attacks upon the Constitution, it can be only when Fundamentals are invaded, nor then unless for absolute Necessity and with great Caution. But these Tarrings and Featherings, these breaking open Houses by rude and insolent Rabbles, in Resentment for private Wrongs or in pursuance of private Prejudices and Passions, must be discountenanced, cannot be even excused upon any Principle which can be entertained by a good Citizen—a worthy Member of Society.[98]

Agreement on the importance of property and the pursuit of happiness was so widespread that examples could be given *ad nauseam*.

While the pursuit of happiness was important for the revolution, like the danger of religious enthusiasm, it was problematic for virtue. Taken to an extreme, the pursuit of happiness could become the vice of luxury. On the issue of luxury, Plato's emphasis on the golden mean, on moderation in all things, had resonance for America's founders:

the mean states of all these habits are by far the safest and most moderate; for the one extreme makes the soul braggart and insolent, and the other, illiberal and base; and money, and property, and distinction all go to the same tune. The excess of any of these things is apt to be a source of hatreds and divisions *[729]* among states and individuals; and the defect of them is commonly a cause of slavery. And, therefore, I would not have any one fond of heaping up riches for the sake of his children, in order that he may leave them as rich as possible. For the possession of great wealth is of no use, either to them or to the state.[99]

Many contemporary Americans reject such thinking. But the founders were well aware of ancient Greek thought and based many of their ideas of civic virtue, as well as civic vice, on such classical sources. They believed that traits of the yeoman, virile, martial virtues, such as "the scorn of ease, the contempt of danger, the love of valor" would make the republic strong; and they feared the effects of luxury, the internal decay, which would corrupt and might destroy the new republic. Luxury "eventually weakened a people and left them soft and effeminate, dissipated cowards, unfit and undesiring to serve the state."[100] So the revolutionaries banned corrupting luxuries, such as plays, horse-racing, and cockfighting.[101]

Adams had a deep fear of luxury; writing to his wife in 1777, he stated that, if Howe's army defeated the American army, "It would cure Americans of their vicious and luxurious and effeminate Appetites, Passions and Habits, a more dangerous Army to American Liberty than Mr. Howes."[102] Months later, in April 1778, John wrote to Abigail from Paris about the "Delights of France" and the "Magnificence" of Paris; but in the same letter he also wrote:

But what is all this to me? I receive but little Pleasure in beholding all these Things, because I cannot but consider them as Bagatelles, introduced, by Time and Luxury in Exchange for the great Qualities and hardy manly Virtues of the human Heart. I cannot help suspecting that the more Elegance, the less Virtue in all Times and Countries.—Yet I fear that even my own dear Country wants the Power and Opportunity more than the Inclination, to be elegant, soft, and luxurious.[103]

Less than two months later, in another letter to his wife, Adams continued on the same theme: "My dear Country men! how shall I perswade you, to avoid the Plague of Europe? Luxury has as many and as bewitching Charms, on your Side of the Ocean as on this—and Luxury, wherever she goes, effaces from human Nature the Image of the Divinity."[104] While Adams thought that, in France, there was a great deal of humanity, charity, and even tenderness for the poor, his Autobiography contains a long section on the luxurious corruption of French society and the dangers inherent in such vice:

What havoc said I to myself, would these manners make in America? Our Governors, our Judges, our Senators, or Representatives and even our Ministers would be appointed by Harlots for Money, and their Judgments, Decrees and decisions be sold to repay themselves, or perhaps to procure the smiles of profligate Females.

The foundations of national Morality must be laid in private Families. In vain are Schools, Academies and universities instituted, if loose Principles and licentious habits are impressed upon Children in their earliest years. The Mothers are the earliest and most important Instructors of youth. . . . The Vices and Examples of the Parents cannot be concealed from the Children. How is it possible that Children can have any just Sense of the sacred Obligations of Morality or Religion if, from their earliest Infancy, they learn that their Mothers live in habitual Infidelity to their fathers, and their fathers in as constant Infidelity to their Mothers.[105]

In the same section Adams argues that earlier republics had been destroyed "when they lost the Modesty and Domestic Virtues of their Women."

The right to pursue happiness did not justify licentious behavior; that does not surprise us. But the modern reader very well might find his view of the importance of women a bit incongruous. Given that these quotations are part of a long disquisition on the evils of Madame de Pompadour, and given Adams's discomfort with Benjamin Franklin's lifestyle in France, one might wonder if Adams were puritanically offended by French sexuality. On the other hand, Withington states that Franklin "led a richly sybaritic life" in France and that "Franklin the persona in *Autobiography* clashed with the historical Franklin." She argues that, rather than showing jealousy, spleen, or prudishness, Adams's reaction to Franklin "reveals the distaste of a republican for a display of values and behavior that flouted republican principles."[106] Franklin participated in activities banned by the revolutionaries and thus was not living a model republican life.

One still wonders how Adams could place so much responsibility on women, when he himself recognized that both male and female infidelity were involved. Perhaps the apparent inconsistency can be explained as an example of that era's common emphasis on the central role of women and the family in fostering republican virtue. On this point, John Adams and his daughter-in-law, Louisa (wife of John Quincy Adams), agreed; she believed that vice in America would be reduced only if women were more successful in practicing and teaching, in the home, "the Christian virtues of love, humility, and selflessness." She thought women could "become latter-day prophetesses" criticizing "the misguided nature of the new economy and government men were designing." She acknowledged "that woman's nature was itself much in need of divine forgiveness," but still thought that "love and compassion, guidance and education should be the concerns of females who, in tackling these responsibilities as respected mothers and wives, might improve the mess men were making of the world."[107] Kerber agrees that the republican mother was seen as having, in her domestic role, an important political function. Through her power over the moral development of her sons and through her influence over her husband, she could serve civic virtue.[108]

Adams clearly saw the dangers of luxury and lack of morality; he understood the importance of women as agents of moral education. But this was not a sexist delegation of responsibility; he realized that he shared this educational function, as is obvious in many of his letters to John Quincy Adams[109] as well as letters to his daughter, Nabby.[110] And he fretted over the impact of his absence on the moral development of his children. Of course, moral development was (and is) much broader than merely avoiding the vice of luxury. Ultimately, the occurrence of the French Revolution confirmed John Adams's fears of the corrupting dangers of luxury.

Jefferson also furnishes a good example of revolutionary era thinking about luxury. He feared commercial avarice; he argued that merchants loved nobody and that commerce bred manipulation and a cold heart, in contrast to the virtues bred by wholesome labor in agriculture. Jefferson was concerned that America would repeat the mistakes of English society, where luxury had debased the commercial-industrial class, which lived off the poor, themselves debased by their work and their poverty.[111] Jefferson distrusted self-interest, which he saw as a danger to the republic. "Commerce and its mentality, like slavery and its corruptions and paper money and its evils, was a snake in the republican garden."[112]

Jefferson was not alone in his connection of commercial self-interest and luxury. Linesch makes it clear that, both during and shortly after the Revolutionary War, there was concern about the prevalence of self-interest at the expense of the common interest; Revolutionary War veterans lamented the virtual disappearance of public spirit. "'Private rage for property suppresses public considerations,' Jay wrote to Washington in 1786, 'and personal rather than national interests have become the great objects of attention.' Virtue, Washington observed sadly from his Mount Vernon retreat, had apparently 'taken its departure from our land.'" Richard Henry Lee thought that civic virtue was declining, and that "there are Mandevilles" in America "who laugh at virtue, and with vain ostentatious display of words will deduce from vice, public good."[113]

Lee's comment about "Mandevilles . . . who laugh at virtue" refers to a thinker who advocated extreme self-interest. Note that he did not refer to Adam Smith, whose *Wealth of Nations* was not yet widely known in revolutionary America;[114] had Lee attributed extreme self-interest to Smith, he would have misinterpreted Smith's thinking. Today, incorrect attribution of extreme self-interest to Smith is very common. The irony is that Smith was very clear in his criticism of luxury. While discussing the negative effects of monopoly, he noted that the high rates of profit inherent in monopolies destroyed the sober virtue known as parsimony. In addition, he criticized luxury for eating into productive capital.[115] Luxury reduced the wealth of society. Smith also agreed with the founders that wealth undermined morality, but thought it was needed to preserve social order: "This disposition to admire, and almost to worship, the rich and the powerful, and to despise, or, at least, to neglect persons of poor and mean condition . . . is, at the same time the great and most universal cause of the corruption of our moral sentiments."[116] So, morality and parsimony are mutually reinforcing, just as lack of parsimony (luxury) can weaken morality.

This discussion of the dangers of luxury and wealth leads to questions about the relationships of individual self-interest, economic activity and virtue, which chapter 6, "Self-Interest and the Economy," examines. The founders regretted that the private pursuit of happiness came at the expense of civic virtue, but the pursuit of happiness was a fundamental principle of a successful revolution.

Equality

Another fundamental value was equality. William Manning, who characterized himself as "a laborer" and whose revolutionary era writings have recently been discovered and reprinted, tied together all the values with justice and equality: "The sole end of government is the protection of the life, liberty, and property of individuals. The poor man's shilling ought to be as much the care of government as the rich man's pound and no more. Every person ought to have justice done to him freely and promptly without delay."[117]

The founders were no less explicit. Equality was at the heart of Adams's political beliefs.[118] In a June 3, 1776, letter to Patrick Henry, Adams was typically colorful and intense about recent egalitarian developments:

The Dons, the Bashaws, the Grandees, the Patricians, the Sachems, the Nabobs, call them by what Name you please, Sigh, and groan, and frett, and Sometimes Stamp, and foam, and curse—but all in vain. The Decree is gone forth, and it cannot be recalled, that a more equal Liberty, than has prevail'd in other Parts of the Earth, must be established in America.[119]

Even though women, blacks, and Amerindians were not considered equal, this ideal was nonetheless revolutionary. It was not, however, a new idea; our founders could trace it to the Greeks, who valued equality of opportunity. And it was this sense of the word that the founders accepted, at least for white males. In other words, equality both ignored large sectors of the population and was not even absolute for those few who were included. McWilliams's discussion of Montesquieu's *The Spirit of the Laws,* clarifies these limits: "Democracy, Montesquieu argued, requires *love of country* and the allied passion of *love for equality*, the latter an inward sentiment, like that praised by traditional thought, which involves a devotion to the good of the whole such that all 'serve with alacrity' even though they cannot serve equally." Equal responsibility for the public good was expected. But "extreme equality" was dangerous because it did not recognize differences in ability; "democratic equality accepts leaders but demands that they be 'none but equals.'"[120] Inequality and equality are thus in a *yin-yang* relationship.

That our founders accepted Montesquieu's point and assumed the continual existence of some types of inequality is stated by Gordon S. Wood; equality was not seen by "even a devout republican like Samuel Adams, as a social leveling." Indeed, equality was to be "'adverse to every species of subordination beside that which arises from the difference of capacity, disposition, and virtue.'" Political office would not be gained because of connections to the monarch; in the new republic "only talent would matter."[121]

However, applying such a differentiated view of equality was problematic. John Adams's political difficulties after his return from European diplomatic duty were partially caused by his attempt to warn his countrymen of the dangers of inequality in an egalitarian country. Congressman Albert Gallatin's criticism of Alexander Hamilton and a monarchist, aristocratic faction in American politics[122] was probably also aimed at Adams, who attracted such criticism because he wrote extensively on the dangers of a natural aristocracy in the United States. However, while Adams believed in equality, he also believed that "there are inequalities which God and nature have planted." These included inequalities of wealth and birth. On the latter he wrote: "The children of illustrious families have generally greater advantages of education and earlier opportunities to be acquainted with public characters and informed of public affairs than those of meaner ones, or even than those in middle life."[123] A February 4, 1794, letter further demonstrates the complexity of his view of equality:

> But man differs by nature from man, almost as much as man from beast. The equality of nature is moral and political only, and means that all men are independent. But a physical inequality, an intellectual inequality, of the most serious kind, is established unchangeably by the Author of nature; and society has a right to establish any other inequalities it may judge necessary for its good. The precept, however, do as you would be done by, implies an equality which is the real equality of nature and Christianity, and has been known and understood in all ages.[124]

Adams's invocation of the golden rule moves the concept beyond mere equality of opportunity. It becomes not just an inalienable right but an active principle: individuals thus have a responsibility to treat others equally.[125]

Adams's use of a religious precept brings us to another aspect of equality. Many Americans believe that each person is a unique child of God. Equality, then, has also meant that all souls are of equal worth in the eyes of God.[126] Or, as Samuel Miller put it, one of the great gospel truths is that "all men are, by nature, equal—children of the same common Father."[127] This idea is consistent with Adams's statement above that the "equality of nature is moral."

While Adams recognized that equality was not absolute, it must be emphasized that neither the advantages of birth nor the reality of physical and intellectual differences among human beings blinded him to the genius of ordinary people. He wrote to Samuel Quincy in 1761, about the creativity of the butcher, the oyster-boat captain, the hunter. "Go on board an Oyster-boat, and converse with the skipper, he will relate as many instances of invention, and intrepidity too, as you will find in the lives of many British Admirals." Adams saw that genius is more common and "much more powerful than is generally thought."[128] In such comments, Adams celebrates equality in the world of work. The new nation overturned the idea of aristocratic leisure and celebrated instead the dignity of labor. In contrast to Europe, equality meant that no class, no order of people, was exempt from work; in America, to live without regular employment was not reputable.[129]

Obviously, then, Adams and other founders did not accept the extreme version of equality which developed after the Revolution, for example the equality that Wood presents when he writes about the world-shaking character of the American Revolution: "Ordinary Americans came to believe that no one in a basic down-to-earth and day-in and day-out manner was really better than anyone else. That was equality as no other nation has ever quite had it."[130] Wood goes on to say that we accept differences among people but believe that all are basically alike.[131] The founders agreed with Adam Smith's belief that human beings are roughly equal in moral and intellectual abilities; Smith attributed the differences which did exist to social conditions and education.[132] But Smith and the founders certainly also believed that there would be inequality in results.

Equality, like religion and property, has been problematic. There are huge inequalities in American society, which can be illustrated by a whole range of diversity issues involving the rights of women, gays, Blacks, Amerindians, Hispanics. Several generations after the founding, the proposition that all are created equal was reemphasized by Lincoln in his Gettysburg Address. Nonetheless, after several additional generations, equality remains a great American unfulfilled promise. In addition, equality has been problematic because it has been weakened by the American individualistic emphasis on liberty.[133]

Liberty: Limited Government

That a country settled by people searching for religious liberty should fight for independence under the banner of "Liberty" is not surprising. The individual right to liberty and the conviction that this required limited government were among the founders' central values.[134] Liberty was threatened by twin dangers: tyranny and anarchy. Government must be limited to prevent tyranny, but government was still valued. The revolutionary generation dreaded anarchy; they wanted "ordered liberty restrained by wholesome laws."[135] Isaac Backus, writing in 1773, stated that many imagine that government interferes with liberty, but "that all nations have found it necessary to submit to some government in order to enjoy any liberty and security at all."[136] Government protected the "natural rights and civil privileges" of the people.[137]

American roots of this differentiated concept of liberty can be traced back to the first governor of the Massachusetts Bay Colony, John Winthrop, who wanted to create an ethical community. "He decried what he called 'natural liberty,' which is the freedom to do whatever one wants, evil as well as good. True freedom—what he called 'moral' freedom, 'in reference to the covenant between God and man'—is a liberty 'to that only which is good, just and honest.'"[138] The religious community, not the individual, must have freedom.[139] This was very different from the individual liberty assumed by Americans today.

A century after Winthrop, the revolutionary generation still saw liberty in terms that he would have appreciated; that generation would not have been comfortable "with the idea that individuals should enjoy freedom from public, and even from familial moral interference."[140] Adams's definition was consistent with Winthrop's: "I would define liberty to be a power to do as we would be done by. The definition of liberty to be the power of doing whatever the laws permit, meaning the civil laws, does not appear to be satisfactory."[141] Adams's use of the golden rule was not unusual; his and Winthrop's distinction between liberty and licentiousness was also common in the revolutionary era.[142] Good government was needed to prevent anarchic licentiousness. The founders wanted both liberty and (limited) government. And that government was intended as a check against what we see today as liberty, but they saw as license.[143] Smith would have agreed. Muller writes that "the tendency of nineteenth-century liberalism and twentieth-century libertarianism to regard the pursuit of self-interest as intrinsically good and government as intrinsically evil . . . was quite foreign to Smith."[144]

Ironically, the founders argued that they fought for independence from Great Britain in order to secure the liberty which was theirs by right under the British constitution. Adams wrote on January 27, 1766: "I shall take for granted, what I am sure no Briton will controvert, viz. that Liberty is essential to the public good, the salus populi. And here lies the difference between the British constitution, and other forms of government, viz. that Liberty is its end, its use, its designation, drift and scope."[145] But how did he define liberty? Retrospectively, in a letter to Benjamin Rush dated February 25, 1808, he stated that in 1774 "liberty meant security for life, liberty, property, and character."[146] But note Shain's contention that the liberty sought in the American Revolutionary War was not individualistic but was "communal and valued corporate goals over individualistic ends."[147]

This value was shared across the political spectrum. Agrippa, an Anti-Federalist, saw free citizens as virtuous, in contrast to people living under absolute rulers: "We accordingly find that in absolute governments, the people, be the climate what it may, are [in] general lazy, cowardly, turbulent, and vicious to an extreme. On the other hand, in free countries are found in general, activity, industry, arts, courage, generosity, and all the manly virtues."[148] Note that, just as equality implied that all should work, liberty resulted in a more industrious people.[149]

Tyranny and liberty also had religious connotations. Tyranny was associated with sin, and liberty with grace. Agrippa's connection of liberty and virtue was commonplace, according to Bloch, who notes that this idea was "usually associated with the secular theories of civic republicanism," but, in addition, "American Protestants usually assumed that true virtue was impossible to achieve without Christian faith."[150]

Important responsibilities were inherent in liberty. Independent citizens (white property-owning males) should serve the state disinterestedly: "According to the classical republican tradition, man was by nature a political being, a citizen who achieved his greatest moral fulfillment by participating in a self-governing republic. Public or political liberty—or what we now call positive liberty—meant participation in government." Such service was not, however, pure altruism, because the citizen thereby received from government protection of his liberty and rights.[151]

The responsibilities of liberty included demonstrating that America's new government was not utopian but actually would work. If the republican form of government were to be attractive to other people, the new republic had to show that liberty and government were compatible. John Jay made this clear in an address in New York in 1788:

> Let us also be mindful that the cause of freedom greatly depends on the use we make of the singular opportunities we enjoy of governing ourselves wisely; for if the event should prove, that the people of this country either cannot or will not govern themselves, who will hereafter be advocates for systems, which however charming in theory and prospect, are not reducible to practice. If the people of our nation, instead of consenting to be governed by laws of their own making, and rulers of their own choosing, should let licentiousness, disorder, and confusion reign over them, the minds of men every where, will insensibly become alienated from republican forms, and prepared to prefer and acquiesce in Governments, which, though less friendly to liberty, afford more peace and security.[152]

Jay's comments reflect a widely shared perspective in the revolutionary era, stemming back to the Puritans, of the United States as a model for all mankind, a "City upon a Hill."[153]

Liberty also assumed knowledge, which required education, a governmental responsibility which John Adams emphasized beginning with his years as the schoolmaster in Worcester, Massachusetts, and continuing throughout his life.[154] In "A Dissertation on the Canon and the Feudal Law" (1765), he wrote:

> Be it remembred, however, that liberty must at all hazards be supported. We have a right to it, derived from our Maker. But if we had not, our fathers have earned, and bought it for us, at the expence of their ease, their estates, their pleasure, and their blood. And liberty cannot be preserved without a general knowledge among the people, who have a right from the frame of their nature, to knowledge, as their great Creator who does nothing in vain, has given them understandings, and a desire to know—but besides this they have a right, an indisputable, unalienable, indefeasible divine right to that most dreaded, and envied kind of knowledge, I mean of the characters and conduct of their rulers.[155]

Adams stated this right in the strongest possible terms and further emphasized that preserving "the means of knowledge, among the lowest ranks" had greater public importance than "all the property of all the rich men in the country."[156] One can hardly imagine a clearer statement. He saw knowledge as a divine right of all classes of the people, an imperative of democratic liberty which must be supported by the government.[157]

However, liberty was not a right possessed by all. What if one were not a white male? If one ignores the eighteenth-century context, one can easily cast moralistic aspersions on the honesty, or at least the lack of intellectual consistency, of the founders. How could they talk about liberty, while continuing to enslave almost 500,000 African-Americans? In contrast, Wood argues that the Revolution was one cause of the eventual emancipation of the slaves. The revolution changed the cultural climate of acceptance of monarchical society's "many calibrations and degrees of unfreedom. . . . The Revolution in effect set in motion ideological and social forces that doomed the institution of slavery in the North and led inexorably to the Civil War." And he notes that the first anti-slavery society in the world was founded in Philadelphia in 1775.[158] Bloch states that leading anti-slavery figures of this period were motivated by religion as well as by the political idea of liberty.[159] Wood also argues that the principles of the Revolution made it possible for women to strive for their own freedom.[160]

Contemporary Americans might wish that John Adams had done more about slavery and the status of women. After all, slavery was anathema to him, even though it was accepted practice in the Boston area. Even his father-in-law (a minister) owned slaves, as did several Boston acquaintances.[161] Adams was against slavery even though he spent thousands of dollars on hired labor for his farm while thinking that he could have reduced his farm expenses had he bought slaves when they were cheap. Parenthetically, Smith also had a strong aversion to slavery,[162] but he disagreed with Adams's perception that free labor was more expensive. Smith stated that "work done by freeman comes cheaper in the end than that performed by slaves. It is found to do so even at Boston, New York, and Philadelphia, where the wages of common labour are so very high.[163] What is important for us is that Adams perceived that he was paying more for free labor, but continued to do so because of his anti-slavery principles.

In private letters, Adams was clear about his abhorrence of slavery. He discussed "the turpitude, the inhumanity, the cruelty, and the infamy of the African commerce in slaves" in one such letter, dated June 8, 1819. In the same letter he showed his foresight by arguing for a balanced approach to emancipation, including providing the victims with the means of sustenance ("the necessary comforts of life") and employment, while taking care not to endanger the lives and property of the slave-owners.[164] But his private views were not translated into public statements, much less public policies.

The issue of the status of women might also lead one to question the extent of John Adams's belief in liberty, given his bantering response rejecting his wife's pleas in her "remember the ladies" letter.[165] Still, the Abigail Adams-John Adams marriage was remarkably ahead of its time, a joint partnership two centuries ago! And the "remember the ladies" exchange does not give a complete picture of John Adams's views of women. From Paris he wrote to Abigail in February, 1779:

> I must not write a Word to you about Politicks, because you are a Woman.
> What an offence have I committed?—a Woman!
> I shall soon make it up. I think Women better than Men in General, and I know that you can keep a Secret as well as any Man whatever. But the World dont know this. Therefore if I were to write any Secrets to you and the letter should be caught, and hitched into a Newspaper, the World would say, I was not to be trusted with a Secret.[166]

Another incident which seems to indicate little concern for the status of women was his vendetta against Mercy Otis Warren. This incident occurred after Adams's retirement and involved sharp criticisms by Adams of the way Warren portrayed him in her history of the American Revolution. Warren had reopened an old wound by accepting the Jeffersonian calumny that John Adams was a crypto-monarchist. The Warren flap can be seen as Adams venting his spleen on a woman, but it can also be seen as John Adams treating a woman precisely as he would (and did) treat any man in similar circumstances. The editors of the

Adams Papers feel he was justified in his reaction. Ellis agrees that Adams was correct, but criticizes him for stating his arguments "in the belligerent style of a wronged defendant rather than in the spirit of accommodation."[167] Before that disagreement, the Warrens and the Adams had been friends and political allies; and he had seen Mrs. Warren as an equal. In a September 26, 1775, letter to her husband, James Warren, Adams wrote that he "never thought either Politicks or War, or any other Art or Science beyond the Line of her Sex." Later in the same letter he credited to Abigail Adams and Mercy Warren "a Share and no small one neither, in the conduct of our American Affairs."[168] He believed that women, either as mothers, wives, or sisters, deserved a large part of the credit for the accomplishments of most famous men.[169] His wife was his most trusted political counselor. And he advocated equal education for women.[170] However, as with slavery, his private views did not result in public action.

Slavery and the status of women were both matters of deep concern to Adams, but he was convinced that priority had to be given to freedom from Great Britain:

> We cannot suddenly alter the Temper, Principles, opinions or Prejudices of Men. The Characters of Gentlemen in the four New England Colonies, differ as much from those in the others, as that of the Common People differs, that is as much as several distinct Natures almost. Gentlemen, Men of sense, or any Kind of Education in the other Colonies are much fewer in Proportion than in N. England. Gentlemen in other Colonies, have large Plantations of slaves, and the common People among them are very ignorant and very poor. These Gentlemen are accustomed, habituated to higher Notions of themselves and the Distinction between them and the common People, than We are, and an instantaneous alteration of the Character of a Colony, and that Temper and those sentiments which, its Inhabitants imbibed with the Mothers Milk, and which have grown with their Growth and stengthend with their Strength, cannot be made without a Miracle. I dread the Consequences of this Dissimilatude of Character, and without the Utmost Caution on both sides, and the most considerate Forebearance with one another and prudent Condescention on both sides, they will certainly be fatal. An alteration of the Southern Constitutions, which must certainly take Place if this War continues will gradually, bring all the Continent nearer and nearer to each other in all Respects.[171]

Today, we take the unity of our country for granted, but Adams could not. Five months later, in March 1776, he stated his fear that the southern colonies would not be willing to join in a republican government of all the colonies:

However, my dear Friend Gates, all our Misfortunes arise from a Single Source, the Reluctance of the Southern Colonies to Republican Government. The success of this war depends upon a Skillfull Steerage of the political Vessell. The Difficulty lies in forming Constitutions for particular Colonies, and a Continental Constitution for the whole, each Colony should establish its own Government, and then a League should be formed, between them all. This can be done only on popular Principles and Maxims which are so abhorent to the Inclinations of the Barons of the south, and the Proprietery Interests in the Middle Colonies, as well as to that Avarice of Land, which has made upon this Continent so many Votaries to Mammon that I Sometimes dread the Consequences.[172]

Similarly, when James Warren wrote that a bill to free the Negroes had been tabled in the Massachusetts legislature and a letter to Congress on the subject had also been diverted, Adams responded on July 7, 1777: "The Bill for freeing the Negroes, I hope will sleep for a Time. We have Causes enough of Jealousy Discord and Division, and this Bill will certainly add to the Number."[173]

In a recent biography, Ferling writes that both Abigail and John Adams thought slavery to be "immoral and contradictory to Christian principles." But in the same paragraph he also writes: "There is no evidence that he ever spoke out on the issue of slavery in any national forum or that he ever entered into a dialogue on the subject with any of his southern friends."[174] Ferling is correct about the essentially private nature of Adams's comments on slavery.[175] But Ferling is missing an important point: given that Adams and other founders had prioritized their political wish list, and that independence was at the top of that list, speaking out nationally and/or entering a dialogue with southern friends on the issue of slavery was clearly incompatible with the unity necessary to obtain independence.[176] One might wish that different priorities had been possible, but the founders established policies consistent with their perceptions of the reality of the eighteenth century. Those policies must be evaluated in that context, not in late twentieth- or early twenty-first century terms.

Even in the founders' terms, as with the other values, liberty was not absolute. How was individual freedom limited? Did liberty allow the strong to oppress the weak? . . . the rich to rob the poor? One theme of the rest of this work is that America has not developed into the just society of the founders' ideals because the concept of liberty has been carried to a dialectical extreme instead of being applied in a *yin-yang* manner. Another way to state this is that absolute government and limited government are not polar opposites. (The opposite of absolute government is no government, anarchy.) Thus limited government includes a wide range from authoritarian to laissez-faire government. The perennial struggle is to determine the optimum amount of government, and therefore the degree of individual freedom. Liberty, important as it is, should not trump democratic equality.[177]

There is a basic paradox in American society. We believe in individual liberty, but that liberty must be constrained. How can one be both bound and free? One possible resolution to this paradox lies in individual virtue. Our forefathers were convinced that their new system would fail if the people were not virtuous.[178] Let us now consider the virtues needed by democratic citizens.

Notes

1. Some definitions are needed here. "Republic" may be defined as indirect democracy, with the people electing representatives. James Madison wrote: "The two great points of difference between a democracy and a republic are: first, the delegation of the government, in the latter, to a small number of citizens elected by the rest; secondly, the greater number of citizens, and greater sphere of country, over which the latter may be extended" (*Federalist*, #10, Madison, 51-2). One of John Adams's definitions of republic came from classic (Greek and Roman) sources and was simply "a government of laws, and not of men" (Robert J. Taylor, ed., *Papers of John Adams*, 2 [Cambridge: Belknap Press of Harvard University Press, 1977], 314). He also defined a republic, in 1790, as "a government in which the people have collectively, or by representation, an essential share in the sovereignty" (David A. Hollinger and Charles Capper, eds., *The American Intellectual Tradition, A Sourcebook*, 2d ed., 1 [New York: Oxford University Press, 1993], 153).

Washington and Adams connected virtue and morality and thus were very close to the second usage for "virtue" in the Oxford English Dictionary: "Conformity of life and conduct with the principles of morality; voluntary observance of the recognized moral laws or standards of right conduct; abstention on moral grounds from any form of wrong-doing or vice."

2. Norman Cousins, *The Republic of Reason: The Personal Philosophies of the Founding Fathers* (San Francisco: Harper and Row, 1988), 69.

3. John Adams, letter to Abigail Adams, February 27, 1783, in Richard Alan Ryerson, et al., eds., *Adams Family Correspondence*, 5 (Cambridge: Belknap Press of Harvard University Press, 1993), 103.

4. John P. Diggins, *The Lost Soul of American Politics: Virtue, Self-Interest, and the Foundations of Liberalism* (Chicago: University of Chicago Press, 1984), 70.

5. Adrienne Koch and William Peden, eds., *The Selected Writings of John and John Quincy Adams* (New York: Alfred A. Knopf, 1946), 119-20.

6. John Adams, letter to Mercy Otis Warren, January 8, 1776, in Taylor, ed., *Papers*, 3, 397-98.

7. John Quincy Adams and Charles Francis Adams, *John Adams* (New York: Chelsea House, 1980), 2, 111.

8. John Adams, letter to Abigail Adams, July 3, 1776, in L. H. Butterfield, ed., *Adams Family Correspondence,* 2 (Cambridge: Belknap Press of Harvard University Press, 1963), 28.

9. Gilbert Chinard, *Honest John Adams* (Gloucester, Mass.: Peter Smith, 1976), 40.

10. Koch and Peden, eds., *Selected Writings of Adams,* 158.

11. John Adams, diary entry of July 16, 1786, in L. H. Butterfield, ed., *The Adams Papers: Diary and Autobiography of John Adams,* 3 (New York: Atheneum, 1964) , 194.

12. Gordon S. Wood, *The Creation of the American Republic 1776-1787* (Chapel Hill: University of North Carolina Press, for the Institute of Early American History and Culture, 1969), 95.

13. Barry A. Shain, *The Myth of American Individualism: The Protestant Origins of American Political Thought* (Princeton: Princeton University Press, 1994), 193-94; see also Ruth Bloch, *Visionary Republic: Millennial Themes in American Thought, 1756-1800* (Cambridge: Cambridge University Press, 1985), 4.

Those who have criticized Adams as pessimistic about human nature are being a bit unfair; Adams thought he was being realistic about human fallibility. Tocqueville had similar views, according to Diggins, *Lost Soul of American Politics,* 232. Diggins traces Adams's views on the depravity of human nature to his Calvinist background (*Lost Soul of American Politics,* 71). But C. Bradley Thompson, *John Adams and the Spirit of Liberty* (Lawrence: University Press of Kansas, 1998), 149, argues that Adams was not a Calvinist and that he did not see men as "evil, wicked, sinful, or even bad by nature"; for Adams, weakness, not evil, defined human nature. Clinton Rossiter, "The Legacy of John Adams," *Yale Review* 46 (1957): 534-35, agrees; he argues that Adams rejected the "dogma of total depravity" and found men to be a blend of virtues and vices.

Note the comment by Jean Bethke Elshtain, *Democracy on Trial* (New York: Basic Books, 1995), xiii, that "the truth is that evil lurks within. Each of us carries in us the capacity for both goodness and hatred, for both creating community and sowing the seeds of petty strife."

14. Wood, *Creation of American Republic,* 395-96.

15. *Federalist,* #55, 174.

16. Herbert J. Storing, ed., *The Anti-Federalist: An Abridgment, by Murray Dry, of the Complete Anti-Federalist* (Chicago: University of Chicago Press, 1985), 16.

17. Melancton Smith, in Storing, ed., *Anti-Federalist,* 337.

18. Herbert J. Storing, in *Friends of the Constitution; Writings of the "Other" Federalists, 1787-1788,* Colleen A. Sheehan and Gary L. McDowell, eds. (Indianapolis: Liberty Fund, 1998), xlix.

19. See Madison's comments to the Virginia Ratifying Convention in Richard Vetterli and Gary Bryner, *In Search of the Republic: Public Virtue and the Roots of American Government,* rev. ed. (Lanham, Md.: Rowman and Littlefield Publishers,

Inc., 1996), 187. Richard C. Sinopoli, *The Foundations of American Citizenship: Liberalism, the Constitution, and Civic Virtue* (New York: Oxford University Press, 1992), 7, argues that Publius expected most citizens and rulers "to be 'virtuous' most of the time." See also 19-20 and 86, where he writes that Madison and Hamilton relied "on virtue in arguing for the proposed Constitution," which "should lead us to doubt a pure 'possessive individualist' interpretation of these thinkers."

20. Ellis Sandoz, ed., *Political Sermons of the American Founding Era, 1730-1805* (Indianapolis: Liberty Press, 1991), xxiv.

21. Thomas L. Pangle, *The Spirit of Modern Republicanism: The Moral Vision of the American Founders and the Philosophy of Locke* (Chicago: University of Chicago Press, 1988), 94.

22. John Adams, letter to James Warren, July 17, 1774, in Taylor, ed., *Papers*, 2, 109.

23. John A. Schutz and Douglass Adair, eds., *The Spur of Fame: Dialogues of John Adams and Benjamin Rush, 1805-1813* (San Marino, Cal.: Huntington Library, 1966), 153.

24. Joseph J. Ellis, *Passionate Sage: The Character and Legacy of John Adams* (New York: W. W. Norton & Company, 1993), 173.

25. Christopher Jencks, "Varieties of Altruism," in *Beyond Self-Interest,* Jane J. Mansbridge, ed. (Chicago: University of Chicago Press, 1990), 58. Jencks is not alone. Dawes, et al., in Mansbridge, ed., 97-98, present some interesting psychological research that there is a role for traditional morality in individual decisions on how to act within a group. Holmes, also in Mansbridge, 268, argues, in the context of a discussion of Smith's finesse in analyzing the human psyche, that we were impoverished, "sometime in the nineteenth century, when Marxism and liberal economics conspired to assert the supremacy of interest and thus to extinguish an older and subtler tradition of moral psychology." In contrast, Robert L. Heilbroner, "The Socialization of the Individual in Adam Smith," *History of Political Economy* 14 (1982): 427-28 and 436, raises the question whether "a virtuous society, not merely a viable one, can be constituted from the socio-psychological premises on which Smith builds both books" [*Theory of Moral Sentiments* and *Wealth of Nations*]? Thomas L. Pangle, *The Ennobling of Democracy: The Challenge of the Postmodern Era* (Baltimore: Johns Hopkins University Press, 1992), 85-89, seems to support Jencks, Dawes, and Holmes on this point.

26. Charles L. Griswold, Jr., Adam *Smith and the Virtues of Enlightenment* (New York: Cambridge University Press, 1999), 20-21. Similarly, Athol Fitzgibbons, *Adam Smith's System of Liberty, Wealth and Virtue* (Oxford: Clarendon Press, 1995), v, writes: "It will transpire that Smith's main intention was to provide liberalism with a workable moral foundation, and that was his theme even in *The Wealth of Nations.*" See also Fitzgibbons, 153-56, and Noel Parker, "Look, no hidden hands: how Smith understands historical progress and societal values," in *Adam Smith's Wealth of Nations: New Interdisciplinary Essays,* Stephen Copley and Kathryn Sutherland, eds. (Manchester: Manchester University Press, 1995), 143.

27. Pangle, *Spirit of Modern Republicanism*, 2.

28. According to Shain, *Myth of American Individualism,* 249-50, the British jurist Blackstone demonstrated that "life, liberty and property were not individual trumps that could ever be exercised against one's legitimately constituted and sovereign people." Community trumps the individual. See also Shain, 25.

29. Henry F. May, *The Enlightenment in America* (New York: Oxford University Press, 1976), 180.

30. Robert N. Bellah, et al., *Habits of the Heart: Individualism and Commitment in American Life* (New York: Harper and Row, 1985), 222.

31. Cousins, *Republic of Reason*, 69; also in John G. West, Jr., *The Politics of Revelation and Reason: Religion and Civic Life in the New Nation* (Lawrence: University Press of Kansas, 1996), 38.

32. West, *Politics of Revelation*, 37.

33. Sandoz, ed., *Political Sermons*, passim.

34. Sandoz, ed., *Political Sermons*, 804-05.

35. Diggins, *Lost Soul of American Politics*, 59.

36. Paul K. Conkin, *Puritans and Pragmatists: Eight Eminent American Thinkers* (New York: Dodd, Mead & Company, 1968), 109. If you are ever in Quincy, Massachusetts, you might enjoy a brief excursion to the Church of the Presidents, on Hancock Street in the center of Quincy. The Adams crypt contains the remains of the second and sixth presidents, and their wives; this is the only site where two United States presidents are buried side by side.

37. Adam Smith, *The Theory of Moral Sentiments,* 6th ed., D. D. Raphael and A. L. Macfie, eds. (Oxford: Oxford University Press, 1976), *19* and 400.

38. For Adams, see Shain, *Myth of American Individualism,* 196; for Smith, see Fitzgibbons, *Smith's System of Liberty,* 94. Ian Simpson Ross, *The Life of Adam Smith* (Oxford: Oxford University Press, 1995), 340, characterizes Smith's moral philosophy as theistic. Adams abhorred the idea of the perfectibility of man; if May, *Enlightenment in America,* 231, is correct that that idea is a central doctrine of deism, Adams could not logically be called deistic.

39. Thomas E. McCullough, *The Moral Imagination and Public Life: Raising the Ethical Question* (Chatham, N.J.: Chatham House Publishers, Inc., 1991), 37. Smith believed that "the laws of society were to be derived from morals" and "that the knowledge of good and evil ultimately emanated from God" (Fitzgibbons, *Smith's System of Liberty,* 37).

40. John Adams, "A Dissertation on the Canon and the Feudal Law," in Taylor, ed., *Papers,* 1, 115.

41. Zoltan Haraszti, *John Adams and the Prophets of Progress* (New York: Grosset and Dunlap, Universal Library, 1964), 61.

42. John Adams, letter to Zabdiel Adams, June 21, 1776, in Butterfield, ed., *Adams Family Correspondence,* 2, 21 (ellipsis in document).

43. Schutz and Adair, eds., *Spur of Fame,* 191-92.

44. Lorraine Smith Pangle and Thomas L. Pangle, *The Learning of Liberty: The Educational Ideas of the American Founders* (Lawrence: University Press of Kansas, 1993), 193-94.

45. West, *Politics of Revelation*, 15.

46. Of course, the importance of religion to American democracy was clear to Tocqueville in the 1830s; see Robert P. Kraynak, "Tocqueville's Constitutionalism," *American Political Science Review* 81 (December 1987): 1194. This point is developed below.

47. Bloch, *Visionary Republic*, ix-xiii.

48. Bloch, *Visionary Republic*, 93 and passim.

49. Ellis Sandoz, *A Government of Laws: Political Theory, Religion, and the American Founding* (Baton Rouge: Louisiana State University Press, 1990), 100.

50. Shain, *Myth of American Individualism*, 195.

51. Vetterli and Bryner, *In Search of the Republic*, 47.

52. Sandoz, *Political Sermons*, 369, states that "over 80 percent of the politically relevant pamphlets" of that era were reprinted sermons or essays by ministers. Other estimates put the figure, much lower, at about one-third (Vetterli and Bryner, *In Search of the Republic*, 241), but that is still a large religious impact. For just one brief example of such sermonizing for the revolution, Abraham Keteltas, "God Arising and Pleading His People's Cause,' in *Political Sermons*, Sandoz, ed., 595, argued that America's fight against Great Britain was "the cause of God." Many Americans agreed with Keteltas.

53. Sandoz, *Political Sermons*, xiv, calls the clergy the "philosophers of the American founding." Shain, *Myth of American Individualism*, xiii-xvi and passim, discusses the three strands of thought and, throughout his book, emphasizes the reformed Protestant intellectual foundations of the young republic. Sandoz, *Government of Laws*, 23, states that any narrowing of the founders' thought to any one "controlling factor is almost certainly misleading if not distorted." Jurgen Gebhardt, *Americanism: Revolutionary Order and Societal Self-Interpretation in the American Republic*, Ruth Hein, trans. (Baton Rouge: Louisiana State University Press, 1993), 106-07, discusses the "radical Protestant dimension of revolutionary republicanism" which was, he writes, typical of leaders as well as "the middle and lower levels of the population." See also Vetterli and Bryner, *In Search of the Republic*, 4-14, and Joyce Appleby, *Liberalism and Republicanism in the Historical Imagination* (Cambridge: Harvard University Press, 1992), 225 and passim. Ronald Takaki, *Iron Cages: Race and Culture in 19th-Century America* (New York: Oxford University Press, 1990), ix-x, discusses the republican and Protestant strands in American social thinking. Sinopoli, *Foundations of American Citizenship*, 4-5 and 40-41, indirectly argues for three strands when he emphasizes the theological component of Locke's writing. But Diggins, *Lost Soul of American Politics*, 16-17, argues that the Christian values were deemphasized after the Revolution.

54. Michael P. Zuckert, "Locke and the Problem of Civil Religion," in *The Moral Foundations of the American Republic,* 3d ed., Robert H. Horwitz, ed. (Charlottesville: University of Virginia Press, 1986), 181.

55. Bellah, *Habits of the Heart,* 223.

56. Diggins, *Lost Soul of American Politics,* 47.

57. Diggins, *Lost Soul of American Politics,* 80, has a differentiated view of religion; he is aware of the positive aspects of universal, non-coerced religion, but critical of the zealotry of doctrinaire, sectarian religion. Also, note Pangle, *Ennobling of Democracy,* 85-86, on Montesquieu's castigation of "the politically destructive moral fanaticism of both religious and atheistic zealots." Still, Montesquieu realized that "no just and humane society could do without a properly tempered religious consciousness."

58. John Adams, letter to John Wentworth, September 1756, in Taylor, ed., *Papers,* 1, 19; see also John Adams, letter to Charles Cushing, October 19, 1756, also in Taylor, ed., *Papers,* 1, 21-22.

59. See Ross, *Life of Adam Smith,* 59, for the bigoted religious climate which Smith most probably observed in Glasgow.

60. *Federalist,* #10, 51.

61. *Federalist,* #51, 163.

62. Sinopoli, *Foundations of American Citizenship,* 96.

63. Griswold, *Smith and Enlightenment,* 280; see also 275-79.

64. Schutz and Adair, eds., *Spur of Fame,* 160.

65. West, *Politics of Revelation,* 39.

66. Steven Forde, "Benjamin Franklin's *Autobiography* and the Education of America," *American Political Science Review* 86 (June 1992): 360.

67. See, for example, Samuel Sherwood, "The Church's Flight into the Wilderness," in Sandoz, ed., *Political Sermons,* 498-99.

68. Elisha Williams, "The Essential Rights and Liberties of Protestants," in Sandoz, ed., *Political Sermons,* 55.

69. John Witherspoon, "The Dominion of Providence over the Passions of Men," in Sandoz, ed., *Political Sermons,* 553-54.

70. Worthington Chauncey Ford, ed., *Statesman and Friend: Correspondence of John Adams with Benjamin Waterhouse, 1784-1822* (Boston: Little, Brown, and Company, 1927), 15.

71. Ford, ed., *Statesman and Friend,* 120.

72. Conkin, *Puritans and Pragmatists,* 109.

73. What Adams suggests is very close to Richard Price's statement that "virtue without knowledge makes enthusiasts; and knowledge without virtue makes devils" (Richard Price, "A Discourse on the Love of Our Country," in *Political Sermons,* Sandoz, ed., 1014). Price was the Adams's family minister when they were in England and a close friend, according to Lynne Withey, *Dearest Friend: A Life of Abigail Adams* (New York: Free Press, 1981), 184. Note Mitchell's argument that Hobbes's vision did not require reason to countermand

revelation, but to *"clear away* false religion so that the true religion may take its rightful place as reason's necessary *supplement"* (Joshua Mitchell, *Not by Reason Alone: Religion, History, and Identity in Early Modern Political Thought* [Chicago: University of Chicago Press, 1993], 47-48).

74. John Adams, letter to Isaac Smith, Sr., May 16, 1780, in L. H. Butterfield and Marc Friedlaender, eds., *Adams Family Correspondence,* 3 (Cambridge: Belknap Press of Harvard University Press, 1973), 349.

75. See, for example, Adam Smith, *An Inquiry into the Nature and Causes of the Wealth of Nations,* R. H. Campbell and A. S. Skinner, eds. (Oxford: Oxford University Press, 1976), V.i.f.61 and V.i.g.1, 788.

76. Griswold, *Smith and Enlightenment,* 237-38 and 273.

77. Griswold, *Smith and Enlightenment,* 194-95.

78. Smith, *Wealth of Nations,* V.i.g.14, 796.

79. Smith, *Wealth of Nations,* V.i.g.15, 796.

80. Griswold, *Smith and Enlightenment,* 151.

81. Schutz and Adair, ed., *Spur of Fame,* 51-52.

82. Schutz and Adair, ed., *Spur of Fame,* 51-52.

83. Ford, ed., *Statesman and Friend,* 123.

84. Appleby, *Liberalism and Republicanism,* 304, has this explanation for Jefferson's substitution of "pursuit of happiness" for "property"; he insisted, she writes, that governments "did not exist to protect property but rather to promote access to property or, more broadly speaking, opportunity."

Without detracting one iota from the grandeur of Jefferson's prose in the Declaration, most analysts agree that the ideas therein were widely shared among the signers. In other words, Jefferson probably did not originate many of the ideas. The committee asked Jefferson to write the document because of his acknowledged facility as a writer.

85. Henry Steele Commager, *Jefferson, Nationalism and the Enlightenment* (New York: George Braziller, 1975), 106.

86. Henry Steele Commager, in Daniel J. Boorstin, ed., *An American Primer* (New York: Penguin Books, 1966), 92.

87. John Adams, "Thoughts on Government," April 1776, in Robert J. Taylor, ed., *Papers of John Adams,* 4 (Cambridge: Belknap Press of Harvard University Press, 1979), 86.

88. Smith, *Theory of Moral Sentiments,* III.5.7, 166.

89. John Adams, "Fragmentary Notes for 'A Dissertation on the Canon and the Feudal Law,'" May-August, 1765, in Taylor, ed., *Papers,* 1, 107.

90. Lester J. Cappon, ed., *The Adams-Jefferson Letters: The Complete Correspondence between Thomas Jefferson and Abigail and John Adams,* 2 (Chapel Hill: University of North Carolina Press, for the Institute of Early American History and Culture, 1959), 492.

91. Israel Evans, "A Sermon Delivered at the Annual Election," in Sandoz, ed., *Political Sermons,* 1074.

92. Shain, *Myth of American Individualism,* 248.

93. Storing, ed., *Anti-Federalist,* 146.

94. Griswold, *Smith and Enlightenment,* 128 and 225.

95. Robert E. Lane, *The Market Experience* (Cambridge: Cambridge University Press, 1991), 527-28, presents a long list of research results demonstrating that money does not buy happiness.

96. Robert H. Webking, *The American Revolution and the Politics of Liberty* (Baton Rouge: Louisiana State University Press, 1988), 44.

97. Pauline Maier, *The Old Revolutionaries: Political Lives in the Age of Samuel Adams* (New York: Random House, 1980), 27.

98. John Adams, letter to Abigail Adams, July 7, 1774, in Butterfield, ed., *Adams Family Correspondence,* 1, 130-31.

99. Plato, *The Dialogues of Plato,* Benjamin Jowett, trans. (Chicago: Encyclopaedia Britannica, Inc., 1952), 728-29.

100. Wood, *Creation of American Republic,* 52-53.

101. The revolutionary generation was hostile to the theater, based on arguments that plays had a large role in corrupting the Athenian republic. Ann Fairfax Withington, *Toward a More Perfect Union: Virtue and the Formation of American Republics* (New York: Oxford University Press, 1991), 21-37 and 199.

102. John Adams, letter to Abigail Adams, September 8, 1777, in Butterfield, ed., 2, *Adams Family Correspondence,* 338. Adams's view here is entirely consistent with the statement by John Witherspoon that "general profligacy" could destroy a nation (in Sandoz, ed., *Political Sermons,* 553).

103. John Adams, letter to Abigail Adams, April 12, 1778, in Butterfield and Friedlaender, eds., *Adams Family Correspondence,* 3, 9-10.

104. John Adams, letter to Abigail Adams, June 3, 1778, in Butterfield and Friedlaender, eds., *Adams Family Correspondence,* 3, 32.

105. John Adams, Autobiography, in Butterfield, ed., *Diary and Autobiography,* 4, 123.

106. Withington, *Toward a More Perfect Union,* 85 and 87.

107. Paul C. Nagel, *The Adams Women: Abigail and Louise Adams, Their Sisters and Daughters* (New York: Oxford University Press, 1987), 281.

108. Linda K. Kerber, *Women of the Republic: Intellect and Ideology in Revolutionary America* (Chapel Hill: University of North Carolina Press, for the Institute of Early American History and Culture, 1980), 229.

109. For examples, see John Adams, letters to Abigail Adams, December 18, 1780, and to John Quincy Adams, May 18, 1781, in Butterfield and Friedlaender, eds., *Adams Family Correspondence,* 4, 56, and 117.

110. For examples, see John Adams, letters to "Nabby" Adams, September 26, 1782, in Butterfield and Friedlaender, eds., *Adams Family Correspondence,* 4, 384, and August 14, 1783, in Ryerson, ed., *Adams Family Correspondence,* 5, 224.

111. Burton Spivak, "Thomas Jefferson, Republican Values, and Foreign Commerce," in *Traditions and Values: American Diplomacy, 1790-1865*, Norman A. Graebner, ed. (New York: University Press of America, 1985), 36-38.

112. Spivak, "Jefferson, Republican Values," in *Traditions and Values*, Graebner, ed., 36-37.

113. Michael Lienesch, *New Order of the Ages: Time, the Constitution, and the Making of Modern American Political Thought* (Princeton: Princeton University Press, 1988), 51-52.

114. But Keith Tribe, "Natural liberty and *laissez faire:* how Adam Smith became a free trade ideologue," in *New Interdisciplinary Essays*, Copley and Sutherland, eds., 29-30, states that Jefferson, Franklin, and Madison drew freely on Smith's writing in the 1780s and 1790s.

115. Smith, *Wealth of Nations*, IV.vii.c.61, 612-13.

116. Smith, *Theory of Moral Sentiments*, I.iii.3.1, 61-62. Similarly, a contemporary critic of neoclassical economics, Amitai Etzioni, *The Moral Dimension, Toward a New Economics* (New York: Free Press, 1988), 53, argues that, to explain increases in savings rates, one must go beyond the economic factors emphasized by neoclassical economists to include moral values.

117. Michael Merrill and Sean Wilentz, eds., *The Key of Liberty: The Life and Democratic Writings of William Manning, "A Laborer," 1747-1814* (Cambridge: Harvard University Press, 1993), 131.

118. Thompson, *Adams and the Spirit of Liberty*, 63.

119. John Adams, letter to Patrick Henry, June 3, 1776, in Taylor, ed., *Papers*, 4, 235. Such egalitarianism was evident in American treatment of the Enlightenment's elitist notion of progress: "Americans . . . democratized and vulgarized the idea. Progress was the welfare of the common man: it was not merely something to delight members of the academies or the courts; it was something to lift the standards of living" (Commager, *Jefferson, Nationalism*, 113). Historically, the United States has been seen as a land of abundance for all, not just for the rich: "We take that for granted, but remember that emigration literature . . . for a hundred years was to exclaim in amazement that Americans ate meat every day, that there was milk enough for the children, that there was white bread on the table" (Commager, *Jefferson, Nationalism*, 150).

120. Quoted by Wilson Carey McWilliams, "On Equality as the Moral Foundation for Community," in *Moral Foundations*, Horwitz, ed., 300-301.

121. Wood, *Creation of American Republic*, 70-71.

122. John R. Nelson, Jr., *Liberty and Property: Political Economy and Policymaking in the New Nation, 1789-1812* (Baltimore: Johns Hopkins University Press, 1987), 104 and 204.

123. John Adams, *A Defence of the Constitutions of Government of the United States of America* [1787] in *The Political Writings of John Adams: Representative Selections*, George A. Peek, Jr., ed. (Indianapolis: Bobbs-Merrill Co., Inc., 1954), 133-34.

124. Adams and Adams, *John Adams*, 2, 161-62.

125. Gregory Vlastos, quoted in Richard Dagger, *Civic Virtues: Rights, Citizenship, and Republican Liberalism* (New York: Oxford University Press, 1997), 27, notes that, in discussions of equality, human worth and human merit are often confused. Adams understood this somewhat but his analysis of this reality did not make him popular in egalitarian America.

126. Elshtain, *Democracy on Trial*, 126.

127. Samuel Miller, "A Sermon on the Anniversary of the Independence of America," in *Political Sermons*, Sandoz, ed., 1156.

128. John Adams, letter to Samuel Quincy, April 22, 1761, in Taylor, ed., *Papers*, 1, 50.

129. Wood, *Creation of American Republic*, 286.

130. Gordon S. Wood, *The Radicalism of the American Revolution* (New York: Alfred A. Knopf, 1992), 234.

131. Wood, *Radicalism of the American Revolution*, 238-39.

132. Griswold, *Smith and Enlightenment*, 199-200.

133. Pangle, *Ennobling of Democracy*, 93; Benjamin R. Barber, "Liberal Democracy and the Costs of Consent," in *Liberalism and the Moral Life*, Nancy L. Rosenblum, ed. (Cambridge: Harvard University Press, 1989), 55, writes: "Rather than permitting democracy to complement liberty, liberty has been given lexical priority over all other principles." I examine this conflict in greater detail in chapter 7.

134. See Paul K. Longmore, *The Invention of George Washington* (Berkeley: University of California Press, 1988), 171-72, for the centrality of the fear of power to American revolutionary thought. While the revolutionaries proposed institutional checks to control power, they also argued that such checks would fail if not supported by public virtue.

135. James M. McPherson, *Abraham Lincoln and the Second American Revolution* (New York: Oxford University Press, 1990), 135. Shain, *Myth of American Individualism*, 317, makes the same point with different words; liberty faced formidable enemies: tyranny and licentiousness.

136. Isaac Backus, "An Appeal to the Public For Religious Liberty," in *Political Sermons*, Sandoz, ed., 334.

137. Moses Mather, "America's Appeal to the Impartial World," in *Political Sermons*, Sandoz, ed., 486.

138. Bellah, *Habits of the Heart*, 28-29.

139. That the Puritans promptly denied religious freedom to Quakers, Baptists, and other heretics points out the danger of religious excess.

140. Shain, *Myth of American Individualism*, 118-19. Joyce Appleby, *Capitalism and a New Social Order: The Republican Vision of the 1790s* (New York: New York University Press, 1984), 16 and 18, states that the most common meaning of liberty in the revolutionary era emphasized community. Further, the least familiar concept of liberty for that age was the common definition today—personal freedom.

141. Koch and Peden, ed., *Selected Writings of Adams*, 208.

142. For other examples, see Isaac Backus and Moses Mather, in *Political Sermons,* Sandoz, ed., 331 and 486; and Fisher Ames, John Dickinson, Noah Webster, and James Wilson in Sheehan and McDowell, eds., *Friends of the Constitution,* 198, 222, 396, and 507.

143. Shain, *Myth of American Individualism,* 166 and passim.

144. Jerry Z. Muller, *Adam Smith: In His Time and Ours* (Princeton: Princeton University Press, 1993), 203.

145. John Adams [*Boston Gazette* letters], January 27, 1766, in Taylor, ed., *Papers,* 1, 167-68.

146. Schutz and Adair, eds., *Spur of Fame,* 104. Consistent with his dissatisfaction with the development of American politics, in the same letter Adams also wrote that liberty "has changed its meaning and signifies [in 1808] money, electioneering, tricks, and libels, and perhaps protection of French armies and British fleets." In short, Adams felt that Americans had not heeded his advice, resulting in problems for both domestic politics and foreign relations.

147. Shain, *Myth of American Individualism,* 241 and 255.

148. Agrippa, in Storing, ed., *Anti-Federalist,* 230.

149. But for modern human beings, there is a huge irony here. Liberty was seen by the founders as supportive of virtues necessary for work. But, if liberty also means equal opportunity to develop one's potential, the American emphasis on the liberty of the corporation as individual conflicts with the liberty of the person as an individual. As Richard Ashcraft, "Class Conflict and Constitutionalism in J. S. Mill's Thought," in *Liberalism and the Moral Life,* Rosenblum, ed., 124, points out, the individuality destroying effects of government bureaucracy, which John Stuart Mill analyzed, apply equally to corporate bureaucracies.

150. Bloch, *Visionary Republic,* 61.

Agrippa was arguing about the proposed Constitution. Abraham Keteltas presented a similar argument in a sermon given in Newburyport in 1777, in which he stated that "Liberty is the grand fountain, under God, of every temporal blessing" and that "it is favorable to the propagation of unadulterated Christianity." Further, he said that "if liberty is thus friendly to the happiness of mankind, and is the cause of the kind parent of the universe; certainly tyranny & oppression are the cause of the devil, the cause which God's soul hates" (Abraham Keteltas, "God Arising and Pleading His People's Cause," in *Political Sermons,* Sandoz, ed., 597-98). For another example, see Sandoz, *Government of Laws,* 153.

151. Wood, *Radicalism of the American Revolution,* 104.

152. Sheehan and McDowell, eds., *Friends of the Constitution,* 153.

153. Bloch, *Visionary Republic,* 84-85 and 230-31, writes of the American revolutionary "universalistic millennial vision" and states that the theme of America "struggling on the behalf of 'all mankind' pervaded revolutionary rhetoric."

154. See, for example, "A Proclamation by the General Court" (in John Adams's hand), January 19, 1776, in Taylor, ed., *Papers,* 3, 385.

155. John Adams, "A Dissertation on the Canon and the Feudal Law," in Taylor, ed., *Papers*, 1, 120-21.

156. John Adams, "A Dissertation," in Taylor, ed., *Papers*, 1, 120-21.

157. Adams was not alone in connecting liberty and education. Moses Mather, preaching in 1775, argued that free government required virtue, which required knowledge and that required education. Further, a free government was incompatible with slavery which he defined as a state of ignorance (in *Political Sermons*, Sandoz, ed., 487-88).

158. Wood, *Radicalism of the American Revolution*, 186-87.

159. Bloch, *Visionary Republic*, 106 and 258. Northern religious leaders connected slavery and the Antichrist in the mid-1770s (Bloch, 100).

160. Wood, *Radicalism of the American Revolution*, 368-69.

161. Abigail and John Adams inherited her father's slaves, whom they promptly freed. That she and John both had a strong aversion to slavery is evident in the vignette Withey relates of Abigail's support for the education of a black servant at a neighborhood school, in the face of some prejudice (Withey, *Dearest Friend*, 246; see also 277).

162. Griswold, *Smith and Enlightenment*, 12-13.

163. Smith, *Wealth of Nations*, I.viii.41, 99; see also III.ii.9, 387-88.

164. Koch and Peden, eds., *Selected Writings of Adams*, 209-10.

165. See the exchange of letters between Abigail and John Adams, dated March 31, 1776, April 14, 1776, and May 7, 1776, in Butterfield, ed., 1, *Adams Family Correspondence*, 370, 382-83, and 402, for this letter and responses. Abigail Adams's concern was to remove the absolute power men held over their wives, power inherited from English laws. What she wanted for women was very important, but hardly radical: education and improved legal and social status, so that women could be better wives and mothers (Withey, *Dearest Friend*, 81-82 and 196). If Mary Wollstonecraft (whom Abigail read and appreciated) is right that the unnatural distinctions in society between men and women "corrupt social relationships and inhibit the development of virtue" (Virginia Sapiro, *A Vindication of Political Virtue: The Political Theory of Mary Wollstonecraft* [Chicago: University of Chicago Press, 1992], 118), then the founders exacerbated the problem of a dearth of citizen virtue by not attacking the gender inequality which contributed to that shortage.

166. John Adams, letter to Abigail Adams, February 13, 1779, in Butterfield and Friedlaender, eds., *Adams Family Correspondence*, 3, 170.

167. Ellis, *Passionate Sage*, 74.

168. John Adams, letter to James Warren, September 26, 1775, in Taylor, ed., *Papers*, 3, 168.

169. John Adams, letter to Abigail Adams, August 11, 1777, in Butterfield, ed., 2, *Adams Family Correspondence*, 306.

170. Ellis, *Passionate Sage*, 186-87.

171. John Adams, letter to Joseph Hawley, November 25, 1775, in Taylor, ed., *Papers*, 3, 316.

172. John Adams, letter to Horatio Gates, March 23, 1776, in Taylor, ed., *Papers*, 4, 59-60.

173. Exchange of letters between James Warren and John Adams dated June 22, 1777, and July 7, 1777, in Taylor, ed., *Papers*, 5, 231, and 242.

174. John Ferling, *John Adams: A Life* (Knoxville: University of Tennessee Press, 1992), 172-73.

175. See also Frederick M. Binder, *The Color Problem in Early National America as Viewed by John Adams, Jefferson and Jackson* (The Hague: Mouton, 1968), 18 and 20-21.

176. Ellis, *Passionate Sage*, 217-18, also states that Adams feared that dealing with the slavery issue at the Continental Congress "would subvert the national co-operation necessary for success in the revolution."

Even though political prudence required avoiding the issues of slavery and inequality of women, that has not prevented some from labeling the American creed hypocritical because of failure to live up to egalitarian ideals; Rogers M. Smith, "Beyond Tocqueville, Myrdal, and Hartz: The Multiple Traditions in America," *American Political Science Review* 87 (September 1993): 587.

177. In this context, it is important to note Holmes's warning about a common error in constitutional theory: "the view that the primary or even sole purpose of a constitution is to secure individual liberty by hamstringing the government and its agents"; in Stephen Holmes, *Passions and Constraint: On the Theory of Liberal Democracy* (Chicago: University of Chicago Press, 1995), 101. He made this comment while discussing state power to control religious fanaticism.

178. A modern political theorist says basically the same thing when he argues: "The liberal state must by definition be broadly tolerant, yet it cannot be wholly indifferent to the character of its citizens" (William A. Galston, "Liberal Virtues," *American Political Science Review* 82 [December 1988]: 1279).

Chapter Three

Virtues for Democratic Citizens

Our founders came from diverse backgrounds and represented different economic interests but shared a concern that both citizens and leaders be virtuous. The father of modern capitalism agreed with the revolutionaries. According to Adam Smith, the reward for industry, prudence, and circumspection was "Success in every sort of business." Truth, justice, and humanity had a different reward: confidence, esteem, and love. "It is not in being rich that truth and justice would rejoice, but in being trusted and believed, recompenses which those virtues must almost always acquire."[1] So, what virtues did our founders believe democratic citizens needed?

Leaders' Virtues

Several of the founding fathers provide us with detailed lists of virtues to be expected of and vices to be avoided by republican citizens and leaders. In some cases, these lists are the analysis of a leader by an observer or an historian; in other cases, the leader himself reflected on the necessary virtues.

One of the earliest revolutionary leaders was Samuel Adams, who chose politics over the ministry. Contemporary Americans may not accept his ascetic values (he was rather puritanical in his personal habits), but he had virtues worthy of emulation. He saw politics as "akin to a religious vocation" and believed that "there was great moral content in the cause of 'Liberty and Truth.'" For Sam Adams, virtue "implied austerity, a 'Sobriety of Manners . . . Temperance, Frugality, Fortitude,' but above all a willingness to sacrifice private advantage for the cause of the community, to subject the self to a greater cause."[2] Many cynics today will read with incredulity that he saw politics as a truthful, moral vocation. Note also that "religious vocation" had (and still has) a connotation that the Almighty is directing one to a particular career.

John Adams characterized his cousin Sam Adams as "always for Softness and Delicacy, and Prudence where they will do . . . but rigid and inflexible, in the Cause." John Adams also wrote of his cousin:

> Adams I believe has the most thorough Understanding of Liberty, and her Resources, in the Temper and Character of the People, tho not in the Law and Constitution, as well as the most habitual, radical Love of it, of any of them—as well as the most correct, genteel and artful Pen. He is a Man of refined Policy, stedfast Integrity, exquisite Humanity, genteel Erudition, obliging, engaging Manners, real as well as professed Piety, and a universal good Character, unless it should be admitted that he is too attentive to the Public and not enough so, to himself and his family.[3]

This hardly fits the radical image of Sam Adams that has come down to us in some versions of American history. Note also the balance John Adams expected. One should serve the public, but one also had personal responsibilities to family. John observed this problem in his cousin's activism, but throughout his own career he himself had difficulty balancing the two.

No grouping of "virtues of the founders" would be complete without George Washington. Wood writes of Washington's fixation on his reputation, which seems egotistical and obsessive to contemporary Americans; but Washington's contemporaries understood him because they believed reputation led to honor and fame, which most of the founders sought. Because of his concern about his reputation as a virtuous leader, he was very sensitive to criticism. He did not want to appear to be "base, mean, avaricious, or unduly ambitious." According to Jefferson, he was deeply concerned about maintaining a reputation for disinterestedness.[4] In addition to disinterest, George Washington embodied the classical ideals of duty, courage, honor, seriousness, manliness, and glory.[5]

In his *Autobiography*, Benjamin Franklin listed thirteen virtues: temperance, silence, order, resolution, frugality, industry, sincerity, justice, moderation, cleanliness, tranquillity, chastity, and humility. He attributed many benefits in his own life to these virtues: health, wealth, a good reputation which, in turn, led his fellow citizens to entrust him with public office; he credited "to the joint Influence of the whole Mass of the Virtues, even in the imperfect State he was able to acquire them, all that Evenness of Temper, & that Cheerfulness in Conversation which makes his Company still sought for, & agreeable even to his younger Acquaintance."[6]

Several years after the end of the Revolutionary War, John Adams noted thirteen virtues in his diary.

> In all Countries, and in all Companies for several Years, I have in Conversation and in Writing, enumerated The Towns, Militia, Schools and Churches as the four Causes of the Grouth and Defence of N. England. The Virtues and Talents of the People are there formed. Their Temperance,

Patience, Fortitude, Prudence, and Justice, as well as their Sagacity, Knowledge, Judgment, Taste, Skill, Ingenuity, Dexterity, and Industry.[7]

Notice the societal sources of virtues: towns, the militia, schools, churches. Throughout the *Adams Family Correspondence* and *Papers of John Adams* series, Adams mentioned other virtues: honesty, honor, benevolence, magnanimity, charity, frugality, simplicity, piety, and ambition. These were more than matters of individual behavior; the founders saw many of these virtues as imperative for the survival of a democratic society.

Throughout his writings, Adams also criticizes a long list of vices: ambition, luxury, corruption, venality, vanity, pride, envy, lying, hypocrisy, sloth, flattery, cruelty, lust, and cowardice. He listed ambition both as a virtue and a vice. He was very much aware of his own passion for distinction; he argued that this passion was "one of the earliest as well as keenest dispositions discovered in the heart of man."[8] He emphasized pride as a crucial aspect of human nature; Peek argues that this concept came largely from Adam Smith's *The Theory of Moral Sentiments* and also states that this was "an expression, in part, of the 'climate of opinion' of 18th and early 19th century America and Europe."[9] Adams was aware that this passion was a two-edged sword. He struggled with this issue throughout his life; he was ambitious and he knew that ambition could be dangerous.

> The principle of Republican Government, is as little understood in America, as its Spirit is felt. Ambition in a Republic, is a great Virtue, for it is nothing more than a Desire, to Serve the Public, to promote the Happiness of the People, to increase the Wealth, the Grandeur, and Prosperity of the Community. This, Ambition is but another Name for public Virtue, and public Spirit. But the Ambition which has Power for its object, which desires to increase the Wealth, the Grandeur, and the Glory of an Individual, at the Expence of the Community, is a very heinous Vice.[10]

The passion for distinction was the virtue of emulation when it was "simply a desire to excel another, by fair industry." But Adams knew it could change from a virtue to a vice, as ambition became jealousy, envy, vanity, or a lust for power.[11]

Adams also felt that too little ambition could be a vice:

> I wish our Uncle [Norton Quincy] has as much Ambition as he has Virtue and Ability. A Deficiency of Ambition is as criminal and injurious as an Excess of it.—Tell him I say so.—How shall We contrive to make so wise and good a Man ambitious? Is it not a sin to be so modest.[12]

Perhaps the uncle was not contributing as much as Adams thought he could to the common good. Liberty has its responsibilities. For John Adams, too little ambition was a vice; the wrong kinds of ambition were also vicious; but ambition to serve the public was virtuous.[13]

Jefferson recommended several virtues to Peter Carr, in a letter dated August 10, 1787: "above all things lose no occasion of exercising your dispositions to be grateful, to be generous, to be charitable, to be humane, to be true, just, firm, orderly, couragious, &c."[14] Since Jefferson believed that man was born for society, these were not purely individual virtues; all had community connotations.

James Madison discussed the republican virtues of patriotism and love of justice in *Federalist # 10*, and contrasted these virtues with the vice of partiality, of faction.[15] Madison also was concerned about war, which he feared would reinforce vice: "The pursuit of 'national splendor and glory' . . . ought never to be our primary objective because war appeals to, and generously rewards, the strongest passions, avarice and ambition, as well as the most dangerous weaknesses of human nature, and links them in the use of force."[16] Adams disagreed with Madison on this. He feared that if a republic were at peace too long, the people would lose their virtue. Ironically, Adams kept the United States out of war during his Presidency, but Madison's first term included the War of 1812.[17]

What can we make of all these lists? First, several of the items are mentioned on only one list; of these, many have more to do with individual character building, such as "taste" on Adams's list, than with civic virtue. (That does not detract from their importance; but it does remove them from our concern.) One item, chastity, was mentioned by a notoriously unchaste leader (which leads to the caveats, below, on the self-promotional and misleading uses of virtue). But four clusters of virtues require examination because of their importance for any democratic polity: moderation-temperance; public spirit-disinterest; universalism; and justice.

Moderation-Temperance

The classical origin of moderation can be seen in Adam Smith's discussion of Aristotle: virtue "lies in a kind of middle between two opposite vices, of which the one offends from being too much, the other from being too little affected by a particular species of objects." As an example, Smith cited magnanimity, which avoided the opposite vices of arrogance and pusillanimity.[18] In the same section as this quotation Smith explicitly tied moderation to reason. Pangle also shows the classical origins of the relationship between reason and passion; he argues that the virtues require "strong support from the sanctions of law, custom, and community opinion." And he lists four "cardinal" virtues: "courage, moderation (meaning especially the proper subordination of the sensual appetites), justice (meaning especially reverence for law, unselfish sharing, and public spirit), and practical wisdom (especially in assisting one's friends and fellow citizens, and taking supervisory care of one's inferiors)."[19] Note that development of virtues requires significant governmental and societal support.

In classical usage, moderation was an antonym of dissipation, and thus meant the tempering of passion by reason. This introduces a community element in that, while individuals reason, individual reasoning does not take place in a vacuum; myriad community factors contribute to the socialization of individuals. Reason is ordinarily based on perceptual systems and norms of logic developed in one's community over many centuries. For example, dialectics and *yin-yang* are different types of perceptual systems from different civilizations.

One such community element is religion. Preaching on Independence Day in 1793, Samuel Miller stated that Christianity requires "temperance and moderation" and that these are important for "political happiness."[20] On the other hand, religious adherents are not always moderate in their actions; many of the founders wanted to control the excesses of religious enthusiasm as well as the political variety. The revolutionary era showed John Adams the importance of taming the excesses of the citizens. The shared concern of Samuel and John Adams, that property be attacked only for just cause, only if there were no other recourse to protect fundamental rights, has already been discussed (in "Property, or the Pursuit of Happiness"). In addition, note what the son and grandson, in their biography of John Adams, reported as his reaction to the Stamp Act riots:

> He perceived, not without serious reflection and concern, even the enthusiasm excited by his own draft of instructions to the representative of the town of Braintree, and he saw that among the most difficult and dangerous of the patriotic duties which he would be called to discharge, that of resisting, and moderating, and controlling the excesses of the people, even in the cause to which he was himself devoted, would become, perhaps, not unfrequently indispensable.
>
> . . . he saw that the end of all popular movements of violence was destruction, and that they were ill adapted, under any circumstances whatever, to the furtherance of justice.[21]

In short, Adams and many colonial leaders feared that popular enthusiasm for the revolution would lead to unrestrained violence which would harm the independence movement. Thus, many revolutionary leaders wanted to maintain order. The revolution would be counter-productive if it went beyond ousting the British.[22]

Furthermore, Adams was convinced that enthusiasm for party or faction could undermine the foundation of morals and mankind's regard for the truth. (Enthusiasm had much more negative connotations for our founders than it has for Americans today.) His relatives report that Adams

> observed that party spirit "seemed to have wrought an entire metamorphosis of the human character. It destroyed all sense and understanding; all equity and humanity; all memory and regard to truth; all virtue, honor, decorum, and veracity." A profound moral sense, a firm unyielding temper, and an

assiduous application to the science of ethics, preserved him from the contamination which he so energetically describes.[23]

In short, the virtue of moderation was needed to counter the vice of enthusiasm, of whatever variety.

Public Spirit-Disinterest

George Washington left the comforts of his plantation for the rigors of serving as Commander-in-Chief; he refused to accept a salary for his service (but he was compensated for his expenses). The patriotism of this example earned him repeated praise from contemporaries.[24] Washington's actions exemplified public spirit, about which Maier writes: "The Americans believed above all that good or 'virtuous' men would subordinate personal considerations to the good of their communities—to the commonweal or *res publica*—which was a more proper object of their thoughts and efforts." Maier also notes that Charles Thomson deleted names of revolutionaries from David Ramsay's history of the Revolution because "To emphasize who did what, it seemed, was to detract attention from their common public mission."[25] Storing reinforces this point: "these eighteenth-century Americans, while sharing with the rest of humankind a curiosity and disposition to gossip about personalities, really did think that what counts most (or at least what ought to count most) in political debate is what is said rather than who said it."[26] This would be the equivalent of contemporary politicians anonymously publicizing arguments for or against an important policy, as Publius, Federal Farmer, Brutus, and many others did in the debates over ratification of the Constitution. In effect, serving the public was more important than individual political posturing. Service to advance the common good was more important than individual or group self-interest. (The common, or public, good is discussed below, in chapter 4.) So this section focuses on the ideal of public spirited, disinterested citizens serving the common good.

Public service was not solely the province of men. In a letter to her husband, Abigail Adams expressed her disappointment that, after eight years of separation, there was still no possibility of determining when he could return home.[27] Her "public" service was to enable John to continue his diplomatic work in Europe. This was only possible because of Abigail's care of the family back home in Massachusetts. Writing a few weeks later, on June 17, 1782, she made a strong argument for women's claim to patriotic laurels:

> Ardently as I long for the return of my dearest Friend, I cannot feel the least inclination to a peace but upon the most liberal foundation. Patriotism in the female Sex is the most disinterested of all virtues. Excluded from honours and from offices, we cannot attach ourselves to the State or Government from having held a place of Eminence. Even in the freest

countrys our property is subject to the controul and disposal of our partners, to whom the Laws have given a soverign Authority. Deprived of a voice in Legislation, obliged to submit to those Laws which are imposed upon us, is it not sufficient to make us indifferent to the public Welfare? Yet all History and every age exhibit Instances of patriotick virtue in the female Sex; which considering our situation equals the most Heroick of yours. "A late writer observes that as Citizens we are calld upon to exhibit our fortitude, for when you offer your blood to the State, it is ours. In giving it our Sons and Husbands we give more than ourselves. You can only die on the field of Battle, but we have the misfortune to survive those whom we Love most."[28]

John was well aware of Abigail's sacrifices. In a letter to Benjamin Rush he wrote about the 1770s as follows: "These were times, my friend, in Boston which tried women's souls as well as man's."[29] Remember also that Adams recognized contributions to the American cause by his wife and by Mercy Warren (discussed above, in chapter 2).

Public service by women was even a topic in a letter of condolence Adams wrote to his wife on the death of her mother. While praising his mother-in-law and seeing her as a model for her grandchildren, he was also mildly critical:

Your Mother had a clear, and penetrating Understanding and a profound Judgment, as well as an honest and a friendly and a charitable Heart.

There is one Thing however, which you will forgive me if I hint to you. Let me ask you rather, if you are not of my opinion? Were not her Talents, and Virtues too much confined, to private, social and domestic Life. My Opinion of the Duties of Religion and Morality, comprehends a very extensive Connection with society at large, and the great Interest of the public. Does not natural Morality, and much more Christian Benevolence, make it our indispensible Duty to lay ourselves out, to serve our fellow Creatures to the Utmost of our Power, in promoting and supporting those great Political systems, and general Regulations upon which the Happiness of Multitudes depends. The Benevolence, Charity, Capacity and Industry which exerted in private Life, would make a family, a Parish or a Town Happy, employed upon a larger Scale, in Support of the great Principles of Virtue and Freedom of political Regulations might secure whole Nations and Generations from Misery, Want and Contempt. Public Virtues, and political Qualities therefore should be incessantly cherished in our Children.[30]

The quotation is important as another example of Adams's concern for his children and also for his community. One could even interpret this as showing his sensitivity to the public's loss of massive amounts of talent because of sexism.

However, in this case one could more reasonably criticize the ordinarily supremely realistic Adams for gross lack of realism. What woman could be so political in that time? According to Kerber, revolutionary women did believe that they had an important community function, which was consistent with the role of mother, but not the public function Adams suggested. Women were not completely depoliticized and powerless. Mercy Warren wrote the following in response to a friend's question of whether women should bother to think about politics:

> "But as every domestic enjoyment depends on the decision of the mighty contest, who can be an unconcerned and silent spectator? Not surely the fond mother, or the affectionate wife who trembles lest her dearest connections should fall victims of lawless power, or at least pour out the warm blood as a libation at the shrine of liberty."[31]

Warren also argued that women's emotional and rational reactions to the political problems of the times were as accurate and as sensitive as men's and that duty to their families required women to take a political position "which they were to arrive at by informed discussion with men and women outside their families." This was justified in order to protect husbands and sons. So, in her letter, she counseled her friend "to resist her husband's constraints on her political conversation, and at the same time assured her that a politically minded woman was not necessarily a threat to family politics."[32] That such a role was highly limited does not indicate any failing on the part of revolutionary mothers. Political thinkers simply had not considered including women among the people. Limited as it was, women's patriotism did emerge during the Revolutionary War, and it was not the passive, admiring, suffering patriotism that men expected. The patriotic woman actively sought sacrifice; she found ways to bring politics into her province, the conditions of daily living.[33]

The revolutionary promise could not be fulfilled, however, until the separation between the woman's domestic world and the man's world of politics and intellect was ended. However, memory of the revolution was a continuing factor in maintaining confidence. Kerber makes it very clear that women, throughout the nineteenth century, thought deeply about the unfulfilled promises of the Republic.[34]

> "Yes, gentlemen," said Elizabeth Cady Stanton to the New York Legislature in 1854, "in republican America . . . we, the daughters of the revolutionary heroes of '76 demand at your hands the redress of our grievances—a revision of your State constitution—a new code of laws." Stanton would wrestle throughout her own career with the contradictory demands of domesticity and civic activism. The ambivalent relationship between motherhood and citizenship would be one of the most lasting, and most paradoxical, legacies of the Revolutionary generation.[35]

Some revolutionary era and nineteenth-century women saw themselves as individuals with responsibility to serve their communities.

One way that all Americans could demonstrate public spirit was by frugality. Abigail Adams perfected this virtue out of necessity. Given the level of compensation for public servants in those days, John could provide little financial support for the family while he was serving in Congress and in Europe. Abigail's frugal management maintained the family so well that John gladly deferred to her judgment in such matters.[36] While frugality was, at first (before the outbreak of fighting with the British), a way to exert economic pressure against Great Britain, it gradually became a virtue in itself. Likewise, luxury became a vice whether or not the source of the luxury had been Great Britain.[37] Frugality and its close relative industry (which we today would label diligence, working hard, industriousness) were republican virtues. But they also had roots in Protestant morality, just as the emphasis on the public service can be traced to religious ideals of individual sacrifice for the common good.[38] John Witherspoon, for instance, clearly connected industry with frugality and public spirit as characteristics of patriots. If these virtues were shared by the people in general, the country would be ready for "the most formidable enemy." Further, he said that industry "is a moral duty of the greatest moment, absolutely necessary to national prosperity, and the sure way of obtaining the blessing of God."[39]

John Adams had strong views on the importance of service to the community. In a 1756 letter to a classmate Adams discussed criteria for choosing a profession. He recognized individual freedom of choice, while emphasizing public service: "But to choose rightly, we should consider in what character we can do the most service to our fellow-men as well as to ourselves. The man who lives wholly to himself is of less worth than the cattle in his barn."[40] Throughout his life, Adams responded positively to the call of duty, but he often did so while regretting the sacrifices he made; lengthy separations from his beloved family and farm and the end of his lucrative career as a lawyer were the sacrifices he mentioned most often. One source of Adams's sense of duty was his family tradition of public service;[41] for example, his father, "Deacon" John Adams, had been a leader in the town of Braintree.[42]

Another example from John Adams is his report of James Otis's speech in the Writs of Assistance case; Otis argued: "'The only principles of public conduct that are worth a gentleman, or a man . . . are, to sacrifice estate, ease, health and applause, and even life itself to the sacred calls of his country. These manly sentiments in private life make the good citizen, in public life, the patriot and the hero.'"[43] That Adams agreed with Otis is clear from Adams's letter to his wife on June 10, 1775: "My Health and Life ought to be hazarded, in the Cause of my Country as well as yours, and all my friends."[44]

Adams's actions demonstrated the ideal of disinterest which he clearly explains in his writing:

my worthy fellow Citizens may be easy about me. I never can forsake what I
take to be their Interests. My own have never been considered by me, in
Competition with theirs. My Ease, my domestic Happiness, my rural
Pleasures, my Little Property, my personal Liberty, my Reputation, my Life,
have little Weight and ever had, in my own Estimation, in Comparison of
the great Object of my Country. I can say of it with great Sincerity, as
Horace says of Virtue—to America only and her Friends a Friend."[45]

While he always responded positively to the call of public duty, he was con-
flicted on this, despite the statement above. He suffered when he was separated
from his beloved family.[46] However, while he missed his family, he was determined that his public service would not be self-interested but would serve the
common good.

Adams's sense of public duty was shaped by his understanding of the
classical republicanism of ancient Greece and Rome.[47] Even more important was
his religious background and his decision to enter the field of law instead of the
ministry. Ellis argues that he saw any conflict between self-interest and the
common good as a test of his morality, that he was dominated by an "other-
worldly ideal" of service. "He was driven by insecurity and self-doubt, not in
the sense of doubting his talent or intelligence, but in the sense of requiring
incessant assurance that what he knew to be his considerable gifts would be
given to a cause larger than himself."[48] For example, Adams wrote to Benjamin
Rush on May 1, 1807: "In every considerable transaction of my public life, I
have invariably acted according to my best judgment for the public good, and I
can look up to God for the sincerity of my intentions."[49]

Revolutionary emphasis on public service was not intended to subordinate
the individual to the state. What John Adams exemplified and what the
Christian ideal meant was "that by purity of soul man ought voluntarily to live
outside himself in genuine interest for the welfare of others and, if the occasion
requires, sacrifice his own interests and desires for the welfare of others."[50] But
individual identity was to be maintained; Adams was possibly the most public
spirited of all the founders, and he most certainly maintained his individual personality.

Thomas Jefferson was aware of a duality of individual and public service; he
thought that the law "'qualifies a man to be useful to himself, to his neighbors,
and to the public.'"[51] Individual motivation is even clearer in a letter to James
Monroe: "'If we are made in some degree for others, yet, in a greater, are we
made for ourselves.'" In the same letter he wrote that he thought "'public
service and private misery inseparably linked together.'"[52] While government
service separated Jefferson from the preferred joys of private life at Monticello,
like Adams, he readily accepted repeated calls to public service. He shared with
Adams and many other founders the Enlightenment idea that "All men of genius
and leisure, all gentlemen, had an obligation to serve the state."[53] Private pleasures were preferred but sense of duty impelled them to serve. And, as Webking

points out, the conclusion of the Declaration of Independence, with the signers mutually pledging to each other their lives, fortunes, and sacred honor, is an example of public spirit, not self-interested motivation.[54]

Public service was not, however, a virtue about which Jefferson was completely sanguine. He feared that the individual aspect of the duality would become dominant. "Jefferson's injunction 'Love your neighbor as yourself, and your country more than yourself' could have an immediate meaning to the citizens. But Jefferson feared that 'our rulers will become corrupt, our people careless.'" Carelessness included an emphasis on individual economic interests. If the people concentrated on making money, tyranny might destroy the republic.[55] As noted above, one ironic result of the revolution was the impetus it gave to just that type of individual economic pursuit.

Benjamin Rush, Philadelphia physician and friend of both Adams and Jefferson, provided another clear statement of how important public service was to the revolutionaries: "Every man in a republic is public property. His time, his talents—his youth—his manhood—his old age—nay more, life, all belong to his country."[56] Rush also connected this view of public service to Christianity, arguing that that religion teaches that "no man 'liveth to himself.'"[57] We have lost this sense that one should be concerned for the public good. Moreover, the Otis-Adams-Rush self-sacrificial view of public service is beyond our comprehension.

The loss of this ideal should not, however, be a surprise because individual subordination to the common good was the exception rather than the rule even during the revolutionary era. Abigail Adams analyzed this in a July 16, 1775, letter to her husband:

> How difficult the task to quench out the fire and the pride of private ambition, and to sacrifice ourselfs and all our hopes and expectations to the publick weal. How few have souls capable of so noble an undertaking— how often are the lawrels worn by those who have had no share in earning them, but there is a future recompence of reward to which the upright man looks, and which he will most assuredly obtain provided he perseveres unto the end.[58]

George Washington understood the scarcity of virtue. His revolutionary service was seen as a model of republican virtue, but he recognized that virtue would not motivate men to fight Great Britain. He thought that those "'who act upon the Principles of disinterestedness, are, comparatively speaking, no more than a drop in the Ocean.'"[59]

Tension between the public spirit and self-interest, as noted by Abigail Adams and George Washington, is still a feature of American politics. The prevalence of self-interested behavior is often blamed on Adam Smith, but this is a misinterpretation of his thought (analyzed in chapter 6) and of liberalism.[60] At this point it is enough to note that the "benevolence" Smith emphasized went far beyond private charity. It was an antonym to self-love and, in its superior manifestations, included participation in public life.[61]

While few citizens exhibited disinterest, this virtue was also problematic because it was subject to political manipulation. John Adams thought it was true that citizens were "oftener deceived and abused in their judgments of disinterested men and actions than in any other." And he was caustic in his comments about LaFayette's parading his disinterest.[62]

As with other virtues public spirit can be manipulated by demagogues. Adams insisted that an essential element of public service, of patriotic duty, was its transcendental foundation: "Without this faith ['a belief in a future state of rewards and punishments'] patriotism can never be anything more than hypocrisy, i.e., ambition, avarice, envy, resentment, lust, or at least the love of fame hidden under a masque. So thinks J. Adams, 1808."[63] Media manipulators can easily manufacture the appearance of public spirit. Only people with a solid core of values will refuse this temptation. However, that still leaves a problem for the electorate. How are voters to distinguish fraudulent public spirit from real disinterest?

Universalism versus Factionalism

Disinterest implied a universalism which many people today do not understand. Wood notes that republican citizens were supposed to be disinterested and states that "Dr. Johnson defined disinterest as being 'superior to regard of private advantage; not influenced by private profit.' We today have lost most of this older meaning."[64] Not only have we lost this older meaning of "disinterest," (which many people confuse with "uninterested") but individual self-interest and its close relative, group self-interest (factionalism), have overwhelmed the universalism of many of our founders. Many revolutionary military leaders shared Washington's cosmopolitan view that "'To be enlightened was to be . . . a citizen of the great republic of humanity at large.'" It was not proper to show favoritism to one's own community.[65] But, even in the eighteenth century, the ideal of universalism was often ignored in practice. Early in the new republic it was evident that factionalism was undermining the public good. John Adams's consistent unhappiness with factionalism is detailed in chapter 5. In this section I simply want to point out that distrust of factions was shared across the political spectrum.[66] In addition, note that Adam Smith was harshly critical of factionalism.[67]

George Washington recognized that the spirit of party (factionalism) was inherent in human nature but still saw it as the worst enemy of popular government. In his Farewell Address, he wrote that even though factions might occasionally serve "popular ends, they are likely in the course of time and things to become potent engines by which cunning, ambitious, and unprincipled men will be enabled to subvert the power of the people, and to usurp for themselves the reins of government."[68] Such a strong aversion was common in that era. Atticus wrote, in favor of adopting the new Constitution, that *"The spirit of all parties is the same, and it ought to be received as a political maxim, that no violent party-man can be a good citizen. "*[69]

Anti-Federalists also wrote about this problem. Federal Farmer (whose identity is not certain—it might have been Richard Henry Lee) wrote:

> Could we get over all our difficulties respecting a balance of interests and party efforts, to raise some and oppress others, the want of sympathy, information and intercourse between the representatives and the people, an insuperable difficulty will still remain, I mean the constant liability of a small number of representatives to private combinations; the tyranny of the one, or the licentiousness of the multitude, are, in my mind, but small evils, compared with the factions of the few.[70]

Federal Farmer's worries about the one, the few, and the many were shared by John Adams and led him to his arguments for balanced government (see chapter 7.) Madison also discussed the prevalence of faction in *The Federalist* but added another type to Federal Farmer's "factions of the few"; while hopeful that the "violence of faction" might be controlled, he was also wary of "the superior force of an interested and overbearing majority."[71]

That the Constitution did not cure the ills of faction is obvious in that parties and interest groups thrive today; but that would be an unfair expectation, since Madison did not assume the end of factions. Whether his solution of counterposing faction against faction serves the nation well is considered further in chapter 5. But note the implication that the public good and majority decisions are not always the same. Madison's concern that the majority might be unjust and might ignore minority rights anticipates similar arguments about the tyranny of the majority in Tocqueville's classic, *Democracy in America.* Also, Madison's fear of unjust majorities is remarkably similar to Federal Farmer's concern about the "licentiousness of the multitude." The founding generation, across the political spectrum, found factionalism to be dangerous for many reasons, not the least of which was the injustice that often resulted from factionalism. That justice was one of their most important virtues reinforced the founders' dislike of factionalism.

Justice

Adams, Franklin, Jefferson, and Madison all included justice in their lists of virtues. It was important to Washington as well. His June 14, 1783, "Circular to the States" listed four things essential to the well-being of the country. "A Sacred regard to Public Justice" was second on the list (after "An indissoluble Union of the States under one Federal Head").[72]

Justice was crucial to John Adams's being. This was not simply because he was a lawyer; it also came from his religion. In 1775 he wrote: "Justice is a

great christian as well as moral duty and virtue, which the clergy ought to incul-
cate and explain."[73] A diary entry of February 22, 1756, included it in a short
list of virtues that would be attributes of the members of a community if everyone regulated his conduct by the precepts of the Bible.[74] Similarly, in a letter to
Jefferson, December 12, 1816, he stated that his religious creed was, for fifty or
sixty years, "contained in four short Words 'Be just and good.'"[75] Policy implications of justice, for Adams, included sharp disagreement with Hamilton's
national bank; he saw the bank as a national injustice because it sacrificed
"public and private Interest to a few Aristocratical Friends and Favourites."[76]
Thompson argues that Adams defined justice in terms of the common good and
the wealth of the people, individually and collectively. Further, justice "defined
as the protection of the free acquisition and exchange of property," was the "sine
qua non of good government."[77] Adams emphasized justice to prevent interests
and factions from destroying the common good.[78]

This virtue was also central to Adam Smith's thinking. He wrote:
"Humanity, justice, generosity, and public spirit, are the qualities most useful
to others."[79] In other parts of the same book, he connected justice and disinterested benevolence with the role of the impartial spectator,[80] even going so far as
to write "that it was benevolence only which could stamp upon any action the
character of virtue."[81] Werhane argues that, for Smith, justice was the main pil-
lar upholding the edifice of human society. She states that the theme of justice is
prominent in his *Theory of Moral Sentiments*, the student transcriptions of his
Lectures on Jurisprudence, and *Wealth of Nations*. Also, she notes that he argued in *Wealth of Nations* that justice was essential to political economy.[82]
Smith emphasized justice as the foundation of any social-political order. In
Wealth of Nations he ranked justice second after international security, but in
Lectures on Jurisprudence he ranked justice as the first function of govern-
ment.[83] Distributive justice (or benevolence, charity, generosity) could "be
morally required of people in their dealings with others." Griswold states that
justice was one part of Smith's virtue theory, which "is the moral foundation of
Smith's political economy, political theory, and 'natural jurisprudence.'"[84]
Ross concludes that, both in *Theory of Moral Sentiments* and in *Wealth of
Nations*, Smith emphasized justice, that Smith believed that happiness of others
is important to human beings, and that freedom, both economic and otherwise,
was "to be exercised with attention to justice to others."[85]

Finally, Smith's emphasis on justice can be illustrated by his argument
that, with regard to virtues such as prudence or generosity, the spirit of the law
was more important than the letter of the law, "But it is otherwise with regard
to justice: the man who in that refines the least, and adheres with the most
obstinate stedfastness to the general rules themselves, is the most commendable,
and the most to be depended upon."[86] Justice was so very important to Smith
that the advocate of individual freedom in economic competition was extremely
wary of individual freedom to interpret the rules of justice.

Of course, justice is also a deeply religious concept which was included in many sermons of the revolutionary age.[87] According to Charles Chauncey, there is no more solemn biblical injunction for civil rulers than justice, which requires that the ruler be above factional interests and "do that which is equal and right."[88] And justice applied to everyone, not only to rulers. Joseph Lathrop preached that all had mutual responsibility for the oppressed and the widow. The first obligation for human beings was justice, which he defined as the golden rule.[89]

Caveats: The Misuse of Virtue

The degree of civic virtue possessed by American citizens has been an issue since the founding of the country. But civic virtue is problematic for another reason as well. Values and virtues are subject to at least three major types of abuse: attempts to impose virtue, demagogic manipulation, and self-righteousness, of both the individual and the group variety.

Some would impose their values on others. But any rational person would agree that you cannot be required by anyone else to be virtuous. Attempts to compel virtue, whether by well-meaning parents, or religious authorities, or anyone else, can result in personal repression and can stunt individual growth; that would be absolutely incompatible with liberty and equality. As an individual you develop your values and virtues with support from myriad community sources, such as family, friends, churches, and schools; but your values are still your individual responsibility. Development of values and virtues cannot be done for you or to you. In the best situation, the family and community play major roles and the shared values of family and community provide powerful models. But family and community cannot compel values and virtues. John Adams provides a good example of how this works. He was born into a relatively strict religious community. His values were heavily influenced by that community, but he also rejected part of his heritage. His father sent him to Harvard to prepare for the ministry, but John Adams rejected that career because he abhorred theological rigidity. While he remained a religious person all his life and was shaped by his family and community, he also developed and maintained his individuality.

Virtues and values can also be cynically manipulated by demagogues. As one example of this, Pangle quotes Trenchard and Gordon: "'Generosity, Self-denial, and private and personal Virtues, are in Politicks but mere Names, or rather Cant-words, that go for nothing with wise Men, though they may cheat the Vulgar.'"[90] Politicians love to manipulate their images so that they appear virtuous. In short, the appearance of virtue can be and has been used for demagogic purposes. Alexander Hamilton, in the *Federalist*, warned of the dangers of demagoguery. The people want to support the public good, Hamilton wrote, but they sometimes make mistakes: "the wonder is that they so seldom err . . . be-set, as they continually are, by the wiles of parasites and sycophants, by the snares of the ambitious, the avaricious, the desperate, by the artifices of men who possess their confidence more than they deserve it."[91] Hamilton was a masterful political tactician, so we should pay careful attention to his warning. Many of the founders feared that unwary citizens could easily be misled by demagogues parading their "virtue."

Adams also astutely analyzed another misuse of virtue: self-righteousness; in an essay, "On Self-Delusion," Adams argued, according to Diggins, "that men think and act from their own egotistical needs and then rationalize their thoughts and actions by deceiving themselves that they are moved by higher motives. The answer to such self-delusion is self-distrust."[92] So, while Adams, with the Puritans, believed that purity of motivation was crucial to integrity,[93] he also knew that one must be cautious about deluding oneself about one's own virtue. Inherent in Adams's approach to dealing with disputants was tolerance and insistence on rational investigation of contested issues. (That his political opponents did not believe his caustic tongue showed much tolerance, does not detract from the importance of this virtue for civil life in any democracy.) Beware the self-righteous; but, even more, beware your own self.[94]

Lincoln also spoke on this subject. According to Diggins, he would not quote Scripture to support his actions, "for to claim to know God's will is the sin of pride."[95] Diggins also makes an extremely important argument about human delusions of capability to destroy evil. Eradicating evil seems to be an attractive idea, but is "psychologically deceptive and pragmatically dangerous." He characterizes it as "a superhuman goal" and "an illusion, a kind of spiritual sickness."[96]

Self-righteousness in one man is obviously dangerous. But this pride is even more dangerous when shared by an entire nation. In a letter to Jefferson, dated November 15, 1813, John Adams commented sarcastically: "Many hundred years must roll away before We shall be corrupted. Our pure, virtuous, public spirited federative Republick will last for ever, govern the Globe and introduce the perfection of Man, his perfectibility being already proved by Price Priestly, Condorcet Rousseau Diderot and Godwin."[97]

None of this negates the importance of values and virtues for a political system. But an unreflective, intolerant, self-deluded politics of virtue produces vicious, not virtuous, results.

Conclusion

Early in the nineteenth century, many of the founders feared that their revolution had failed. Ordinary Americans could not understand such fears. Their pursuit of happiness in a democratic country had made America a different world, one where the founders' views had been ignored: "We cannot rely on the views of the founding fathers anymore, Martin Van Buren said in 1820. We have to rely on our own experience, not on what they said and thought. They had many fears, said Van Buren, fears of democracy, that American experience had not borne out."[98] Van Buren was right about democracy but wrong in implicitly ignoring the founders' emphasis on virtue.

Virtue has been a problem in the United States because of a fundamental ambivalence on the subject. Diggins argues that liberalism and Christianity have been competing for "the soul of America." Moreover, while liberalism has given this country a "dynamic energy," it has reinforced "ambition, envy, and self-satisfaction, all the cardinal offenses of Christian religion."[99] Perhaps the split is a bit more complex than what Diggins presents because Christians are also split between rule-bound moralizers on the one hand, and on the other hand those who try to adhere to the "spirit of the law" of a loving God, to say nothing of differences on the first part of the dichotomy ("labor, competition, and self-help").

In chapter 6 we will return to the issue of the liberal impact on virtue in the United States. But, for now, note that modern distortions of Adam Smith's capitalism played a major role in further undermining civic virtue; during the nineteenth century, American capitalism overwhelmed such virtues as love, humanity, magnanimity, humility, sacrifice, and forgiveness.[100] In chapter 6, I argue in great detail that the American version of capitalism is a perversion of what was intended by Smith. In effect, American capitalism has undermined civic virtues, those virtues which are necessary for democracy and, ironically, are also crucial to Smith's type of capitalism.[101]

Our founders' reasons for wanting a virtuous citizenry are still important for our government and society. That civic virtue has declined in this country hurts all of us. So, think about this question: what virtues (individual, civic) are important for our modern age? From our history, what can we learn about virtues for people of a new millennium?

Now, let us discuss a concept which seems extremely strange to modern readers: how one maintains one's individuality within communities. The founders lived in a much more community-oriented age then we do today. And public spirit was one of their fundamental ideals. We live in a less community-oriented age than the founders, but could learn how to strengthen both our individuality and our communities.

Notes

1.   Adam Smith, *Theory of Moral Sentiments*, 6th ed., D. D. Raphael and A. L. Macfie, eds. (Oxford: Oxford University Press, 1976), III.5.8, 166-67.

2.   Pauline Maier, *The Old Revolutionaries: Political Lives in the Age of Samuel Adams* (New York: Random House, 1980), 32.

3.   John Adams, diary entry of December 23, 1765, in L. H. Butterfield, ed., *The Adams Papers: Diary and Autobiography of John Adams,* 1 (New York: Atheneum, 1964), 271.

4.   Gordon S. Wood, *The Radicalism of the American Revolution* (New York: Alfred A. Knopf, 1992), 206-07. See Paul K. Longmore, *The Invention of George Washington* (Berkeley: University of California Press, 1988), 47, for a discussion of the impact of disinterest on George Washington. As a logical result of the shift from a monarchical politics of deference to a republican impartiality, he devoted increased attention to merit for the appointments and promotions for which he was responsible.

5.   John P. Diggins, *The Lost Soul of American Politics: Virtue, Self-Interest, and the Foundations of Liberalism* (Chicago: University of Chicago Press, 1984), 23.

6.   Benjamin Franklin, *The Autobiography and Other Writings* (New York: Penguin Books, 1986), 90-91 and 100.

7.   John Adams, diary entry of July 21, 1786, in Butterfield, ed., *Diary and Autobiography*, 3, 195.

8.   George A. Peek, Jr., ed., *The Political Writings of John Adams: Representative Selections* (Indianapolis: Bobbs-Merrill Co., Inc., 1954), 176.

9.   Peek, ed., *Political Writings of Adams*, xxi.

10.   John Adams, letter to Unknown, April 27, 1777, in Robert J. Taylor, ed., *Papers of John Adams,* 5 (Cambridge: Belknap Press of Harvard University Press, 1983), 163.

11.   Peek, ed., *Political Writings of Adams,* 177-78.

12.   John Adams, letter to Abigail Adams, June 16, 1776, in L. H. Butterfield, ed., *Adams Family Correspondence*, 2 (Cambridge: Belknap Press of Harvard University Press, 1963), 12.

13.   In contrast, Washington did not have a differentiated view of ambition since he did not see it as virtuous; he tried, successfully, to keep his own ambitions hidden (Longmore, *Invention of Washington*, 67).

14.   Merrill D. Peterson, ed., *The Portable Thomas Jefferson* (New York: Penguin Books, 1975), 425.

15.   *Federalist*, #10, 52.

16.   Quoted by Robert J. Morgan, "Madison's Analysis of the Sources of Political Authority," *American Political Science Review* 75 (September 1981): 624.

17.   In addition to the founders' lists of virtues, here are two from more modern writers. Michael Novak, a somewhat conservative commentator, suggests virtues needed by democratic citizens in contrast to citizens of authoritarian societies: "enterprise more than resignation, civic virtue more than familial piety; respect for law and lawmaking rather than mere submission to command; self-improvement and self-realization more than contentment with an assigned station; skills in practical compromise and loyal opposition rather than in unbending moral absolutism"; see Michael Novak, *Free Persons and the Common Good* (New York: Madison Books, 1989), 114.

William Galston's list of virtues includes courage, law-abidingness, loyalty, independence, tolerance, discernment (of others' rights and of the character of candidates), moderation in demand for services, willingness to pay for services demanded, patience, and, in leaders, ability to narrow the gap between popular demands and wise action, among others. He also lists some vices of liberal polities: propensity to gratify short-term desires, inability to act on unpleasant truths, and earning popularity by pandering to popular, but immoderate, demands (William A. Galston, "Liberal Virtues," *American Political Science Review* 82 [December 1988]: 1281-84).

18. Smith, *Theory of Moral Sentiments*, VII.ii.1.12, 270-71.

19. Thomas L. Pangle, *The Spirit of Modern Republicanism: The Moral Vision of the American Founders and the Philosophy of Locke* (Chicago: Univer-sity of Chicago Press, 1988), 55.

20. Samuel Miller, "A Sermon on the Anniversary of the Independence of America," in *Political Sermons of the American Founding Era, 1730-1805,* Ellis Sandoz, ed. (Indianapolis: Liberty Press, 1991), 1159.

21. John Quincy Adams and Charles Francis Adams, *John Adams,* 1 (New York: Chelsea House, 1980), 99.

22. Pauline Maier, *From Resistance to Revolution: Colonial Radicals and the Development of American Opposition to Britain, 1765-1776* (New York: Random House, 1972), xv.

23. Adams and Adams, *John Adams,* 1, 110-11.

24. Longmore, *Invention of Washington,* 177.

25. Maier, *Old Revolutionaries,* xiv.

26. Herbert J. Storing, ed., *The Anti-Federalist: An Abridgment, by Murray Dry, of the Complete Anti-Federalist* (Chicago: University of Chicago Press, 1985), 25.

27. Abigail Adams, letter to John Adams, April 10, 1782, in L. H. Butterfield and Marc Friedlaender, eds., *Adams Family Correspondence,* 4 (Cambridge: Belknap Press of Harvard University Press, 1973), 306.

28. Abigail Adams, letter to John Adams, June 17, 1782, in Butterfield and Friedlaender, eds., *Adams Family Correspondence,* 4, 328.

29. John A. Schutz and Douglass Adair, eds., *The Spur of Fame: Dialogues of John Adams and Benjamin Rush, 1805-1813* (San Marino, Calif.: Huntington Library, 1966), 142.

30. John Adams, letter to Abigail Adams, October 29, 1775, in Butterfield, ed., *Adams Family Correspondence,* 1, 316-17.

31. Linda K. Kerber, *Women of the Republic: Intellect and Ideology in Revolutionary America* (Chapel Hill: University of North Carolina Press, for the Institute of Early American History and Culture, 1980), 83-84.

32. Kerber, *Women of the Republic,* 83-84.

33. Kerber, *Women of the Republic,* 110-11.

34. Kerber, *Women of the Republic,* 276-78.

35. Kerber, *Women of the Republic,* 287-88.

36. Lynne Withey, *Dearest Friend: A Life of Abigail Adams* (New York: Free Press, 1981), 60 and passim.

37. Ann Fairfax Withington, *Toward a More Perfect Union: Virtue and the Formation of American Republics* (New York: Oxford University Press, 1991), 96.

38. Ruth Bloch, *Visionary Republic: Millennial Themes in American Thought, 1756-1800* (Cambridge: Cambridge University Press, 1985), 109.

39. John Witherspoon, "The Dominion of Providence over the Passions of Men," in *Political Sermons,* Sandoz, ed., 556-57. Charles L. Griswold, Jr., *Adam Smith and the Virtues of Enlightenment* (New York: Cambridge University Press, 1999), 184-85, lists prudence, industry, frugality, moderation, and self-control as Smith's virtues of the selfish passions; see also 203-04.

40. John Adams, letter to Charles Cushing, April 1, 1756, in Taylor, ed., *Papers,* 1, 12.

41. Peter Shaw, *The Character of John Adams* (Chapel Hill: University of North Carolina Press, for the Institute of Early American History and Culture, 1976), 11.

42. During Adams's life, the towns of Randolph and Quincy split off from Braintree; the Adams's properties are in what is now Quincy, which calls itself the City of Presidents, but which cannot claim to be the birthplace of the same two presidents because both were born in what was still Braintree when they were born.

43. Shaw, *Character of Adams,* 61.

44. John Adams, letter to Abigail Adams, June 10, 1775, in Butterfield, ed., *Adams Family Correspondence,* 1, 213. John R. Howe, Jr., *The Changing Political Thought of John Adams* (Princeton: Princeton University Press, 1966), 30, emphasizes this same point; he states that, for Adams, virtue "meant, above all, a concern for the welfare of society as a whole as opposed to one's own purely selfish interests."

45. John Adams, letter to Abigail Adams, March 19, 1776, in Butterfield, ed., *Adams Family Correspondence,* 1, 363.

46. Withey, *Dearest Friend,* 70.

47. Bruce Miroff, *Icons of Democracy: American Leaders as Heroes, Aristocrats, Dissenters, and Democrats* (New York: Basic Books, 1993), 50.

48. Joseph J. Ellis, *Passionate Sage: The Character and Legacy of John Adams* (New York: W. W. Norton & Company, 1993), 52. Barry A. Shain, *The Myth of American Individualism: The Protestant Origins of American Political Thought* (Princeton: Princeton University Press, 1994), 40-41, argues that John Adams's dual sources of the concept of the public good, religion and republicanism, applied to many Americans. For Americans in general, the Bible was the main source of ideas of virtue, including public service and benevolence; see Richard Vetterli and Gary Bryner, *In Search of the Republic: Public Virtue and the Roots of American Government,* rev. ed. (Lanham, Md.: Rowman & Littlefield Publishers, Inc., 1996), 50-51. Vetterli and Bryner also argue that benevolence, or the golden rule, was the cornerstone of the founders' ideal of virtue (61). And Richard Hofstadter, *Social Darwinism in American Thought* (Boston: Beacon Press, 1983), 204, writes: "that there is nothing in nature or a naturalistic philosophy of life to make impossible the acceptance of moral sanctions that can be employed for the common good."

49. Schutz and Adair, ed., *Spur of Fame,* 83-84.

50. Vetterli and Bryner, *In Search of the Republic*, 79.

51. Wood, *The Radicalism of the American Revolution*, 346.

52. Quoted by Pangle, *Spirit of Modern Republicanism*, 121.

53. Wood, *The Radicalism of the American Revolution*, 104.

54. Robert H. Webking, *The American Revolution and the Politics of Liberty* (Baton Rouge: Louisiana State University Press, 1988), 108.

55. Robert N. Bellah, et al., *Habits of the Heart: Individualism and Commitment in American Life* (New York: Harper and Row, 1985), 30-31.

56. Colleen A. Sheehan and Gary L. McDowell, eds., *Friends of the Constitution; Writings of the "Other" Federalists, 1787-1788* (Indianapolis: Liberty Fund, 1998), 5.

57. Quoted in Ellis Sandoz, *A Government of Laws: Political Theory, Reli-gion, and the American Founding* (Baton Rouse: Louisiana State University Press, 1990), 132.

58. Abigail Adams, letter to John Adams, July 16, 1775, in Butterfield, ed., *Adams Family Correspondence*, 1, 246.

59. Diggins, *Lost Soul of American Politics*, 23.

60. Stephen Holmes, *Passions and Constraint: On the Theory of Liberal Democracy* (Chicago: University of Chicago Press, 1995), 24, for example, argues that liberals are not motivated purely by self-interest. Indeed he characterizes the accusation that liberals see humans as "propelled by rational self-interest alone, as if benevolence, love of others, and devotion to the common good were wholly unreal motivations" as "reckless." Stephen Macedo, *Liberal Virtues: Citizenship, Virtue and Community in Liberal Constitutionalism* (Oxford: Clarendon Press, 1990), 274-75, makes a related point: "The judicial virtues are those that allow people to stand back from their personal commitments and projects and judge them from an impersonal point of view." Macedo's point seems very close to Adam Smith's "impartial spectator."

61. Athol Fitzgibbons, *Adam Smith's System of Liberty, Wealth and Virtue* (Oxford: Clarendon Press, 1995), 105.

62. Schutz and Adair, eds., *Spur of Fame*, 97 and 92.

63. Zoltan Haraszti, *John Adams and the Prophets of Progress* (New York: Grosset and Dunlap, 1964), 62-63.

64. Wood, *The Radicalism of the American Revolution*, 104-05.

65. Wood, *The Radicalism of the American Revolution*, 220-21. Universalism, in short, was an antonym for self-interest and factionalism. Universalism was inclusive, concerned for the common good, in contrast to local, parochial, partial interests. Universalism included all of humanity, although Adams and Smith both knew that this sentiment weakened with both relational and geographic distance.

At least one politician at the end of the nineteenth century was still averse to parochialism, the "over-exaltation of the little community"; Theodore Roosevelt, *American Ideals and Other Essays, Social and Political* (New York: G. P. Putnam's Sons, 1897), 19. And see 46 for Theodore Roosevelt's approving comments on disinterest.

66. Pennsylvanians probably had the strongest aversion to faction. While they understood that politics involved contention, they highly valued political harmony; factionalism was a serious vice, according to Alan Tully, *William Penn's Legacy: Politics and Social Structure in Provincial Pennsylvania, 1726-1755* (Baltimore: Johns Hopkins University Press, 1977), 122.

67. Smith, *Theory of Moral Sentiments*, III.3.43, 155-56.

68. Daniel J. Boorstin, ed., *An American Primer* (New York: Penguin Books, 1966), 219-20.

69. Sheehan and McDowell, eds., *Friends of the Constitution*, 331 (italics in original).

70. Federal Farmer, in Storing, ed., *Anti-Federalist*, 78.

71. *Federalist*, #10, 49.

72. Sheehan and McDowell, eds., *Friends of the Constitution*, 15.

73. John Adams, fourth Novanglus letter, February 13, 1775, in Taylor, ed., *Papers*, 2, 266-67.

74. John Adams, diary entry of February 22, 1756, in Butterfield, ed., *Diary and Autobiography*, 1, 9.

75. Lester J. Cappon, ed., *The Adams-Jefferson Letters: The Complete Correspondence between Thomas Jefferson and Abigail and John Adams*, 2 (Chapel Hill: University of North Carolina Press, for the Institute of Early American History and Culture, 1959), 499.

76. Cappon, ed., *Adams-Jefferson Letters*, 2, 401-02.

77. C. Bradley Thompson, *John Adams and the Spirit of Liberty* (Lawrence: University Press of Kansas, 1998), 190-91.

78. Jurgen Gebhardt, *Americanism: Revolutionary Order and Societal Self-Interpretation in the American Republic*, Ruth Hein, trans. (Baton Rouge: Louisiana State University Press, 1993), 113.

79. Smith, *Theory of Moral Sentiments*, IV.2.9, 190.

80. Smith, *Theory of Moral Sentiments*, Book VI, Conclusion, 262-63, and Book VII, Section ii, especially 267-68 and 300 ff.

81. Smith, *Theory of Moral Sentiments*, VII.ii.3.7, 302.

82. Patricia H. Werhane, *Adam Smith and His Legacy for Modern Capitalism* (New York: Oxford University Press, 1991), 12 and 179.

83. Adam Smith, *An Inquiry into the Nature and Causes of the Wealth of Nations*, R. H. Campbell and A. S. Skinner, eds. (Oxford: Oxford University Press, 1976) V.i.a.1, 689.

84. Griswold, *Smith and Enlightenment*, 231-32 and 181; see also 237-38.

85. Ian Simpson Ross, *The Life of Adam Smith* (Oxford: Oxford University Press, 1995), 419. Holmes, *Passions and Constraint*, 268-69, sees such values as justice, peace, rational discussion, and human diversity as important counterweights against the destructive loyalties of faction. He also emphasizes equalitarian justice as an important liberal tenet (241-42).

86. Smith, *Theory of Moral Sentiments*, III.6.10, 175.

87. Jacob Cushing, "Divine Judgments upon Tyrants," in *Political Sermons,* Sandoz, ed., 614-15, preached that people who were just, temperate, industrious, and zealous for the public good prospered. See also Samuel Miller, in *Political Sermons,* 1158; Samuel Sherwood, in *Political Sermons,* 382-83; and John Winthrop, in Boorstin, ed., *American Primer,* 28-29.

88. Charles Chauncey, "Civil Magistrates Must Be Just, Ruling in the Fear of God," in *Political Sermons,* Sandoz, ed., 141, 145-46 and passim.

89. Joseph Lathrop, "A Sermon on a Day Appointed for Publick Thanksgiving," in *Political Sermons,* Sandoz, ed., 875.

90. Pangle, *Spirit of Modern Republicanism,* 31.

91. *Federalist,* #71, 214-15.

92. Diggins, *Lost Soul of American Politics,* 92.

93. Shaw, *Character of Adams,* 24.

94. On the point of purity of personal motivation, a quotation from Reinhold Niebuhr is worth repeating: "No virtuous act is quite as virtuous from the standpoint of our friend or foe as it is from our standpoint" (quoted by Diggins, *Lost Soul of American Politics,* vii).

95. Diggins, *Lost Soul of American Politics,* 344.

96. Diggins, *Lost Soul of American Politics,* 345-46.

97. Cappon, ed., *Adams-Jefferson Letters,* 2, 1959, 400. Many American diplomatic historians have commented on the foreign relations problems inherent in the American crusading spirit, our conviction that we have the answers for all the world's ills. Also, throughout our history, nonconformists in domestic politics have felt the effects of such self-righteousness.

98. Wood, *The Radicalism of the American Revolution,* 368-69.

99. Diggins, *Lost Soul of American Politics,* 326.

100. Diggins, *Lost Soul of American Politics,* 341.

101. I am not the only contemporary political scientist who argues the need for renewed attention to virtue. Galston is one example of contemporary scholars arguing for a renewed attention to citizen virtue.

> The claim is . . . that the operation of liberal institutions is affected in important ways by the character of citizens (and leaders) and that at some point the attenuation of individual virtue will create pathologies with which liberal political contrivances, however technically perfect their design, simply cannot cope. To an extent difficult to measure but impossible to ignore, the viability of liberal society depends on its ability to engender a virtuous citizenry.
>
> . . . to the extent that the liberal virtues are not simply consistent with individual self-interest, processes of forming and maintaining them will come into conflict with other powerful tendencies in liberal life (William A. Galston, "Liberal Virtues," *American Political Science Review* 82 [December 1988]: 1279).

Here Galston is using liberal in its traditional sense. Note also that I interpret the last sentence as including virtues for democratic citizens. In other words, society might need to make special efforts to develop civic virtues which are important to communities, but which individuals, focusing on their own desires, might neglect. See also William Galston, "Civic Education in the Liberal State," in *Liberalism and the Moral Life,* Nancy L. Rosenblum, ed. (Cambridge: Harvard University Press, 1989), 89-101.

Robert P. Kraynak, "Tocqueville's Constitutionalism," *American Political Science Review* 81 (December 1987): 1175, argues that "constitutional government must go beyond the mere concern with constraining power through institutional mechanisms and take a deliberate interest in the moral education of citizens."

For other examples, see Amy Gutmann, "Undemocratic Education," in *Liberalism and the Moral Life,* Rosenblum, ed., 79, and Daniel R. Sabia, Jr., "Political Education and the History of Political Thought," *American Political Science Review* 78 (December 1984): passim.

Chapter Four

Individuality within Communities

Americans are, on the whole, dialectical extremists who emphasize individualism at the expense of communities. A *yin-yang* approach, individuality within communities, would result in a better society. One point, however, must be clarified before supporting that contention. The intent is not to emphasize community at the expense of individuals. Such a reading of the title and the substance of this chapter would be a dialectical misinterpretation of a *yin-yang* argument. Both individuals and communities suffer when either is overemphasized. The pendulum in this country has swung to the extreme of individualism; I do not advocate the opposite extreme. I argue for restoration of a necessary balance. Bellah and his collaborators make a similar point: "We do not argue that Americans should abandon individualism—that would mean for us to abandon our deepest identity." However, they insist on critical analysis of individualism, in particular, of "those tendencies that would destroy it from within."[1] Bellah, et al., argue for a balance of individual and community. On that point I agree, but I think different terminology is needed. Basically, I use Tocqueville's distinction between individualism and individuality.[2] Individualism, connoting excess, underemphasizes or ignores community; this type of individualism has been called anomic individualism or atomistic individualism by various scholars. In contrast, throughout this work "individuality" represents individuals in a healthy relationship to community. A healthy relationship means individual identity is maintained within a community context. This symbiotic relationship results in stronger individuals and stronger communities.[3]

Please note that this chapter emphasizes governmental aspects of community. But community and government are not synonyms; government is only one aspect of community. Churches, synagogues, mosques, clubs, fraternal organizations, unions, are examples of the multiple, overlapping manifestations of community. Government is an important aspect, but only one part of a heterogenous mixture.

Another dimension of this chapter involves the scholarly debate over the role of individualism versus civic virtue in the American Revolution. Pangle presents one aspect of this debate in his discussion of the complex duality of classical thought. Human nature leads us "to social existence by way of the needs of the body and above all the need for survival" but it also includes "longing for a meaningful existence that would transfigure mere comfortable self-preservation."[4] This classical approach differs from what has actually occurred in the United States. Diggins agrees with the classical argument in political philosophy that a constitutional republic requires adherence to its first principles if it is to maintain itself; but he questions whether Americans have ever agreed on the individualist or pluralist variant of liberalism for their first principles: "One expression of liberalism valued freedom, autonomy, and the sufficiency of the individual, the other power, stability, and the efficacy of the state. Both identified happiness with property and material pleasure; neither committed America to political ideals that appealed to man's higher nature."[5] In short, Diggins argues that America has not aimed for "a meaningful existence that would transfigure mere comfortable self-preservation."

There are indications that this debate over the historical role of civic virtue versus individual rights is being replaced by an awareness that both were important in shaping American revolutionary politics.[6] The extreme individualist view, alone, does not provide an adequate explanation of how the polity functions: "The resources of the American tradition uphold more complex and more democratic conceptions of leadership than are available in theories that employ the classical capitalist market as the master model for politics."[7] The issue is, of course, more complex than liberalism versus civic virtue, as I argued in chapter 2. Religion must be added to the mix. And the religious foundation of revolutionary America strongly supported community values. So, one result of mixing all three strands is that we expect our leaders to be public servants, not self-interested individuals. But the struggle will continue, so long as the extreme individualist misinterpretation of Adam Smith's capitalism dominates the political economy.

Individuals are more than atoms of pure self-interest; individuality, as used in this work, is incompatible with both extreme individualism and overbearing community. When we understand this, we can move beyond dialectics to individuals within communities, a move that would be consistent with the community-oriented individuality of the founders.

The Founders on Community

At the end of the eighteenth century religious values strongly supported community against licentiousness.[8] And it appears that Adam Smith also saw the connection of religion, values, and community. Griswold writes that "Smith agrees with the Platonic tradition that religion is and ought to be a permanent natural feature of the human landscape and that when properly structured it is essential to sustaining community based on a shared notion of the virtues."[9] This connection helps explain the large difference between our founders' view of government and the contemporary view. They did not see government as a referee among competing interests; factionalism was a vice (see the next section). They were certain that our republic would survive only if the citizens were "animated by a spirit of virtue and concern for the public good."[10]

Emphasis on the importance of community in the development of the United States is not simply a liberal political bias. Irving Kristol, a neoconservative commentator, writes that the founders knew that citizens did not uniformly and universally possess virtues; yet "They understood that republican self-government could not exist if humanity did not possess—at some moments, and to a fair degree—the traditional 'republican virtues' of self-control, self-reliance, and a disinterested concern for the public good."[11] Of course, contemporary (political) liberals and conservatives would disagree on what concrete actions are inherent in the founders' virtue of "disinterested concern for the public good." So, let us briefly examine the historical background of the public good and then look at how the founders evaluated it.

Historical Sources

The roots of the founders' concern for the public good go back to the first European settlers. The Mayflower Compact, with its emphasis on the good of the colony and with the settlers' promise of "all due submission and obedience" to the colony is a prime example.[12] John Winthrop wrote in 1630 that "the care of the publique must oversway all private respects" and "perticuler estates cannott subsiste in the ruine of the publique."[13] The Puritans wanted to preserve the independence of their corporation (their society). The individual was secondary, the corporation, primary. The corporate conscience and the corporate conduct were to be free and untrammelled, but not necessarily the conduct and conscience of the individual.[14] Diggins agrees that the Puritans believed that the liberty of the commonwealth, of the community, was more important than individual liberty.[15] Individual members of Puritan communities were expected to work for the public good.[16]

Social cohesion and community authority were important to colonists in both Connecticut and Massachusetts throughout the seventeenth century.[17] Tully, while recognizing the "latent individualism and egalitarianism of the 'inner light,'" states that mutuality and community were strong characteristics of mid-eighteenth century Pennsylvania Quakers.[18] In short, throughout the colonies over many decades from initial settlement up to the revolutionary era, Americans were very community oriented, much more so than contemporary Americans.

Had the founders been sensitive to the settlers who predated the Puritans, they would have found Amerindian precedents for community as well. Zinn, looking at the age of exploration, notes the Amerindian belief in sharing and their acceptance of the universe of all things.[19] The community orientation of the Amerindians was still present in late colonial America. Crevecoeur, a Frenchman who lived in the United States during the revolutionary era and wrote about his impressions of the new country, stated that thousands of Europeans were Indians, had been assimilated into Indian tribes, but there were no examples of aborigines becoming Europeans by choice; so, he wondered if there was something in the Indians' social bond which was superior to anything the Europeans had.[20] Even if this incredible statement were true for only a few hundred Europeans, it would be a strong argument for the importance of community.

Eighteenth-century radicals, both in America and Europe, were also a source for the founders' ideas about the common good. The radicals believed that pre-revolutionary governments sacrificed the public good to the greed of monarchs and the monarchs' supporters. Josiah Quincy reflected this concern when he said, in 1774: "'Strange as it may seem . . . what the many through successive ages have desired and sought, the few have found means to baffle and defeat.'"[21] The common good "became for the Americans, as one general put it, their 'Polar Star.'" This idea was "shared not only by Hamilton and Paine . . . but by any American bitterly opposed to a system which held 'that a Part is greater than its Whole; or, in other Words, that some Individuals ought to be considered, even to the Destruction of the Community, which they compose.'"[22]

From this perspective, the American Revolution was against partiality shown to any special interest; government was to represent the whole people, to work for the common good. However, the Revolution did not resolve this issue. One theme throughout the remainder of this work is the perennial struggle between the rights of the many and the power of the few, whether that power be labeled monarchy, aristocracy, interest group liberalism, factionalism, or something else; whatever it is called, it is still with us in the third century of American independence.

Rugged Individualism in the American Revolutionary Era

Any consideration of individuality within communities must examine liberty, because communities can stifle individuals. Liberty was seen by the founders in terms remarkably similar to John Winthrop's view of freedom (see chapter 2). They contrasted it to licentiousness, the freedom to do anything, and insisted that true liberty required consideration of one's neighbor's happiness as well as one's own. For some revolutionaries, the state should completely dominate the individual: "Ideally, republicanism obliterated the individual. 'A Citizen,' said Samuel Adams, 'owes everything to the Commonwealth.' . . . . 'No man is a true republican,' wrote a Pennsylvanian in 1776, 'that will not give up his single voice to that of the public.'" [23] Americans today would see in such quotations an overemphasis on community, the virtual disappearance of the individual. Crevecoeur similarly disliked the dangerous power of community he observed during the revolution. He wrote of revolutionary governments easily overpowering individuals to raise militia. Another example of the excess he abhorred was the Patriots' mistreatment of Tories.[24]

While I do not advocate returning to that revolutionary era submersion of the individual in the community, note that wars (hot and cold) have that tendency. One reality of the revolution was that many individuals subordinated themselves to the state so that they and their posterity might have individual liberty. So where were the rugged individualists? In the revolutionary generation, few such people existed; the norm was individuals within communities. Most people of that era simply could not have comprehended the modern concept of individualism.

Winthrop's distinction between true liberty (roughly, individuals in communities) and the liberty of the state of nature (roughly, absolute individual freedom, or the survival of the fittest in a war of all against all) was accepted by John Jay, who further argued that the citizen's economic well-being was connected directly to respect for the law. Lerner presents Jay's thinking as follows: "'Let each man consider, that his liberty and his property cannot be secured without forming a common interest with all the other members of the society to which he belongs.'" [25] Jay presents an economic motivation for community (in addition to the security motivation mentioned in the quotation). The law of the jungle prevents sustained economic growth for the vast majority (while allowing a few to prosper, a situation which is economically inefficient as well as destructive of democracy—see chapters 6 and 7 for elaboration on these two points). John Adams also exemplifies our founders' balanced view of individual liberty within a community context.

John Adams

Adams was well aware that he was part of a community. He consistently emphasized what he called the human being's social affection. In a 1775 letter to his wife, he described this as encompassing the entire species, faintly it is true, but still a universal affection. This affection became stronger and stronger as one considered one's nation, county, town, family. Adams's circle of affections perspective on the universality of community is remarkably similar to a statement in Adam Smith's *Theory of Moral Sentiments*.[26] Typical of Adams's continual introspection, he also included in the same letter a self-criticism for having too much attachment to his own area, an "overweening Prejudice in favour of New England."[27] Wood places Adams's view in a broader context as an example of widely accepted views of the moral science of his time.[28]

That Adams believed that public interests must have primacy over private interests was clearly stated in an April 16, 1776, letter to Mercy Warren:

> Public Virtue cannot exist in a Nation without private, and public Virtue is the only Foundation of Republics. There must be a possitive Passion for the public good, the public Interest, Honour, Power, and Glory, established in the Minds of the People, or there can be no Republican Government, nor any real Liberty. And this public Passion must be Superiour to all private Passions. Men must be ready, they must pride themselves, and be happy to sacrifice their private Pleasures, Passions, and Interests, nay their private Friendships and dearest Connections, when they Stand in Competition with the Rights of society.[29]

The context of this quotation was a discussion of the importance of religion and morality as supports for government.

While Adams's sense of the public good included a strong sense of the social responsibility of leaders, he also had important thoughts about the population at large:

> Our proper Business in this Life is, not to accumulate large Fortunes, not to gain high Honours and important offices in the State, not to waste our Health and Spirits in Pursuit of the Sciences, but constantly to improve our selves in Habits of Piety and Virtue. Consequently, the meanest Mechanick, who endeavours in proportion to his Ability, to promote the happiness of his fellow men, deserves better of Society, and should be held in higher Esteem than the Greatest Magistrate, who uses his power for his own Pleasures or Avarice or Ambition.[30]

This quotation should not lead one to believe that Adams was a critic of capitalism: far from it! His similarities with Adam Smith on free trade will be discussed below; here it is important to note that he viewed commerce as demonstrating a community reality, a view he still held fifty years later: "Now commerce, the instrument of an universal alliance . . . renders it visible to the grossest eyesight that we are made for one another, that our destination is to be useful reciprocally, that we are members of the same body and children of the same family."[31]

For all of his emphasis on the common good, Adams still had a balanced position on individuality within communities. His sense of public duty (discussed in chapter 3) was so strong that he sacrificed the joys of private life time and again to serve first his town, then his beloved Massachusetts, and finally his nation. But, whenever he could, he returned to his Quincy farm. Adams understood that there was an individual element in life. He even wrote: "Private good does not always depend on the public. The happiness of every individual does not always depend on the happiness of society."[32] He made a similar statement in chapter 3 that his cousin, Samuel Adams, was perhaps too attentive to public duty at the expense of himself and his family and note his letter to his classmate, Charles Cushing (also in chapter 3), which discussed both "service to our fellowmen as well as to ourselves" as criteria for choosing a career. Adams constantly struggled with himself to find the right balance between community welfare and individual rights.[33]

Other Founders

Thomas Jefferson emphasized the individual pursuit of happiness. But that should not lead one to believe that he advocated the atomistic individualism so common today.[34] Jefferson and Adams had similar views of the public good. In a June 13, 1814, letter to Thomas Law, Jefferson discussed man as a "social animal." And he criticized self-love as "the sole antagonist of virtue, leading us constantly by our propensities to self-gratification in violation of our moral duties to others."[35] Jefferson thought that "'the brightest gem'" in human character was the "'moral instinct'" to help others. In addition, individuals experience pleasure when they help others. Why? "'Because nature hath implanted in our breasts a love of others, a sense of duty to them.'"[36] While Jefferson believed the social sense to be an inherent part of one's moral being, he also knew that people were concerned for themselves, had selfish passions. As Lorraine and Thomas Pangle state, there were two contradictory elements in Jefferson's moral reasoning: happiness based on independence, self-reliance, and domestic life was in tension with his teaching of "harmony and respect for the feelings and opinions of others in a community of ordinary men."[37]

Debates on adoption of the new constitution furnish additional examples of the founders' thinking about community. John Dickinson believed that "our Creator designed men for society" and that men could not be secure, free, or happy without society.[38] James Wilson added that man needed society and government "for his perfection and happiness as well."[39] John Marshall said that "The American way was so to blend public and private interests that all men (or most) would have a sense of their stake in society. When the American 'promotes his own [interest], he promotes that of the community. When we consult the common good, we consult our own.'"[40] The *yin-yang* nature of Marshall's statement is also true for the views of many of the founders.[41]

The Federalist makes an extremely important point about the relationship between leaders and communities, as reported by Lerner:

> Adherence to the republican principle, to the spirit of a government wholly popular, in no way entails "an unqualified complaisance to every sudden breeze of passion, or to every transient impulse which the people may receive from the arts of men, who flatter their prejudices to betray their interests." Publius, like Rousseau, knew that while "the people commonly *intend* the PUBLIC GOOD," they do not always *"reason right* about the *means* of promoting it." Indeed, we may say that the deepest justification of a separate and independent judiciary is the expectation that, more often than is politically safe, "the interests of the people are at variance with their inclinations." If the "republican principle demands, that the deliberate sense of the community should govern the conduct of those to whom they entrust the management of their affairs," it also imposes a "duty" on "the guardians of those interests" to call the people to their senses or at least to give the people the chance to come to their senses.[42]

John Adams also indicated a desire to promote public happiness without flattering popular prejudices.[43] The people have a right to the pursuit of happiness which government should support. However, a good leader would limit that support to what was just, reasonable, and in the long-term interests of the whole community. Sometimes, a leader must disagree with popular demands in order to serve the common good.

Political Philosophers

Philosophers have long been interested in the interrelationships of individuals in communities. Many of them have shared with the founders a concern for the common good. Enlightenment thinkers certainly understood the duality of individuals in communities. "To a degree perhaps unknown in the previous history of thought, Locke, together with Hobbes, teaches that human beings must strive to accommodate themselves to others." In addition, Locke believed that "men have an overriding moral obligation to live with a view to 'getting along' with one another."[44] Note the normative nature of this statement; because human beings are individualistic, they must struggle to meet their *moral* obligation to maintain community. Locke also argued, according to Pangle, that humans need society in order to survive. Humans cope with the chaotic state of nature by surrendering some freedom to gain order and security.[45] Other scholars agree; Mitchell, for example, states that we misread Hobbes and Locke when we find individualism in their works. Community is preeminent.[46]

Adam Smith has often been interpreted as a supporter of individualism. But such arguments distort Smith by ignoring the social dimensions of his thought. The opening sentence in *Theory of Moral Sentiments* makes this clear: "How selfish soever man may be supposed, there are evidently some principles in his nature, which interest him in the fortune of others, and render their happiness necessary to him, though he derives nothing from it except the pleasure of seeing it." He also wrote that man "has a natural love for society," that nature "formed man for society," and that man "can subsist only in society. . . . All the different members of it [society] are bound together by the agreeable bands of love and affection, and are, as it were, drawn to one common centre of mutual good offices."[47] Love and assisting others ("mutual good offices") are hardly the stuff of atomistic individualism. But Smith makes an even stronger comment:

> In directing all our actions to promote the greatest possible good, in submitting all inferior affections to the desire of the general happiness of mankind, in regarding one's self but as one of the many, whose prosperity was to be pursued no further than it was consistent with, or conducive to that of the whole, consisted the perfection of virtue.
>
> Self-love was a principle which could never be virtuous in any degree or in any direction. It was vicious whenever it obstructed the general good.[48]

Several scholars have criticized the individualist misinterpretation. For example, Werhane writes that in Smith's *Theory of Moral Sentiments* "the social passions are motivating forces equal to the selfish passions," and in his *Wealth of Nations* "the social passions are the sources of cooperation and coordination without which no economy could operate. Therefore, in both works . . . the social passions and interests are as important as is self-interest."[49] However, according to Werhane: "Smith gives primary importance to the individual rather than the social order, and so it is not incorrect to label him as a moderate individualist." But this individualist perspective is qualified by one of the natural qualities of human beings, "their desire for approval by others and their desire 'of being what ought to be approved of.'"[50] Human individuality was very important to Smith but he was also aware of human social passions. For him, human beings were both individuals and social beings.[51]

Both of Smith's works provide myriad examples of the interrelationship of individual and community. The most obvious is that the title of his more famous work is not "Wealth of Individuals" but *An Inquiry into the Nature and Causes of the Wealth of Nations*. In that work he clearly stated: "But the great object of the political oeconomy of every country is to encrease the riches and power of that country."[52] Some might discount that quotation because it comes in a section dealing with free trade. Such a criticism would miss the point, in my view, because Smith's purpose in advocating free trade was to increase the wealth of all the people. And there are other, clearer statements. Smith proposed that the two goals for political economy should be to enrich the people and the state: "first, to provide a plentiful revenue or subsistence for the people, or more properly to enable them to provide such a revenue or subsistence for themselves; and secondly, to supply the state or commonwealth with a revenue sufficient for the publick services."[53] It is true that Smith recognized that such objectives were often attained as the unintended result of self-interested individual economic behavior (which is a quick definition of "the invisible hand").

Nevertheless, even the "invisible hand" illustrates the social orientation of Smith's thinking. *Wealth of Nations* uses that phrase only once.

> As every individual, therefore, endeavours as much as he can both to employ his capital in the support of domestick industry, and so to direct that industry that its produce may be of the greatest value; every individual necessarily labours to render the annual revenue of the society as great as he can. He generally, indeed neither intends to promote the publick interest, nor knows how much he is promoting it. By preferring the support of domestick to that of foreign industry, he intends only his own security; and by directing that industry in such a manner as its produce may be of the greatest value, he intends only his own gain, and he is in this, as in many other cases, led by an invisible hand to promote an end which was no part of his intention. Nor is it always the worse for the society that it was no part of it. By pursuing his own interest he frequently promotes that of the society more effectually than when he really intends to promote it.[54]

In the only *Theory of Moral Sentiments* paragraph containing that phrase, Smith contrasted the rich and the poor, commented on the unintended benefits for the poor that result from the rapacity and vanity of the rich, and concluded: "In what constitutes the real happiness of human life, they [the poor] are in no respect inferior to those who would seem so much above them."[55] Note that while Smith recognized that even rapacious individuals provide benefits for society, he still harshly criticized the rich. Note, also, the basic egalitarianism of his conclusion.

So far, the "invisible hand" quotations from Smith's two books might appear to support individualism, not individuality within communities. But, the "invisible hand" should not be interpreted as supporting unvarnished individualism. The editors of the Glasgow edition of the works and correspondence of Adam Smith suggest that commentators may be overemphasizing the "invisible hand" which Smith used so rarely. In that same series, the editors of *Theory of Moral Sentiments* argue that in both of Smith's published books the context for discussion of the "invisible hand" is "the Stoic idea of harmonious system, seen in the working of society." They insist that the philosophical foundation for both of Smith's books was a combination of Stoic and Christian virtues and that the chief sources for Smith's Stoic ideas were Romans who "closely connected men's moral duties with their legal obligations as citizens."[56] In short, both of the major sources for the philosophy of this systematic thinker support a balanced view of individuals in communities. The "invisible hand" is about individuals meeting their responsibilities for harmonious community.

Smith's *Theory of Moral Sentiments* concept of the "impartial spectator," a much more important concept than the "invisible hand,"[57] is inherently community oriented. That community orientation is seen in the way conscience counteracts self-love.

> It is he [the impartial spectator] who, whenever we are about to act so as to affect the happiness of others, calls to us, with a voice capable of astonishing the most presumptuous of our passions, that we are but one of the multitude, in no respect better than any other in it; and that when we prefer ourselves so shamefully and so blindly to others, we become the proper objects of resentment, abhorrence, and execration. It is from him only that we learn the real littleness of ourselves, and of whatever relates to ourselves, and the natural misrepresentations of self-love can be corrected only by the eye of this impartial spectator. It is he who shows us the propriety of generosity and the deformity of injustice; the propriety of resigning the greatest interests of our own, for the yet greater interests of others, and the deformity of doing the smallest injury to another, in order to obtain the greatest benefit to ourselves.[58]

The impartial spectator is fundamentally determined by community influences. And, in turn, the impartial spectator controls selfishness, so that individuals do not harm other individuals. The final sentence illustrates the complexity of the interaction; the individual desire to maintain one's character prevents selfish behavior. This concept is remarkably like the founders' quest for distinction; both Washington and Adams had a passion for distinction. They were ambitious, yet this was a virtuous ambition because their quest for fame led them to disinterested public service.

Werhane states that Smith's "impartial spectator" enables one to make disinterested moral judgments:

> in moral decision making, Smith's impartial spectator asks (1) whether a particular judgment would be the kind of judgment that society would deem appropriate to that kind of situation, (2) whether it is the kind of decision that others should make, all things considered, and (3) whether that decision embodies a rule that could serve as a general rule for other similar cases.[59]

This is quite similar to Immanuel Kant's categorical imperative. (Would you like to see your individual action generalized to society as a whole? Would you like to see everybody doing what you are doing?)

An everyday example might help to make the point about generalizing individual behavior. You are downtown, walking to an appointment, and worried that you might be late. At a crosswalk the pedestrian light clearly states "Don't Walk." But there in no oncoming traffic. Is any community interest harmed by your walking against the light? Let's change the scenario a bit: there is oncoming traffic. Do you still step out into the crosswalk and cause traffic to slow down and/or stop? Does such action harm any community interest? Obviously, if you cause an accident, you have harmed community interests to say nothing of the broken bones you, yourself, have most probably suffered. But what if you successfully cross the street, and as a result are on time for your appointment? Does it make any difference if you impeded the flow of traffic for only one car, or several? Would society deem your judgment appropriate? Should others make the same decision? Could your decision be the basis for a generalization applicable to similar cases? How would you feel if you were one of the drivers slowed down by the impatient pedestrian? In short, how do you balance your self-interest with community interests?

Many other philosophers could be cited as examples of the importance of community.[60] But I think the point has been made that the founders' emphasis on the public interest was (and still is) part of a broad tradition. Now let us return to the American scene and examine what various scholarly observers have to say about individuals in communities.

Other Commentators

Earlier I referred to Crevecoeur, an astute observer of revolutionary era America. Even though Crevecoeur understood and abhorred governmental power to repress individuals, he argued quite strongly for the importance of community, both in a parable and in comments on actual social practice in rural America. His parable of the bees described the success of a hive resulting from the solidarity and community action of the bees and, in contrast, the failure of individual bees that went out on their own. He also wrote about the social practice of communal barn-raising, part of our heritage about which many contemporary Americans are aware. But few today know that barn-raising was only one example of the more general practice of making bees. That custom included helping widows and orphans, and providing neighbors with reciprocal help for major projects, such as hauling firewood, building a house, or clearing swamps.[61] That the practice of bees had so many applications in addition to barn-raising shows that early settlers were even more community oriented than many of us have thought.

Life for most eighteenth-century Americans was community oriented. Shain argues that "a dozen or so elite nationalists" were extremely individualistic but that the "vast majority of Americans lived voluntarily in morally demanding agricultural communities shaped by reformed-Protestant social and moral norms." Family and community were the defining agencies.[62] Throughout his book Shain argues that, although the individual was subordinated to society, s/he was not obliterated. Americans served the "collective good first" as "the precondition for the subsequent exercise of a measured amount of autonomous individual freedom."[63]

In the nineteenth century Charles Darwin wrote his works on the evolutionary survival of the fittest. His writings were sometimes interpreted as supporting rugged individualism. But Hofstadter argues that Darwin believed that the sociability of man was "of enormous importance in his survival."[64]

Community is a moral imperative for some contemporary scholars who connect public service and our religious heritage. Remember Pangle's statement above that Locke and Hobbes argued that maintenance of community was a moral obligation. You may also recall from chapter 3 that Samuel Adams considered his political work to be similar to a religious vocation. Bellah argues that the idea of vocation ("the calling") comes from both our biblical and republican traditions; however, it is very uncommon in contemporary America:

> But the calling not only links a person to his or her fellow workers. A calling links a person to the larger community, a whole in which the calling of each is a contribution to the good of all. . . . The calling is a crucial link between the individual and the public world. Work in the sense of the calling can never be merely private.[65]

In addition, Bellah states that interviewees basically agreed that community was important to happiness, self-esteem, and moral worth. Note his balanced view of the issue: "And the positive side of our individualism, our sense of the dignity, worth, and moral autonomy of the individual, is dependent in a thousand ways on a social, cultural, and institutional context that keeps us afloat even when we cannot very well describe it."[66]

Such a balanced view is also obvious in Etzioni's *The Moral Dimension, Toward a New Economics,* an extended argument for economics based on an "I-We" model. He challenges "the entrenched utilitarian, rationalistic-individualistic, neoclassical paradigm which is applied not merely to the economy but also, increasingly, to the full array of social relations, from crime to family." Further, he argues that, while individuals are able to act rationally on their own, this ability "is deeply affected by how well they are anchored within a sound community and sustained by a firm moral and emotive personal underpinning—a community they perceive as theirs, as a '*We,*' rather than as an imposed, restraining 'they.'"[67] In Etzioni's work, a balanced and inextricable relationship of individuals and community is emphasized.[68] We would be better off economically if we recognized that we are individuals in communities.

Barber, a political scientist, argues for "strong democracy." He points out that our private rights exist because of the law, that we can be individuals only because the community protects our rights. "Autonomy is not the condition of democracy, democracy is the condition of autonomy." Further, he states that people cannot "become individuals" without taking part in community life. "Freedom, justice, equality, and autonomy are all products of common thinking and common living; democracy creates them."[69] Similarly, Dagger states that "autonomy and civic virtue are complementary" because human beings are interdependent.[70] And Sinopoli writes that liberals must work "to weaken the centrifugal forces that are embedded in liberal ideology and to strengthen those that tend toward community and civic virtue."[71]

Both Barber and Etzioni warn of the dangers of extreme individualism. Barber argues that "the great aberrations of twentieth-century political culture—majoritarian tyranny, mass society, and totalitarianism—have resulted more from the thinness of liberalism than from the participatory aspirations of strong democracy." He also states that individuals alone are easy targets for authoritarianism.[72] Similarly, Etzioni emphasizes the importance of community for anyone with a deep commitment to liberty, pointing out that anomic individuals are "vulnerable to totalitarian movements" and easily manipulated by demagogues.[73]

Scholars studying differences in male and female self-perceptions have developed an argument about gender differences in individual-community views. Hirschmann states that there is empirical support for the argument that females see themselves as connected to others, and males see themselves as separate. Thus, males reason more in terms of individual rights while females see relationships and overlapping responsibilities.[74] Hirschmann then argues that such perceptions have important implications for the priority that liberalism assigns to freedom:

> Thus, a feminist method profoundly alters the very terms of the discourse. Beginning with the self as separate, liberal voluntarist obligation seeks to find areas and modes of connection that are safe—that can provide for needs without risking the loss of self. This feminist model, beginning with connection, tries to determine how to carve out a space for the self without violating care. While freedom is certainly achievable in the context of human relationships, it must *be achieved*, it is not a given. Freedom is an entity that must be created, as an individual carves out space for him—or herself. And since freedom is created by a stepping away from, or out of, obligations, freedom must also be justified.[75]

In this balanced argument, freedom is important, but it must exist within the context of responsibility for relationships. The individual is valued, but is not supreme. Hirschmann also states that men and women "are often in fact nonconsensually bound more tightly than our public discourse admits."[76] In short, many relationships tie us to one another, but our ideology of individualism ignores this important reality of connection.

Libertarians would probably disagree with that conclusion. However, some conservatives might disagree with libertarians on this. For example, Novak distinguishes between individuals and persons, intimating that individuals are like animals, slaves to events, while a person is more than an individual. Note what he argues about persons and community: "Analogously, on earth and in time, the common good of persons is to live in as close an approximation of unity in insight and love as sinful human beings might attain." But, he also states, it is difficult to know what the common good is and to achieve it.[77]

Thus we see, from many different perspectives, the importance of individuals in communities. I believe these sources show that humans are both individual and social beings. The founders' thinking on this issue was not aberrant. Moreover, many contemporary thinkers still agree on this fundamental point. Given all this, why has individualism overwhelmed individuality within communities?

Disappearing Community

Factors which help answer that question have roots in the revolutionary era. Early in the new republic, Jefferson understood that the public good was endangered by personal economic concerns. Both Adams and Jefferson feared the corrupting effects of commerce. (In this context, remember the founders' fears of the corrupting tendencies of luxury, in the "Pursuit of Happiness" section of chapter 2.) Pangle notes that Jefferson warned that Americans "absorbed by commerce, would more and more exhibit a syndrome of apathetic withdrawal into petty personal spheres, preoccupied with material comfort and the promotion of narrow and dependent economic interests."[78]

Perhaps unintentionally, Benjamin Franklin reinforced the self-interested economic fixation the founders feared, although it is possible that he did not personally agree with the popular emphasis on individual economic interest. In his *Autobiography* he emphasized philanthropy, passionate concern for one's fellow man, and ardor for the common good.[79] Similarly, Forde argues that Franklin was not an "unregenerate materialist," that he was concerned about virtues and wanted to direct people to a "much fuller vision of human happiness and the well-lived life."[80] For example, Franklin wrote the following about good works:

For my own Part, when I am employed in serving others, I do not look upon myself as conferring Favours, but as paying Debts. In my Travels, and since my Settlement, I have received much Kindness from Men, to whom I shall never have any Opportunity of making the least direct Return. And numberless Mercies from God, who is infinitely above being benefited by our Services. Those Kindnesses from Men, I can therefore only Return on their Fellow Men; and I can only show my Gratitude for these mercies from God, by a readiness to help his other Children and my Brethren. For I do not think that Thanks and Compliments, tho' repeated weekly, can discharge our real Obligations to each other, and much less those to our Creator.[81]

But Diggins has a much more individualistic interpretation; while recognizing Franklin's public service, he states that "Franklin taught Americans that the true path to virtue lies not in subordinating one's interest to the state but in pursuing wealth and fortune as a self-reliant individual."[82] In a similar vein, Bellah writes that Franklin's "image contributed much to this new model of human life."[83] If this interpretation is correct, Franklin is a major source of the extreme, self-interest school of American capitalism.

Social bonds were destroyed by the revolutionary quest for liberty. Sociologists frequently discuss anomie in modern societies. One might argue that anomie also existed in late-eighteenth-century America, produced by that "apathetic withdrawal into petty personal spheres" which Jefferson feared. (Note that in this context, apathy refers to the public sphere; Americans in the early republican era were by no means apathetic about their individual interests.) Shortly after the revolution, individual emphasis on self-interest, supported by political leaders, produced anomie or something remarkably similar to it. Charles Nisbet, a Scotsman who arrived in America in 1787, complained of "'a new world . . . unfortunately composed . . . of discordant atoms, jumbled together by chance, and tossed by unconstancy in an immense vacuum.'" Leaders were telling the people "'to pursue their own happiness,'" and that each person should "'be his own master in all respects.'"[84] The version of self-interest Charles Nisbet observed in 1787 was a marked change from the revolutionary era. Shain states that Americans of the revolutionary generation saw "self-interest, selfishness, self-centeredness, and self-love" as "forms of personal pathology."[85]

Decline in public spirit was also affected by the ready availability of new land, which contributed to farmers' proclivity to sell their farms and start over again. American farmers did not settle down in one place with the intention of remaining for generations. Of course, repeated buying and selling and moving weakened social ties and made it difficult to maintain community.[86] Jefferson had believed in the virtues of the independent farmer. But the farmer, seeking his own self-interest, was profiting from land sales at the expense of developing communities. The end of the frontier would eventually force farmers into more stable land-holding, but that would not alleviate the problem because very few Americans are now farmers, and in general, Americans are still a restless people. In this century, that restlessness has been reinforced by corporate policy. Bellah describes the case of one man for whom community commitments were very important but who said he was "losing his sense of social commitment because of the pressure to leave his community for a higher echelon job in his bank."[87] Establishing stable communities is very difficult, given that many Americans move from community to community, often from one state to another, several times in their lives, to say nothing of the amorphousness of community in modern megalopolitan society.

Was the frontier a major contributor to the decline of community values? This question has been the subject of some academic debate. Merriam argued that social and economic conditions on the frontier produced self-reliance, independence, and individuality.[88] But Diggins, analyzing Frederick Jackson Turner's thought, disagrees, arguing "that significant participation in local town affairs took place in western communities."[89] Such community cooperation began with the wagon trains; it was not very safe for individual families to cross the Great Plains alone. While Diggins insists that frontier conditions required individuals to participate in their communities, he also states that Turner saw the loss of the frontier as a problem for American society.[90]

Individualism was reinforced by Transcendentalism. In his 1841 essay, "Self-Reliance," Ralph Waldo Emerson wrote of economic responsibility as focused on the self: "'Then again, do not tell me, as a good man did to-day, of my obligation to put all poor men in good situations. Are they *my* poor?'"[91] American discomfort with welfare programs has been strengthened by such views. Diggins comments that the Transcendentalists "privatized the concept of virtue," devalued the public good, and "rejected as immaterial three of the greatest questions in political philosophy: What makes society possible? What makes the state legitimate? And why should man obey either?"[92] Muller agrees; he sees the Emersonian tradition and also the Romantic ideal as individualistic conceptions of the good life that Adam Smith "would have found abhorrent if not incomprehensible."[93]

Thus, economic self-interest, physical factors (easy availability of land and the end of the frontier), political expediency (politicians' emphasis on liberty, which reinforced individualism at the expense of individuality within communities), and cultural currents (Transcendentalism) all contributed to the reduction in public spirit.

Caveats

Given this range of factors contributing to a decline in concern for the common good, anyone attempting to restore the public interest to the preeminence which the founders gave it must be prepared for powerful resistance. In addition, such restoration must be done with sensitivity, because there are dangers in emphasizing community. The immense conformity pressures of community taken to an extreme are antithetical to individual liberty. The reality of the traditional American small town was that many Americans felt imprisoned. Bellah is aware of this: "We thus face a profound impasse. Modern individualism seems to be producing a way of life that is neither individually nor socially viable, yet a return to traditional forms would be to return to intolerable discrimination and oppression."[94] Etzioni states that we do not want to "backpedal" to the constraining and authoritarian traditional communities but to develop a balance of "diversity and unity."[95] Similarly, Tocqueville forcefully warned us of the dangers of "tyranny of the majority." And Pangle, commenting on uneasiness in Western democracies about the decline of civic concern warns about a "cynical passivity" on the one hand and, on the other "an insistent hope or demand for a kind of democratic politics of 'participation' that would not respect the limits imposed by the nature and the historical development of modern liberalism."[96]

Historically, small communities were often repressive of individuality, as the comments above indicate. But modern Americans do not generally live in such isolated communities. We are now members of multiple communities, with churches, families, and many other associations added to the usual political mix of cities, counties, states, and nations.[97] This gives individuals an escape hatch, if one particular community becomes repressive. Or, as Rosenblum puts it, pluralism limits vulnerability; shifting involvements among various spheres is a self-defense mechanism against public authority and private despotisms.[98] Thus, we need a liberalism that offers a healthy politics of community[99] and there is reason to believe that it is attainable, in spite of the historical difficulties with the concept. Individuals are not powerless; we can build viable communities which need not be repressive. However, the twentieth century has witnessed many totalitarian states, and provides many concrete examples of how easy it is to convince people that dictatorial methods are the most efficient means of achieving worthy goals, with the inevitable result that those goals are perverted. Liberalism has defended us against twentieth-century totalitarianisms as well as the repression of the small, closed community.[100] But, just because absolute communities are pathological should not lead us to reject healthy, liberal communities.

A second concern is that appeals to the common good can be used by factions to manipulate elected officials. An Anti-Federalist writer feared that even when legislators refused to be bribed, the special interests would use "specious and false reasoning" to convince honest legislators that the private interest was really for the public good.

> It is not to be expected that a legislature will be found in any country that will not have some of its members, who will pursue their private ends, and for which they will sacrifice the public good. Men of this character are, generally, artful and designing, and frequently possess brilliant talents and abilities; they commonly act in concert, and agree to share the spoils of their country among them; they will keep their object ever in view, and follow it with constancy. To effect their purpose, they will assume any shape, and Proteus like, mould themselves into any form. . . . Those who are acquainted with the manner of conducting business in public assemblies, know how prevalent art and address are in carrying a measure, even over men of the best intentions, and of good understanding.[101]

In this quotation, Brutus described one of the results of factions. Chapter 5 examines the problem of factionalism in greater detail.

Conclusion

The revolutionary slogan, "Eternal vigilance is the price of liberty," seems to be the battle cry of some American individualists who fear any constraint. That rugged individualists view any suggestion of strengthening community with a jaundiced eye can be somewhat understood, given the dangers of excessive community. Such individualists seem to believe that any limits on freedom would have the same result that Enlightenment thinkers attributed to classical Stoic and orthodox Christian doctrines: repression of egoism, which inevitably produced tyranny.[102] This is a dialectically extreme position.

A recent, excellent Adams biography is somewhat flawed in that the author seems close to this extreme position; Ellis criticizes Adams for having a "premodern or pre-liberal" vision and writes that Adams's "orientation was inherently social and collectivistic" rather than assuming "that the individual was the sovereign unit in the social equation." Ellis further characterizes Adams as assuming that individual interests "must naturally and necessarily be subordinated to public imperatives if the human potential unleashed by the American Revolution were to achieve its fullest realization."[103] I believe that Adams understood some fundamental truths about society which we need to relearn today. One of the most important of these truths is that the absolute freedom inherent in the extreme individualist position is impossible today, just as it was impossible in the revolutionary era. The difficulty is in protecting the individual while strengthening the community. How does one develop a strong symbiosis of individuality within communities, while avoiding the dialectical dangers of anomic individualism on the one hand and absolutist community repression of individual freedom on the other?

Such symbiosis would not violate the principles of our founders because the United States was founded on an assumption of individual-community duality. Pangle states that patriotism is not "simply loyalty to what is one's own, that it must also express loyalty to what is good," and that there may be a tension between the two.[104] But he is much more optimistic than Diggins, who writes that the idea of community, that private interests should be subordinate to the common good "was an idea that could not be translated into politics."[105] Diggins is overgeneralizing. Indeed, making community work is difficult; self-interest is tenacious. But, while American history has many examples of heavily self-interested action, there have also been more community-oriented periods, such as the New Deal. Community ideals have been translated into politics by both Democrats and Republicans. In addition to the New Deal, remember Republican President Dwight D. Eisenhower's Interstate Highway program. Remember, also, the massive support for science and technology under presidents of both parties in the post-World War II period. The founders' belief in strong government has been implemented at various times in the twentieth century during both Republican and Democratic presidencies (see chapter 6).

Just as changing conditions contributed to the decline of community in the United States, so additional changes may lead us back to community. Note that the examples above were governmental responses to changing circumstances. Barber writes about other changes requiring community response:

> The new pressures of ecology, transnationalism, and resource scarcity in combination with the apparent bankruptcy of privatism, materialism, and economic individualism—the pathologies and the ambivalent promises of our modernity—create conditions more inviting to the generation of public purposes and a public spirit than any America has ever known.[106]

Barber, of course, does not predict when these pathologies will have developed to the point of generating a renewal of concern for the public good. However, individual initiative supported by governmental leadership might help.

Pope John XXIII had a definition of the common good which connects individual and government: "'the common good . . . embraces the sum total of those conditions of social living, whereby men are enabled more fully and more readily to achieve their own perfection.'" He also states that two factors require balancing: "'(1) the freedom of individual citizens and groups of citizens to act autonomously, while cooperating one with the other; (2) the activity of the State whereby the undertakings of private individuals and groups are suitably regulated and fostered.'"[107] The second point leads us to the governmental aspect of maintaining individuality within communities.

Notes

1. Robert N. Bellah, et al., *Habits of the Heart: Individualism and Commitment in American Life* (New York: Harper and Row, 1985), 142.
2. Thomas E. McCollough, *The Moral Imagination and Public Life: Raising the Ethical Question* (Chatham, N.J.: Chatham House Publishers, Inc., 1991), 66 and 93.
3. One example of the excessively individualistic approach can be seen in Thomas C. Cochran's contrast between early America and Europe; Americans valued the following "more than, or differently from" Europeans: "individual initiative and responsibility, self-determination, private rights, material success, belief in an immanent God, and impatience with apparently nonutilitarian activities or learning, and white male supremacy" (Thomas C. Cochran, *Challenges to American Values: Society, Business, and Religion* [New York: Oxford University Press, 1985], 4). This is a clear example of the bias of many Americans in favor of individualism, to say nothing of the anti-egalitarian white male chauvinism of the statement. I agree with individual responsibility and belief in God. But his list omits some attributes which have been, historically, very important. He does not list early American civic virtues, such as public spirit and disinterest. To be fair to Cochran, he later notes that American individualism included a cooperative element (Cochran, *Challenges to American Values*, 19), but I think he understates the community orientation of revolutionary America. His list is biased toward individualism, at the expense of communities; however, his awareness of early American cooperation demonstrates the importance of this chapter's examination of the relationships of individuals and communities.
4. Thomas L. Pangle, *The Spirit of Modern Republicanism: The Moral Vision of the American Founders and the Philosophy of Locke* (Chicago: University of Chicago Press, 1988), 212.
5. John P. Diggins, *The Lost Soul of American Politics: Virtue, Self-Interest, and the Foundations of Liberalism* (Chicago: University of Chicago Press, 1984), 5.
6. Bruce Miroff, *Icons of Democracy: American Leaders as Heroes, Aristocrats, Dissenters, and Democrats* (New York: Basic Books, 1993), 350-51; Richard Dagger, *Civic Virtues: Rights, Citizenship, and Republican Liberalism* (New York: Oxford University Press, 1997), 12-13 and passim. Steven B. Smith, "Hegel's Critique of Liberalism," *American Political Science Review* 80 (March 1986): 122, presents a related argument.
7. Miroff, *Icons of Democracy*, 350.
8. Ruth Bloch, *Visionary Republic: Millennial Themes in American Thought, 1756-1800* (Cambridge: Cambridge University Press, 1985), 224-25.
9. Charles L. Griswold, Jr., *Adam Smith and the Virtues of Enlightenment* (New York: Cambridge University Press, 1999), 286-87.

10. Bellah, *Habits of the Heart,* 253. The public good is another value Americans inherited from their Puritan ancestors (Bloch, *Visionary Republic,* 4).

11. Irving Kristol, Martin Diamond, and G. Warren Nutter, *The American Revolution: Three Views* (New York: American Brands, Inc., 1975), 29.

12. In Daniel J. Boorstin, ed., *An American Primer* (New York: Penguin Books, 1966), 21.

13. John Winthrop, "A Model of Christian Charity," in *The American Intellectual Tradition, A Sourcebook,* 2d ed., 1, David A. Hollinger and Charles Capper, eds. (New York: Oxford University Press, 1993), 14; also in Boorstin, ed., *American Primer,* 28-38.

14. Charles Edward Merriam, *A History of American Political Theories* (New York: Augustus M. Kelley, 1969), 24.

15. Diggins, *Lost Soul of American Politics,* 150.

16. John Ferling, *John Adams: A Life* (Knoxville: University of Tennessee Press, 1992), 44.

17. Joyce Appleby, *Liberalism and Republicanism in the Historical Imagination* (Cambridge: Harvard University Press, 1992), 144.

18. Alan Tully, *William Penn's Legacy: Politics and Social Structure in Provincial Pennsylvania, 1726-1755* (Baltimore: Johns Hopkins University Press, 1977), 143-45. Some people may think that the greater community orientation of the settler and revolutionary generations was a necessity for survival which is no longer pertinent to contemporary Americans. I believe that our community needs today are similar in degree, although different in kind.

19. Howard Zinn, *A People's History of the United States* (New York: Harper and Row, 1980), 1 and 515.

20. J. Hector St. John de Crevecoeur, *Letters from an American Farmer and Sketches of Eighteenth-Century America* (New York: Penguin Books, 1981), 214.

21. Quoted by Gordon S. Wood, *The Creation of the American Republic 1776-1787* (Chapel Hill: University of North Carolina Press, for the Institute of Early American History and Culture, 1969), 54.

22. Wood, *Creation of American Republic,* 55. Wood explains that the founders' distrust of factions stemmed from their view of the common interest, which they saw in a corporate, holistic sense. The existence of clashing interests was seen as a perversion, as a sign of "sickness in the body politic." The common good was "an entity in itself, prior to and distinct from the various private interests of groups and individuals. . . . [P]olitics·was conceived to be not the reconciling but the transcending of the different interests of the society in the search for the single common good" (Wood, *Creation of American Republic,* 58-59). This holistic view is not appreciated in contemporary America; indeed, the concept has been lost; see Bernard Grofman and Scott L. Feld, "Rousseau's General Will: A Condorcetian Perspective," *American Political Science Review* 82 (June 1988): 568-69. Instead, we usually act as if the common good is merely the sum of individual and factional interests.

23. Wood, *Creation of American Republic,* 60-61.

24. Crevecoeur, *Letters from an American Farmer,* passim.

25. Ralph Lerner, *The Thinking Revolutionary: Principle and Practice in the New Republic* (Ithaca, N.Y.: Cornell University Press, 1979), 100-101.

26. Here is Adam Smith's "circle of affections" statement:

Among those primary objects which nature had recommended to us as eligible, was the prosperity of our family, of our relations, of our friends, of our country, of mankind, and of the universe in general. Nature, too, had taught us, that as the prosperity of two was preferable to that of one, that of many, or of all, must be infinitely more so (Adam Smith, *The Theory of Moral Sentiments,* 6th ed., D. D. Raphael and A. L. Macfie, eds. [Oxford: Oxford University Press, 1978], VII.ii.I.18, 274).

Smith continued this statement arguing that our own interest should yield to the common interest. He emphasized the prosperity of the whole, not the individual.

27. John Adams, letter to Abigail Adams, October 29, 1775, in L. H. Butterfield, ed., *Adams Family Correspondence,* 1 (Cambridge: Belknap Press of Harvard University Press, 1963), 318.

28. Gordon S. Wood, *The Radicalism of the American Revolution* (New York: Alfred A. Knopf, 1992), 220-21. A common view at that time was that individuals cannot be happy without communities, and that self-love, benevolence, and individual happiness were all interrelated parts of a system.

29. John Adams, letter to Mercy Otis Warren, April 16, 1776, in Robert J. Taylor, ed., *Papers of John Adams,* 4 (Cambridge: Belknap Press of Harvard University Press, 1979), 124-25.

30. John Adams, diary entry of April 29, 1756, in L. H. Butterfield, ed., *The Adams Papers: Diary and Autobiography of John Adams,* 1 (New York: Atheneum, 1964), 23.

31. John Adams letter to Benjamin Rush, December 22, 1806, in John A. Schutz and Douglas Adair, eds., *The Spur of Fame: Dialogues of John Adams and Benjamin Rush, 1805-1813* (San Marino, Calif.: Huntington Library, 1966), 71.

32. Zoltan Haraszti, *John Adams and the Prophets of Progress* (New York: Grosset and Dunlap, 1964), 72-73.

33. Paul K. Conkin, *Puritans and Pragmatists: Eight Eminent American Thinkers* (New York: Dodd, Mead and Company, 1968), 131. Or, to use Elshtain's formulation: "The great challenge for the Founders was to form a political body that brought people together and created a 'we,' but also enabled people to remain separate and to recognize and respect one another's differences. Modern democrats face the same challenge" (Jean Bethke Elshtain, *Democracy on Trial* [New York: Basic Books, 1995], 66).

34. Garry Wills, *Inventing America: Jefferson's Declaration of Independence* (New York: Random House, 1978), 187-88, argues that, on this issue, Jefferson was affected by Scottish thinkers. Thomas Reid, whose *Inquiry into the Human Mind* was published in 1764, was one of those thinkers. As part of his communitarian morality,

Reid "held that community is a necessary guide and corrective for all thought" and saw "common" sense "as a *communal* sense, the shared wisdom of the community." Note the similarity to Jefferson's statement: "I have great confidence in the common sense of mankind in general" (Wills, *Inventing America,* 190).

Wills further argues that Jefferson basically agreed with another Scotch Enlightenment thinker, Francis Hutcheson, on social bonds, social connections, always being bonds of affection, not of submission or oppression. Thomas Jefferson agreed with this conception of social cohesion and also agreed with the "Scottish belief in government as an expression of man's basic sociability" (Wills, *Inventing America,* 290 and 292). In other words, laissez-faire, individualist interpretations of Jefferson fall far from the mark, according to Wills.

Historians of political thought debate Wills on this point. Diggins, *Lost Soul of American Politics,* 10-11, for instance, agrees that Scottish thought influenced our founders but also argues that the Scottish approach minimizes the essential individualism of the American, seen by Tocqueville and continuing today.

35. Hollinger and Capper, eds., *American Intellectual Tradition,* 1, 183-84.

36. Pangle, *Spirit of Modern Republicanism,* 120.

37. Lorraine Smith Pangle and Thomas L. Pangle, *The Learning of Liberty: The Educational Ideas of the American Founders* (Lawrence: University Press of Kansas, 1993), 263-64.

38. Colleen A. Sheehan and Gary L. McDowell, eds., *Friends of the Constitution; Writings of the "Other" Federalists, 1787-1788* (Indianapolis: Liberty Fund, 1998), 67.

39. Sheehan and McDowell, eds., *Friends of the Constitution,* 9.

40. Lerner, *Thinking Revolutionary,* 117.

41. Joyce Appleby, *Liberalism and Republicanism,* 228, states that recent historical research has shown the importance of "a form of community" in framing the Constitution; she also characterizes self-interest as "dysfunctional." It is also a significant indicator of the importance of community that the 1780 Massachusetts Constitution changed the name of that state from the "State of Massachusetts Bay" to the "Commonwealth of Massachusetts." Belief in the importance of the common good was widely shared among the delegates to that convention, according to Oscar Handlin and Mary Flug Handlin, *Commonwealth: A Study of the Role of Government in the American Economy, Masssachusetts, 1774-1861,* rev. ed. (Cambridge: Belknap Press of Harvard University Press, 1969), 30.

42. Lerner, *Thinking Revolutionary,* 129.

43. Lester J. Cappon, ed., *The Adams-Jefferson Letters: The Complete Correspondence between Thomas Jefferson and Abigail and John Adams,* 1 (Chapel Hill: University of North Carolina Press, for the Institute of Early American History and Culture, 1959), 176.

44. Pangle, *Spirit of Modern Republicanism,* 228.

45. Pangle, *Spirit of Modern Republicanism,* 244.

46. Joshua Mitchell, *Not by Reason Alone: Religion, History, and Identity in Early Modern Political Thought* (Chicago: University of Chicago Press, 1993), ix. In addition, Mitchell criticizes some modern readers of Hobbes and Locke for a "procrustean reflex"; instead, he argues that "the self is constituted neither by itself nor by the community, and action is decidedly not wholly self-assumed" (132-33). See also Stephen Holmes, *Passions and Constraint: On the Theory of Liberal Democracy* (Chicago: University of Chicago Press, 1995), 240; Stephen Macedo, *Liberal Virtues: Citizenship, Virtue, and Community in Liberal Constitutionalism* (Oxford: Clarendon Press, 1990), 254; Oren M. Levin-Waldman, *Reconceiving Liberalism: Dilemmas of Contemporary Liberal Public Policy* (Pittsburgh: University of Pittsburgh Press, 1996), xvi and passim.

47. Smith, *Theory of Moral Sentiments* I.i.1.1, 9; II.ii.3.6, 88; III.2.6, 116; II.ii.3.1, 85.

48. Smith, *Theory of Moral Sentiments,* VII.ii.3.11-12, 303.

49. Patricia H. Werhane, *Adam Smith and His Legacy for Modern Capitalism* (New York: Oxford University Press, 1991), 11; see also 127 for a similar statement.

50. Werhane, *Smith and His Legacy,* 27-28.

51. In addition to Werhane, see Griswold, *Smith and Enlightenment,* 78, who states that the "general issue of harmonizing self and other is fundamental to both" of Smith's books; also, Jerry Z. Muller, *Adam Smith: In His Time and Ours* (Princeton: Princeton University Press, 1993), 2.

Wills argues that "Smith was conscripted to individualist uses by nineteenth-century liberalism," but he was "a good communitarian of the Scots school." Part of Wills's argument is based on the economic concept of the division of labor; for Smith competition is a form of cooperation between producers and buyers, preventing "a small faction from thwarting the designs of the community" (Wills, *Inventing America,* 232).

52. Adam Smith, *An Inquiry into the Nature and Causes of the Wealth of Nations,* R. H. Campbell and A. S. Skinner, eds. (Oxford: Oxford University Press, 1976), II.v.31, 372.

53. Smith, *Wealth of Nations,* IV, Introduction, 428.

54. Smith, *Wealth of Nations,* IV.ii.9, 456.

55. Smith, *Theory of Moral Sentiments,* IV.I.10, 184-85.

56. Smith, *Theory of Moral Sentiments,* 7. Stoic sources of Smith's thought are detailed on *5-10.*

57. See chapter 1, footnote 8, for a definition of the "impartial spectator."

58. Smith, *Theory of Moral Sentiments,* III.3.4, 137.

59. Werhane, *Smith and His Legacy,* 38-39. See also Ian Simpson Ross, *The Life of Adam Smith* (Oxford: Oxford University Press, 1995), 166, for the social nature of the impartial spectator. Holmes, *Passions and Constraint,* 27, argues that fairness overrides self-interest for the ideal-typical liberal; and he explains fairness as playing "by rules which apply equally to all."

60. For just a few examples, see Paul Tillich, *The Socialist Decision,* Franklin Sherman, trans. (New York: University Press of America, 1977), 6, for his discussion of the "I-Thou" relationship and justice, a discussion quite like Martin Buber's "I-Thou" relationship, and note David L. Norton, *Democracy and Moral Development* (Berkeley: University of California Press, 1991), 137-38, for the "I-Thou" relationship and community; Werner Picht, *The Life and Thought of Albert Schweitzer* (New York: Harper and Row, 1964), 114-15, on Albert Schweitzer; W. R. Newell, "Heidegger on Freedom and Community: Some Political Implications of His Early Thought," *American Political Science Review* 78 (September 1984): 775, who makes an interesting argument that Heidegger's man is "primordially a social and communal and historical being"; and Grofman and Feld, "Rousseau's General Will," 568-72, on individual-community duality in Rousseau.

61. Crevecoeur, *Letters from an American Farmer,* 20-21, 239, 277-78.

62. Barry A. Shain, *The Myth of American Individualism: The Protestant Origins of American Political Thought* (Princeton: Princeton University Press, 1994), xvi.

63. Shain, *Myth of American Individualism,* 23 and passim.

64. Richard Hofstadter, *Social Darwinism in American Thought* (Boston: Beacon Press, 1983), 91-92. At least one rugged individualist at the turn of the twentieth century seemed to agree. In a book review written in 1895, Theodore Roosevelt, *American Ideals and Other Essays, Social and Political* (New York: G. P. Putnam's Sons, 1897), 311-22, harshly criticized selfishness.

65. Bellah, *Habits of the Heart,* 66.

66. Bellah, *Habits of the Heart,* 84.

67. Amitai Etzioni, *The Moral Dimension, Toward a New Economics* (New York: Free Press, 1988), ix-x.

68. For Etzioni, the importance of balance in the individual-community relationship is crystal clear.

> The term *responsive community* is used to accord full status both to individuals and to their shared union. A responsive community is much more integrated than an aggregate of self-maximizing individuals; however, it is much less hierarchical and much less structured and "socializing", than an authoritarian community. . . . *Individuals and community are both completely essential, and hence have the same fundamental standing.*
>
> From this synthesis there results an unavoidable, indeed a deeply productive tension between the two basic elements of the responsive community. Individuals may pull to diminish the community; the community may pull excessively to incorporate individuals. But if neither element gains ascendancy, and if the excesses of one are corrected by shoring up the other, a balanced, responsive community may be sustained. (Etzioni, *Moral Dimension,* 8-9, italics in original).

69. Benjamin R. Barber, *Strong Democracy: Participatory Politics for a New Age* (Berkeley: University of California Press, 1984) xv; see also 25, 42, 70-71, 90,

213, and 216-17; see also Norton, *Democracy and Moral Development*, 8 and 113; McCollough, *Moral Imagination*, 58.

70. Richard Dagger, *Civic Virtues: Rights, Citizenship, and Republican Liberalism* (New York: Oxford University Press, 1997), 17-18 and 39.

71. Richard C. Sinopoli, *The Foundations of American Citizenship: Liberalism, the Constitution and Civic Virtue* (New York: Oxford University Press, 1992), 33.

72. Barber, *Strong Democracy*, 92 and 101.

73. Etzioni, *Moral Dimension*, 138.

74. Nancy J. Hirschmann, "Freedom, Recognition, and Obligation: A Feminist Approach to Political Theory," *American Political Science Review* 83 (December 1989): 1231.

75. Hirschmann, "Freedom, Recognition, and Obligation," 1242.

76. Hirschmann, "Freedom, Recognition, and Obligation," 1242. Similarly, Marilyn Friedman, "Feminism and Modern Friendship: Dislocating the Community," in *Communitarianism and Individualism*, Shlomo Avineri and Avner De-Shalit, eds. (New York: Oxford University Press, 1992), 101-04, states that many feminists have posed the concept of the "social self" in contrast to the "abstract individualism" of some liberal theory. She also criticizes communitarians for being oblivious to the oppression of women in many communities. And see Virginia Sapiro, *A Vindication of Political Virtue: The Political Theory of Mary Wollstonecraft* (Chicago: University of Chicago Press, 1992), 166-67 and 173, for the patriarchal and masculinist aspects of individualist liberalism.

77. Michael Novak, *Free Persons and the Common Good* (New York: Madison Books, 1989), 34-35.

78. Pangle, *Spirit of Modern Republicanism*, 98.

79. Pangle, *Spirit of Modern Republicanism*, 18-19.

80. Steven Forde, "Benjamin Franklins' *Autobiography* and the Education of America," *American Political Science Review* 86 (June 1992): 358-59.

81. Benjamin Franklin, *The Autobiography and Other Writings* (New York: Penguin Books, 1986), 248.

82. Diggins, *Lost Soul of American Politics*, 21.

83 Bellah, *Habits of the Heart*, 33.

84. Wood, *Radicalism of the American Revolution*, 305-06. Michael Kammen, *A Machine That Would Go of Itself: The Constitution in American Culture* (New York: Alfred A. Knopf, 1987), 207, quotes David Jayne Hill on the Constitution; it changed liberty from the previous group concept to "something inherent in each individual as a moral personality." Similarly, Appleby, *Liberalism and Republicanism*, 182-83 and 338, discussing the changing concept of self-interest, states that the colonial elite despaired at the pervasiveness of the vice, but that self-interest was seen "by their inferiors as an extension of individual freedom."

85. Shain, *Myth of American Individualism*, 100, but he dates the change somewhat later. He cites Tocqueville's comments on laws restraining citizens as an

indication that American had a "corporate and communal understanding of civil liberty" well into the nineteenth century (288).

86. Wood, *Radicalism of the American Revolution*, 128.

87. Bellah, *Habits of the Heart*, 197.

88. Merriam, *History of American Political Theories*, 177.

89. Diggins, *Lost Soul of American Politics*, 122. Amitai Etzioni, *The Spirit of Community: The Reinvention of American Society* (New York: Simon and Schuster, 1993), 118, differentiates the community orientation of Western agricultural areas from the "rampant individualism" of mining towns and trading posts.

90. Diggins, *Lost Soul of American Politics*, 123.

91. Quoted by Bellah, *Habits of the Heart*, 56.

92. Diggins, *Lost Soul of American Politics*, 228.

93. Muller, *Adam Smith*, 193.

94. Bellah, *Habits of the Heart*, 144.

95. Etzioni, *Spirit of Community*, 12.

96. Pangle, *Spirit of Modern Republicanism*, 48.

97. Macedo, *Liberal Virtues*, 28. See also Etzioni, *Spirit of Community*, 32.

98. Nancy L. Rosenblum, "Pluralism and Self-Defense," in *Liberalism and the Moral Life*, Nancy L. Rosenblum, ed. (Cambridge: Harvard University Press, 1989), 222-23.

99. Benjamin Barber, "Liberal Democracy and the Costs of Consent," in *Liberalism and the Moral Life*, Rosenblum, ed., 61.

100. See Stephen Holmes, "The Permanent Structure of Antiliberal Thought," in *Liberalism and the Moral Life*, Rosenblum, ed., 227-28, on parallels between current antiliberal thought and the writings of European fascists, and 251 for his reminder that liberals are not against all community, only communities with arbitrary authority. And Robyn Dawes, et al., "Cooperation for the Benefit of Us—Not Me, or my Conscience," in *Beyond Self-Interest*, Jane J. Mansbridge, ed. (Chicago: University of Chicago Press, 1990), 110, remind us that the Nazis had a strong group identity. We all know the horrible results of their attempts to construct a restricted community.

101. Brutus, writing to the citizens of New York, in Herbert J. Storing, ed., *The Anti-Federalist: An Abridgment, by Murray Dry, of the Complete Anti-Federalist* (Chicago: University of Chicago Press, 1985), 128-29.

102. Pangle, *Spirit of Modern Republicanism*, 31.

103. Joseph J. Ellis, *Passionate Sage: the Character and Legacy of John Adams* (New York: W. W. Norton and Company, 1993), 229.

104. Pangle, *Spirit of Modern Republicanism*, 278.

105. Diggins, *Lost Soul of American Politics*, 150.

106. Benjamin R. Barber, "The Compromised Republic: Public Purposelessness in America," in *The Moral Foundations of the American Republic*, 3d ed., Robert H. Horwitz, ed. (Charlottesville: University of Virginia Press, 1986), 60.

107. Novak, *Free Persons*, 215-16.

Chapter Five

Government and Self-Interest

Adam Smith and the founders would have agreed on the importance of individuality within communities, but still unresolved is the issue of what should be the scope of government. This remains a bone of contention today, with the common political meanings of "liberal" and "conservative" roughly indicating the nature of the split. Thomas Jefferson's discussion of some principles of a "wise and frugal government" in his first inaugural address, March 4, 1801, illustrates the horns of the dilemma. Within the context of making "a happy and prosperous people," he advocated restraining "men from injuring one another" while leaving citizens "free to regulate their own pursuits of industry and improvement."[1] In this speech, Jefferson advocated liberty. On the other hand, advancing the happiness and prosperity of the people and preventing injury implies a strong government. Jefferson's desire to restrain citizens from injuring one another leads us to the issue of justice, the provision of which is largely a government responsibility. Thus, this chapter examines the views of the founders and Smith on resolving the dilemma of establishing a government strong enough to provide justice for all its citizens but not strong enough to threaten liberty.

Justice

One of the prime virtues for the founders was justice. But justice had broader connotations for them than it has today. Pangle states that the classical definition for justice was "reverence for law, unselfish sharing, and public spirit."[2] In another work he discusses the culmination of classical political philosophy in "the exploration of the problem of justice, or the common good."[3]

These definitions gave justice economic and community meanings which most Americans today would not understand as aspects of justice, because we are now so focused on the legal-juridical connotations of the word. Similarly, for Smith, justice was balanced between fair play for others (the community) and protection of individual rights. His principle of justice included:

> (1) not harming another or oneself; (2) engaging in fair play or, alternative-ly, not engaging in activities that are unfair; and (3) not engaging in conduct that violates perfect rights. Perfect rights include the natural rights not to be harmed, the right to personal liberty and personal reputation, and the adventitious right to property.[4]

By "adventitious right to property" Smith was saying that one has the right to own property, but the terms of that ownership can be established by society (that is, by the government).[5]

Both Federalists and Anti-Federalists agreed on the need for government to promote justice. Jefferson's concern for restraining "men from injuring one another" is consistent with an argument of Publius that "Justice is the end of government. It is the end of civil society. It ever has been and ever will be pur-sued until it be obtained, or until liberty be lost in the pursuit."[6] In the same paragraph, the author establishes the government's responsibility to protect the weak against the strong. Also, Madison wanted to control factions because "they often promote injustice."[7]

One Anti-Federalist assumed that humans would act unjustly toward each other and thus made a point, which can be generalized to all governmental regu-lation of economy and society.

> If they [mankind] had been disposed to conform themselves to the rule of immutable righteousness, government would not have been requisite. It was because one part exercised fraud, oppression, and violence on the other, that men came together, and agreed that certain rules should be formed, to regulate the conduct of all, and the power of the whole community lodged in the hands of rulers to enforce an obedience to them. But rulers have the same propensities as other men; they are as likely to use the power with which they are vested for private purposes, and to the injury and oppression of those over whom they are placed, as individuals in a state of nature are to injure and oppress one another. It is therefore as proper that bounds should be set to their authority, as that government should have at first been instituted to restrain private injuries.[8]

If people were ethical, government regulation would not be needed. Note the similarity to *Federalist* # 51: "But what is government itself but the greatest of all reflections on human nature. If men were angels, no government would be necessary."[9] Government is necessary to enforce justice, but government must also be controlled to prevent it from becoming an instrument of injustice.

Justice does not occur automatically; it requires an enforcement agent, and that brings us back to the role of government. Smith wrote that government, for one of its functions, was responsible, for "protecting, as far as possible, every member of the society from the injustice or oppression of every other member of it."[10] In contrast to extreme advocates of laissez-faire, Smith was well aware of a harsh aspect of reality which necessitated such governmental enforcement; he understood that "few of us internalize the ideal of fair play." Few of us deliberately try to hurt others, but Smith knew that businessmen colluded against others. Capitalists exploit others if the government does not establish a legal system to prevent exploitation.[11] Similarly, Holmes insists that for liberals, including Smith, state power is necessary as a remedy for "private injustice and oppression." He states that Smith "thought the interests of the grasping few must be forcibly sacrificed to the interest of the great majority of the people."[12] One could argue that Smith believed human nature to be so unethical that only law kept society from degenerating into a war of all against all.

Critics contend that such arguments place too much reliance on Smith's *Theory of Moral Sentiments*, that his *Wealth of Nations* does not emphasize such concerns. Such critics often see a massive disjunction between *Theory of Moral Sentiments* and *Wealth of Nations*. This view is part of an argument which can be traced back to 1848, with the publication of the first mention of the "Adam Smith Problem." The critics charged that, in *Wealth of Nations*, Smith changed from the virtuous, benevolent, and altruistic human nature of *Theory of Moral Sentiments* to an egoistic, materialistic theory.[13] On the critics' side of the issue, the question is: "Why does altruistic man of his *Theory of Moral Sentiments* behave egoistically in *Wealth of Nations*? Each of his books presents one model of man and forgets the other," according to Kolm. But for Kolm to read Smith as advocating an ideology of "individualization of society" he must grossly distort Smith.[14] He falsely attributes to Smith an idea Smith abhorred, an eighteenth-century fallacy no longer appropriate if democracy is to exist in the twenty-first. It appears that Kolm uses a twentieth-century lens to read an eighteenth-century thinker.

It is indeed true that Smith was quite critical of the powers available to governments in his day. But those governments were functioning according to the mercantile system. Rejecting massive government intervention in the economy did not require Smith to go to the opposite pole of an egoistic society with little government power. It is indeed true that he emphasized the benefits for society of individual initiative; that is not incompatible with an altruistic awareness of one's connections and debts to society. The editors of the 1976 Glasgow edition of *Theory of Moral Sentiments* sharply reject the "Adam Smith problem" as "a pseudo-problem based on ignorance and misunderstanding." They write:

> Anybody who reads TMS, first in one of the earlier editions and then in
> edition 6, will not have the slightest inclination to be puzzled that the
> same man wrote this book and WN, or to suppose that he underwent any
> radical change of view about human conduct. Smith's account of ethics and
> of human behavior is basically the same in edition 6 of 1790 as in edition 1
> of 1759. There is development but no fundamental alteration. . . . Who
> would suppose this to imply that Adam Smith had come to disbelieve in the
> very existence or the moral value of benevolence? Nobody with any
> sense.[15]

The editors further argue that Smith himself "regards WN as continuing the
sequence of thought set out in TMS."[16] In other words, advocates of the "Adam
Smith Problem" seem to ignore the systematic nature of his thinking and
writing. He saw himself as a philosopher, explaining an interdependent, coherent
world. The *Wealth of Nations* editors state that Smith had "a great capacity for
model-building," that his ethics, jurisprudence, and economics were "an attempt
to delineate the boundaries of a single system of thought," and that *Wealth of
Nations* includes "the elements of economics against a philosophical and
historical background."[17] Further, the concept of justice is not located only in
Theory of Moral Sentiments but is central to the arguments of the *Wealth of
Nations*. His emphasis on the liberty of the individual to compete, "to pursue
his own interest his own way" is preceded by the qualifier: "as long as he does
not violate the laws of justice."[18] Also, Fitzgibbons writes: "There is no bio-
graphical evidence that Smith's philosophic principles changed over time. . . . If
anything, Smith emphasized the continuity of his ideas over the decades of his
adult life."[19]

Justice is not a disembodied ideal. It is central to the efficient functioning of
capitalism. Smith's free market mechanism works well only when individual
actions are taken within a context of a just community; it works "when people
operate with restrained self-interest in cooperation with others under the precepts
of justice." Werhane also states that Smith's theory of justice "plays a more
important role in the *WN* than is sometimes thought."[20] Justice and fair play
permeate Smith's writings. He was certainly aware that individual action could
produce unintended good for a community. But his analysis of the role of government, his repeated criticisms of actions of businessmen, and his concern for
the working classes provide an important balance.[21] Self-interest must be balanced with justice. (For those who are still skeptical, see chapter 6 for discussion of Smith's critique of market failures, monopolies, and the working and
living conditions of laborers; most, if not all, of these problems can be seen as
failures of fair play.)

The version of unlimited capitalist individualism which has been widely
propagated in the United States does not reflect the balanced approach for which
Adam Smith argued. In *Theory of Moral Sentiments*, he clearly stated that we
must not harm our neighbor, "even to prevent our own ruin." In competing for

wealth, a person should work hard: "he may run as hard as he can, and strain every nerve and every muscle, in order to outstrip all his competitors. But if he should justle, or throw down any of them, the indulgence of the spectators is entirely at an end. It is a violation of fair play, which they cannot admit of."[22] Human actions are based on selfish, unsocial, and social motives. But no matter the motive, Smith labeled any self-interested action which harms anyone, oneself included, an evil.[23]

Smith assumed that the results of free market competition would be unequal. Some would prosper and others would not. What one earns from one's own skill and hard work and cooperation with others, in other words through justice and fair play, is acceptable. But inequality is a vice if it is a result of domination of others.

How are we to reach the goals of justice and the happiness of the people? Individual by individual, group by group, or as a whole? The history of the United States has given a decidedly individual and small group answer to that question. However, when individuals take self-interest to an extreme, community and government functions suffer and, more than any other type of political system, democratic government suffers most of all. Extreme individualists can exist in anarchical situations, but democracy requires a virtuous citizenry, with public spirit among the prime virtues. Therefore, in this chapter, we examine first the founders' attempts to provide justice through a democratic system which would withstand the pressures of individualism and factionalism, and, second the results of the founders' efforts.

Crafting a Democratic System

When the American Constitution was written, the representatives in Philadelphia tried to avoid two dangers: the excesses of popular passions and the excesses of absolute government. Fear of popular passions was probably not common among the working classes. At least one Massachusetts "laborer,"[24] William Manning, responded as follows to an anonymous person who charged that the masses ("the Many") were dangerous in republics:

> But I am very far from thinking as he doth that the destruction of free governments arises from the licentiousness of the Many or their representatives. On the contrary, I shall endeavor to prove that their destruction always arises from the unreasonable dispositions and combinations of the Few, and the ignorance and carelessness of the Many.[25]

In addition to ignorance, Manning criticized the people for "their readiness to hear and follow the schemes of great men without examining and seeing themselves."[26] John Adams made similar statements.

But the experienced men of affairs who were delegates to the Constitutional Convention had a different perspective. Their Calvinistic conviction of human evil, according to Hofstadter, had been reinforced by their observations of life; they had seen human nature "in all its frailty. To them a human being was an atom of self-interest. They did not believe in man, but they did believe in the power of a good political constitution to control him." The founders, "intellectual heirs of seventeenth-century English republicanism with its opposition to arbitrary rule and faith in popular sovereignty," wanted to craft their government carefully to avoid tyranny.[27] In short, they wanted a democratic government but feared tyranny by the majority; and their experience as subjects of the British monarchy also led them to fear control by one person.

The problem was complicated by an inherited attitude toward government; the Americans had a reputation for "unruliness and contempt for authority." Wood also writes that eighteenth-century Englishmen in general were known for "their stubborn unwillingness to be governed."[28] In his autobiographical fragment,[29] John Adams reports a vignette which illustrates this attitude:

> An Event of the most trifling nature in Appearance, and fit only to excite Laughter, in other Times, struck me into a profound Reverie, if not a fit of Melancholly. I met a Man who had sometimes been my Client, and sometimes I had been against him. He, though a common Horse Jockey, was sometimes in the right, and I had commonly been successfull in his favour in our Courts of Law. He was always in the Law, and had been sued in many Actions, at almost every Court. As soon as he saw me, he came up to me, and his first Salutation to me was "Oh! Mr. Adams what great Things have you and your Colleagues done for Us! We can never be gratefull enough to you. There are no Courts of Justice now in this Province, and I hope there never will be another!". . . . Is this the Object for which I have been contending? said I to myself, for I rode along without any Answer to this Wretch. Are these the Sentiments of such People? And how many of them are there in the Country? Half the Nation for what I know: for half the Nation are Debtors if not more, and these have been in all Countries, the Sentiments of Debtors.[30]

Thus, our founders had the unenviable task of forming a government for a people who distrusted any government. This attitude still survives; the "Live Free or Die" aphorism on New Hampshire license plates is an example.

One reason this attitude remains popular is a common misinterpretation of Adam Smith's economics. Some admirers presented him as opposed "to *all* government action"; but his position was quite different.[31] How could someone be against all government and still willingly serve government? Yet that is exactly what Smith did both as an advisor to various British officials and as a Commissioner of Customs in Scotland, a position he actively sought and happily filled the last twelve years of his life. In his classic *Wealth of Nations,* Smith clearly listed three types of governmental duties: external defense, justice, and public works.[32] Note that he defined public works to include education and facilitation of commerce, through infrastructure projects, such as roads, bridges, harbors, canals, navigable rivers, in addition to those public works needed for defense and administering justice.[33] And remember that justice, broadly conceived, was central to Smith's thought. Also, Muller points out Smith's fascination with the unintended consequences of human action but insists that "Smith did not intend this as a call to quietism: the purpose of social science was to aid the legislator in preserving, reforming, or designing institutions that channel the motives of men toward socially beneficent ends."[34]

Smith believed government action was necessary in many spheres of life. While arguing for competition among banks, he also argued for various types of banking regulation. In addition to what we would today call patent and copyright protection for intellectual properties, he believed in governmental financial incentives, premiums, for artisans and manufacturers in order to encourage dexterity and creativity. He wrote that the public could impose education requirements. Government could use taxation policy to enforce socially useful behavior. He thought that compelling frugality through sumptuary laws (taxes on "luxuries" like tobacco, liquor, tea, sugar, chocolate) might increase the ability of poorer people to raise their families by making it less likely that they would waste resources needed for their families.[35] Smith's emphasis on liberty, then, was a subtle one, allowing much more scope for governmental action than the belief in absolute liberty some have attributed to him.

Smith and the founders would have agreed that government must be strong enough to fulfill its functions but limited so that its power could not diminish the rights of citizens.[36] The founders knew that any government must require the people to surrender some of their liberty in order for that government to have the power necessary to govern.[37] Power, however, was a large part of the problem. Americans from colonial times to the present have had an enormous distrust of power, "'power in the abstract, wherever it existed and under whatever name it was known,'" in the hands of any one person or any group.[38] John Adams was aware of this fear and of its abuse by demagogues:

Popular orators are generally opposite to the present Administration, blaming public Measures, and despizing or detesting Persons in Power, whether wise or foolish, wicked or upright, with all their Wit, and Knowledge, merely to make themselves the Idols of a slavish, timid People, who are always jealous and invidious of Power and therefore devoted to those that expose, ridicule or condemn it. Eloquence that may be employed wisely to persuade, is often employed wickedly to seduce, from the Eloquence of Greece and Rome down to the rude speeches of our American Town Meeting.[39]

Such comments indicate concern that crass demagogues could easily use the people's unthinking fear of power against the public interest. Adams was deeply distrustful of power as a corrupting force; much of his writing analyzed the control of power.

Adams's notes for an oration at Braintree, Spring, 1772, contain the following: "There is Danger from all Men. The only Maxim of a free Government, ought to be to trust no Man living, with Power to endanger the public Liberty."[40] Forty-three years later he made the same point in another way, writing to Jefferson on November 13, 1815: "The fund[a]mental Article of my political Creed is, that Despotism, or unlimited Sovereignty, or absolute Power is the same in a Majority of a popular Assembly, an Aristocratical Counsel, an Oligarchical Junto and a single Emperor. Equally arbitrary cruel bloody and in every respect diabolical."[41] Throughout his life he consistently distrusted unchecked power. But he also believed in exercising power as is shown by his long career in public service. Power was necessary, but if it was not checked or if it was exercised by leaders lacking in virtue, it was dangerous. In short, Adams did not possess a dialectical aversion to power, but saw it dualistically; power must be controlled, yet when it was controlled, power could be used to promote the common good.[42]

Strong Government

By the time of the Constitutional Convention, many leaders were convinced that the United States needed a strong government. Cotton Tufts, Abigail's uncle, wrote to John Adams, then serving as American Ambassador to Great Britain, in August, 1785: "The Want of a sufficient Power in Congress to regulate the national Concerns of the United States is now pretty generally seen and has been severely felt."[43] Two years earlier Adams had commented on the problems caused by disunity: debate over responsibility for the public debt was leading to default; there was no uniformity in dealing with foreign commerce, including import duties; the coast was not uniformly defended; and the new nation was losing respect from other nations.[44] He wrote his *Defence of the Constitutions of Government of the United States of America* (1787) because he perceived that the new country's difficulties could be "traced to one source, the want of energetic government."[45] This was not a new concern for Adams; in 1777 he had concerns about insufficient energy in the governments of the various states and the possibility that that lack of energy might cause defeat in the revolutionary struggle.[46] Similarly, George Washington argued in his 1783 "Circular to the States" that the Revolutionary War could have been won in less time and at much less expense if the continental government had had "adequate authority" and more energy.[47]

Most political scientists would agree with Merriam's statement that revolutionary era thinkers saw government's purpose as responsibility for the welfare of the people, with the understanding that maintaining civil liberty was a central part of that mission.[48] But liberty was not an absolute value for the founders. "Liberty viewed as an unchecked or unsubordinated end is found in and characterizes the state of nature."[49] Our founders were not interested in returning to a state of nature; thus, they insisted on establishing a strong government. Any government inherently controls liberty; our country was founded on the principle of liberty, but not in a dialectical sense: not absolute liberty, but liberty and government. (See chapter 2 for additional discussion of this view of liberty.)

Thomas Jefferson believed in both democracy and the potential of government to assist in the pursuit of happiness; he knew that there were good uses for governmental power, but he also knew that such power could be abused.[50] "Freedom he conceived not as a void or as freedom from evil, but as a positive condition in human society that might sustain continued social improvement and would afford expression of man's best nature."[51] But some readers might wonder how Jefferson could advocate a strong government and also argue for a democratic right to rebel. His position is evident in his reaction to Shay's Rebellion, in a letter to Madison, January 30, 1787:

> Even this evil is productive of good. It prevents the degeneracy of government, and nourishes a general attention to the public affairs. I hold it that a little rebellion now and then is a good thing, and as necessary in the political world as storms in the physical. Unsuccessful rebellions indeed generally establish the incroachments on the rights of the people which have produced them. An observation of this truth would render honest republican governors so mild in their punishment of rebellions, as not to discourage them too much. It is a medicine necessary for the sound health of government.[52]

In other words, if the people cannot protect their rights through the established rules of the system, they have the right to go outside the system, to rebel, to protect their rights. And when attempts to protect rights fail, when rebellions are unsuccessful, those rights are diminished; the "incroachments" are "established"; the government has reduced the rights of the people. It should be noted here that "Jefferson's" right of rebellion closely followed eighteenth-century Whig arguments for the right of resistance.[53]

The right of rebellion does not contradict the desire for strong government. The authors of the Constitution wanted to provide effective government. Rebellion is the last resort against ineffective government. The founders wanted both strong government and sufficient checks built into the system to prevent a cause of rebellion: governmental injustice resulting from concentrated power. If checks and balances and all other remedies failed, the final check was the right to rebel. But if people have a right to rebel, why did Shay's Rebellion elicit such a strong national reaction? One might think that, once the rebellion was defeated, the issue would have disappeared.

Jefferson might have advocated the right of resistance. But that did not mean most politically active Americans would accept rebellion with equanimity. Also, the issue did not disappear because many founders connected Shay's Rebellion to legal acts in various state assemblies, acts which the founders perceived as attacks on property and order. Rhode Island had enforced a law undermining contracts and the security of property. Other states had legislated monetary policies which frightened men of great wealth.[54] Madison believed that life, liberty, and property were endangered by a despotic majority and by a lack of energy and stability in the governments established under the Articles of Confederation.[55]

Hamilton favored strong government, arguing that "Energy in the Executive" is a major aspect of "the definition of good government." He believed it was necessary for international security, for the fair administration of law, to protect property and to defend liberty "against the enterprises and assaults of ambition, of faction, and of anarchy."[56] Note that Hamilton (and many other founders) connected justice with protection of property. Wood also points out that Hamilton questioned a fundamental tenet of laissez-faire ideology. He characterized the belief that private interests would regulate themselves as a wild speculative paradox, "'contrary to the uniform practice and sense of the most enlightened nations. . . . It must be rejected by every man acquainted with commercial history.'" [57] Hamilton was known for his belief in strong government.

Replacement of the Articles of Confederation by the Constitution is irrefutable evidence of the proposition that the framers desired strong government. That issue was one of the defining differences between Federalists and Anti-Federalists. Bourgin states this very clearly:

> Laissez-faire did not fit the purposes of the Constitution makers, for it was against the laissez-faire policy of the confederation that the Constitution was struck. . . . Had the Constitution makers really favored laissez-faire, it is difficult to see why they should have desired any change from the inactive policy of the Confederation.[58]

There were disagreements within the Federalist camp on some aspects of government, but they agreed on the need for energetic government. Storing writes: "To acknowledge the need for a *government* is to acknowledge the need for power and compulsion."[59] Many Federalist pieces written during the debate over ratification of the Constitution support Storing's point.[60] What Atticus wrote is just one example: "Too, too long it hath been the humour of our countrymen, to be so fearful of giving their rulers power to do hurt, that they never have given them power to do good."[61] And Adams and Jefferson, two of the founders who were not involved in framing the Constitution because they were serving as diplomats in Europe, also desired strong government (as noted earlier in this section).

Nevertheless, ratification of the Constitution did not resolve the issue of the legitimate scope of government, as the following statement by Supreme Court Chief Justice John Jay makes clear: "'It cannot be too strongly impressed on the minds of us all how greatly our individual prosperity depends on our national prosperity, and how greatly our national prosperity depends on a well organized, vigorous government.'"[62] He was also careful to assert that such government was compatible with individual liberty. Such a statement from the leader of the highest court in the land, the apex of the court system set up by the new Constitution, would have been unnecessary if the principle of strong government had been widely accepted. Indeed, debate on this principle was one of the important differences between the Federalist and Republican parties in the early republic, with the Republicans seeing a powerful government as one of the worst of evils.[63]

Distrust of power was, and continues to be, endemic in this country. The "great dilemma of America's constitutional democracy" was and still is how to craft a system with sufficient power to fulfill its functions, but not so much as to endanger individual liberty.[64] As a response to this dilemma the Constitution placed limits on national governmental power, such as checks and balances and the federal division of powers between state and national governments. The founders crafted a system which fragmented power and thus facilitated factional power at the expense of the common interest.

Factions versus the General Welfare

One of the major ironies of the American system is that the Constitution's checks and balances contributed to development of one of the vices the founders feared: faction. What is a faction? A good place to start is James Madison's definition: "a number of citizens, whether amounting to a majority or minority of the whole, who are united and actuated by some common impulse of passion, or of interest, adverse to the rights of other citizens, or to the permanent and aggregate interests of the community."[65] In this context, remember that revolutionary war leaders abhorred parochialism. They valued the general welfare, the good of the whole community, in contrast to only a particular, limited part of the community. And note well that when individuals join in factions their actions are the antithesis of the goal of individuality within communities. The founders thought the government should be responsible for the general welfare, not for the interests of individuals or factions.

Clearly within Madison's definition of faction was the group John Adams called a "natural aristocracy." In a December 6, 1787, letter to Jefferson, Adams wrote: "You are afraid of the one—I, of the few. We agree perfectly that the many should have a full fair and perfect Representation.—You are Apprehensive of Monarchy; I, of Aristocracy."[66] Adams and other founders knew that the United States did not have an aristocracy in the European sense, an aristocracy by birth. What Adams did not like was special privilege for anyone, the one and the many also included. He feared that tyranny by a few (an elite, an aristocracy), was a greater danger than monarchical tyranny, tyranny by one.

This was a theme of *A Defence of the Constitutions of Government of the United States of America,* in which he wrote that the masses support politicians based "too often on artifices and tricks, on hypocrisy and superstition, on flattery, bribes, and largesses." A few pages later he wrote "that the multitude have always been credulous and the few are always artful."[67] A quarter of a century later (July 9, 1813) he was still complaining to Jefferson of the wiles of the aristocrats, subtle enough to secure support from the ordinary citizen in order to thwart honest plans to control their special privilege.[68] And in a letter of November 15, 1813, Adams wept at the stupidity of the multitude because they became dupes of the aristocracy and "love to be Taken in by their Tricks."[69] He was also aware that the many were dangerous; he agreed with Madison that they could be a faction. In his *Defence of the Constitutions* Adams wrote:

> If a majority are capable of preferring their own private interest or that of their families, counties, and party to that of the nation collectively, some provision must be made in the constitution in favor of justice to compel all to respect the common right, the public good, the universal law, in preference to all private and partial considerations.[70]

No matter the label—party, aristocracy, or faction—Adams's dislike of special privilege did not change over time. Howe clearly shows that Adams's definition of faction included political parties as a prime example of that vice: "Parties accentuated the struggle for political spoils and made personal ambition rather than social virtue the touchstone of political success."[71] His dislike of parties was long-standing and even included strong concerns about the nature of the struggle for independence. He wrote to his wife in July 1774 about the slander, defamation, and libels propagated by both sides in the struggle over British rule. The letter continued:

> These Bickerings of opposite Parties, and their mutual Reproaches, their Declamations, their Sing Song, their Triumphs and Defyances, their Dismals, and Prophecies, are all Delusion.
> We Very seldom hear any solid Reasoning. I wish always to discuss the Question, without all Painting, Pathos, Rhetoric, or Flourish of every Kind. And the Question seems to me to be whether the american Colonies are to be considered, as a distinct Community so far as to have a right to judge for themselves, when the fundamentals of their Government are destroyed or invaded?[72]

This is more than John Adams, lawyer, wanting citizens to focus on the heart of the issue. He hoped support for the cause would come from logic and reasoning, not from emotional appeals. The irony here is that John Adams certainly demonstrated the full range of human emotions. And he knew that it was human nature to be swayed both by the heart and the head.

Still, his opposition to parties as factions was consistent over time. A 1763 letter to the *Boston Gazette* criticized factions for going beyond the truth: "Many of the ablest tongues and pens, have in every age been employ'd in the foolish, deluded, and pernicious flattery of one set of partisans; and in furious prostitute invectives against another."[73] In a letter to Jefferson fifty years later (July 9, 1813) Adams wrote about the governmental problems caused by the party strife, the factionalism, sometimes caused by the one, sometimes by the few, sometimes by the many:

> "The same political parties which now agitate U.S. have existed through all time." Precisely. And this is precisely the complaint in the preface to the first volume of my defence. While all other Sciences have advanced, that of Government is at a stand; little better understood; little better practiced now than 3 or 4 thousand Years ago. What is the Reason? I say parties and Factions will not suffer, or permit Improvements to be made. As soon as one Man hints at an improvement his Rival opposes it. No sooner has one Party discovered or invented an Amelioration of the Condition of Man or the order of Society, than the opposite Party, belies it misconstrues it, misrepresents it, ridicules it, insults it, and persecutes it.[74]

He worried that American elections were being corrupted by parochial interests. In an August 25, 1776, letter Adams wrote: "A Sober, conscientious Habit, of electing for the public good alone must be introduced, and every Appearance of Interest, Favour, and Partiality, reprobated, or you will very soon make wise and honest Men wish for Monarchy again, nay you will make them introduce it into America."[75] He was not advocating an American monarchy in 1776 nor did he advocate one twenty years later. He was reasoning by historical analogy. He was very aware that earlier republics in England, France, Holland, Switzerland, and Venice had fallen, corrupted by "commerce, luxury, and avarice." Adams also wrote: "When public virtue is gone, when the national spirit is fled, when a party is substituted for the nation and faction for a party, when venality lurks and skulks in secret . . . the republic is lost in essence, though it may still exist in form."[76]

For Adams, election politics should be about serving the national interest, not about winning at all costs. He held this view of politics consistently throughout his life but it was also shaped by his own problems with the Hamilton faction within the Federalist party (the chicanery of the Hamilton faction in both 1796 and 1800, denying him a second term—see chapter 1). Adams always argued for the primacy of the common good and criticized parochialism in whatever form it appeared. As president, he tried to remain above political parties, thus adding to Hamiltonian dissatisfaction with his administration because he did not support some of their policies. So, it is easy to understand why Adams repeatedly stated that faction was "the greatest Evil."[77] Adams's problems with the Hamiltonians are also ironic in that Hamilton believed a strong executive and an energetic central government were needed to control factions, especially majority factions.[78] Yet the Hamiltonians fought John Adams's strong presidential initiatives time and again.[79]

Morgan presents Madison's fears of distortions in public opinion because of the actions of faction and wealth:

> Opinion, Madison observed, is malleable as well as naturally diverse. He warned that, because the American people occupy an extended territory, they are likely to be influenced for some time to come by the "misrepresentations" of "interested men." Three years later he repeated this warning, saying, the "larger a country is, the less easy for its real opinion to be ascertained, and the less difficult for it to be counterfeited." . . . . Clever persons had made dupes of both the public and other honest but gullible legislators by "veiling . . . and varnishing sophistical arguments" in order to disguise their real objectives. It was scarcely worth the effort to reform Congress, if the people chose their own representatives only to find eventually that a clever, enterprising and "moneyed few" profited personally from every new regulation of commerce and finance at a cost paid by the "industrious and uninformed mass."[80]

Some Anti-Federalist critics of the proposed constitution had a similar fear; Federal Farmer, Centinel, Brutus, and Melancton Smith argued that the new constitution would establish an aristocracy over free men.[81]

Whether special privilege was extended to an aristocracy of wealth or to some small group (an interest group or a faction), the founders abhorred it. The constitution of Vermont stated that "'the common benefit, protection, and security of the people, nation, or community, and not the particular emolument or advantage of any single man, family or set of men who are a part only of that community,' is the proper end of government." Merriam also notes an anti-special privilege clause from Massachusetts as another example of similar constitutional statements from many of the states.[82] Of course, defining the "common benefit . . . of the people" remains one of the perennial issues of politics.

The founders' abhorrence of faction was widely shared in that era.[83] In early eighteenth-century Great Britain, most political writers considered parties to be "indisputably evil."[84] Adam Smith caustically criticized factionalism in *Theory of Moral Sentiments*.

A true party-man hates and despises candour; and, in reality, there is no vice which could so effectually disqualify him for the trade of a party-man as that single virtue. The real, revered, and impartial spectator, therefore, is, upon no occasion, at a greater distance than amidst the violence and rage of contending parties. To them, it may be said, that such a spectator scarce exists any where in the universe. Even to the great Judge of the universe, · they impute all their own prejudices, and often view that Divine Being as animated by all their own vindictive and implacable passions. Of all the corrupters of moral sentiments, therefore, faction and fanaticism have always been by far the greatest.[85]

If anything, he was even more critical in *Wealth of Nations*. He thought that the thirteen American colonies had been protected by the mother-country from "virulent factions" which would become "ten times more virulent than ever" if the colonies gained their independence.[86]

His criticisms of monopoly showed a singular distaste for the ability of that type of faction known as businessmen to influence legislation for private gain. "Whenever the legislature attempts to regulate the differences between masters and their workmen, its counsellors are always the masters."[87] This parliamentary leverage was used to influence prices (in other words, factional power subverted the free market). He was acerbic in his criticism of factional resistance to free trade; private interests were often able to "intimidate the legislature." And he continued:

The member of parliament who supports every proposal for strengthening this monopoly, is sure to acquire not only the reputation of understanding trade, but great popularity and influence with an order of men whose numbers and wealth render them of great importance. If he opposes them, on the contrary, and still more if he has authority enough to be able to thwart them, neither the most acknowledged probity, nor the highest rank, nor the greatest publick services can protect him from the most infamous abuse and detraction, from personal insults, nor sometimes from real danger, arising from the insolent outrage of furious and disappointed monopolists.[88]

In analyzing the power of woolen manufacturers, at the expense of wool growers, he wrote: "To hurt in any degree the interest of any one order of citizens, for no other purpose but to promote that of some other, is evidently contrary to that justice and equality of treatment which the sovereign owes to all the different orders of his subjects."[89] He criticized similar factional excesses in several other sectors of the economy as well as commerce in general.[90]

Given the widely shared aversion to special privilege in the eighteenth century, how is it that the American system today is so controlled by those factions known as interest groups? Part of the answer is in the Constitution itself. One of the leading drafters of the Constitution, James Madison, was among those thinkers who were convinced that faction could not be avoided; he hoped instead to craft the Constitution so that it would control factions. He wanted the Constitution to set passion against passion, ambition against ambition.[91] Madison also argued that it would not be safe to depend on virtuous leaders to counter the vice of faction: "It is in vain to say that enlightened statesmen will be able to adjust these clashing interests, and render them all subservient to the public good. Enlightened statesmen will not always be at the helm." Thus, what was needed was a governmental structure to control inevitable factionalism: "The inference to which we are brought is, that the *causes* of faction cannot be removed, and that relief is only to be sought in the means of controlling its *effects*."[92]

Madison and the Federalists succeeded in obtaining their Constitution with all its checks and balances. But, in the long run, they were not the winners. Ironically, some Anti-Federalists, who looked like the losers, won. The pluralist, interest-group politics we now have closely reflects a populist concern which was often supported by Anti-Federalists. According to Wood, Anti-Federalists believed that, "given the variety of competing interests and the fact that all people had interests, the only way for a person to be fairly and accurately represented in government was to have someone like himself with his same interests speak for him; no one else could be trusted to do so."[93]

However, this American system of representing interest groups, instead of the people, leaves a major question: is anyone sufficiently disinterested to speak for the common good? That question assumes, of course, that the public interest is more than the sum of its parts. The founders did assume that there was a common good which was different from the sum of the interests of multitudinous factions.[94] Let us now jump ahead 200 years and examine the results of the new constitutional system.

Mixed Results

Certainly the longevity of our Constitution is worthy of praise. The United States has the oldest continuously functioning written constitution of any nation in the world. So why are the results only "mixed"?

What were the founders' goals? Justice? Happiness of the people? Prosperity? Activist but democratic government? The results are mixed because we have today a government dominated by interest groups instead of a democratic government. We have an oligarchy, a "natural aristocracy," the type of system Adams and Smith vigorously opposed. This American oligarchy resists activism in government when activism would provide economic justice (for example, health insurance for all) but supports activism for the benefit of economically powerful, well-connected interest groups. Such influence by a few was excoriated by Smith and is precisely the type of imbalance against which Adams inveighed. Such restrictions on activist government call into question the degree of democracy in our government and inevitably affect the other goals.

But, you say, American prosperity in the twentieth century has been the envy of the rest of the world. I agree that there is some truth in this, but note that, over the past twenty years the earnings gap between rich and poor has been increasing; add the recent economic stagnation of the middle class and one has good reasons to call into question the justice of that prosperity.[95] Prosperity for the few, to the exclusion of the many, is not what Adams meant by balance and is not what Smith aimed for as the wealth of the nation. Such prosperity is not just; nor does it conduce to the happiness of the many. Oligarchs view justice, happiness, prosperity for the few as legitimate goals and have for centuries been adept at using governments to advance their self-interest, quite often disguising their selfishness behind a facade of the common good. But they see the use of government power to make justice, happiness, prosperity available for all as illegitimate. We have forgotten that one truly revolutionary concept of the American founding was equality in the pursuit of happiness.

Conservatives would disagree with that word "activist" in the fourth goal and with the strong government argument throughout this chapter. For example, Novak argues that, since the people are sovereign, the citizens must take responsibility for achieving the common good. To do this, the citizens will sometimes use government but government "cannot take full responsibility for the common good," because its powers are "expressly limited." Thus, "large and historically unprecedented scope must be left to free citizens, alone and in their associations, to achieve those many aspects of the common good that lie beyond the limited powers of the state."[96] From the same democratic base which Jefferson emphasized, Novak comes to a radically restricted role for government. But Novak begs the question of limits. After all, who decides the limits? I grant that limited government is necessary to prevent tyranny (and I certainly do not want tyranny), and I agree that individual responsibility is very important; but must fear of power push us into atomistic individualism? Novak goes too far in that direction, even though he is not an extreme individualist. A more balanced approach is needed.

Novak's comment about associations assumes that free individuals cannot be disconnected social atoms. He often refers to the importance of "mediating structures" in society. Such structures, including churches and interest groups, were recognized early in the republic as an important check against a potentially despotic government. Bellah and company (who come from a very different ideological perspective) note that Tocqueville saw associations as the best protection against a dangerous weakness: "the mass society of mutually antagonistic individuals, easy prey to despotism."[97]

The thoughtful reader might now interject: you were arguing against factions and now you seem to be endorsing them under a different name. It sounds like associations are just another word for factions. It is fair to infer that I advocate associations. Various community structures, mediating organizations are certainly necessary if individuals are to have any impact in our mass society. However, when I attack factions, I am criticizing them for parochialism. I agree with a criticism by Crozier, a contemporary French observer of the American scene, who believes that the community structures which Tocqueville observed in 1830s America have broken down. He argues that the American emphasis on equality has weakened social structures, that the voluntary associations which Tocqueville witnessed as a major strength of America are now simply defensive interest groups.[98] In short, when associations become interested only in their own selfish goals, when they lose sight of the common good, they are factions. In this context, remember what chapter 2 said about tolerance of the truths of others and about the dangers of enthusiasm. However, an even more fundamental issue is that large groups of Americans are not equally represented in our pluralist politics. This has always been a failing of what Lowi labeled "interest-group liberalism." So some factions, aristocrats, oligarchs, prosper while the anomic many are virtually excluded from the system. Citizens need groups to overcome anomie and to gain and exercise power. Interest groups and parties are problematic only when they act as factions.

Crozier also argues that the American emphasis on proper procedures exacerbates the American situation and that Americans suffer from a kind of anarchy; "their feudal power bases, endlessly quarreling with one another, are nonetheless practically untouchable."[99] Our litigious society, our emphasis on problem-solving through application of judicial procedures, impedes a cooperative approach. Crozier's comment about "feudal power bases" is directed at our interest groups, which are the most powerful factions in our current political system. Forget the political parties, which are now merely hired guns for interest groups. Also, you can ignore campaign rhetoric against special interests; each party has its favored special interests and each party has interests it prefers to attack, but both are playing the same interest group game. Remember, also, that Crozier's comments about our litigious society apply not only to individuals but also to interest groups because they work through the courts as well as by lobbying legislators.

So, no one is watching the shop. Everyone seems to be concerned only about self-interest (contemporary interest group factionalism is a variant of individual self-interest); the result is that the common good is forgotten.[100] But let us not blame the founders for failure to foresee the development of interest groups and political parties. These developments would have dismayed them. The issue is not where to assess blame, but what to do about a formerly democratic system that has been transformed into an interest group oligarchy (or an aristocracy, to use Adams's term).

Conclusion

The founders wanted to have a strong democratic government but factions are destroying that democracy. This destructiveness comes from an extremely appealing argument, an argument for freedom. Tillich, using "liberalism" in its older connotation of individual freedom, makes the following connection:

> Liberalism prevails, in bourgeois society, among the groups that require the free play of forces for their development, and for whom the idea of harmony provides justification for their unlimited economic aspirations, i.e., among individual entrepreneurs in commerce, industry, and finance. When commercial interests are combined into power groups, however, the idea of harmony becomes merely an ideology serving to protect the power structures from governmental interference. . . . Among the large cartels, the Enlightenment's paradoxical concept of harmony is being more and more transformed into the feudal, stratified concept of organism espoused by political romanticism. *This is the way from liberalism to the new feudalism.*[101]

Tillich's use of "the free play of forces" refers to free market economics. Free markets have been enormously powerful as engines of economic growth. But at what cost do we purchase that growth? To determine whether we are to continue toward a new feudalism or move toward an improved democratic system, it is necessary to examine the political implications of capitalism, in the next chapter.

Notes

1.   Merrill D. Peterson, ed., *The Portable Thomas Jefferson* (New York: Penguin Books, 1975), 293.

2.   Thomas L. Pangle, *The Spirit of Modern Republicanism: The Moral Vision of the American Founders and the Philosophy of Locke* (Chicago: University of Chicago Press, 1988), 55.

3.   Thomas L. Pangle, *The Ennobling of Democracy: The Challenge of the Postmodern Era* (Baltimore: Johns Hopkins University Press, 1992), 9.

4.   Patricia H. Werhane, *Adam Smith and His Legacy for Modern Capitalism* (New York: Oxford University Press, 1991), 179.

5.   James Q. Wilson, "The Moral Sense," *American Political Science Review* 87 (March 1993): 5, discusses the vast body of research demonstrating, compellingly, the importance of fairness, defined as distributive justice, proportionality. Howard Zinn, *Declarations of Independence: Cross-Examining American Ideology* (New York: HarperCollins, 1990), 109, defines justice as "fair treatment of all human beings, the equal right of all people to freedom and prosperity." He also cautions that

1016

Chapter 5

justice might be impeded by citizens committed to absolute obedience to law, when justice requires instead adherence to a higher law, "the law of morality" (119).

Remember, also, the sermons in chapter 3 connecting justice and the golden rule. A twentieth-century German theologian, Paul Tillich, *The Socialist Decision,* Franklin Sherman, trans. (New York: University Press of America, 1977), 6, also defines justice in terms of the golden rule, although he does not use that label:

> The demand is directed towards the fulfillment of the true origin. Now a person experiences an unconditional demand only from another person. The demand becomes concrete in the "I-Thou" encounter. The content of the demand is therefore that the "thou" be accorded the same dignity as the "I"; this is the dignity of being free, of being the bearer of the fulfillment implied in the origin. This recognition of the equal dignity of the "Thou" and the "I" is justice.

Note the similarity between this passage and Martin Buber's "I-Thou" relationship. Also, this is certainly compatible with Smith's concern with fair play as one aspect of justice.

6. *Federalist,* #51, 164.

7. Richard C. Sinopoli, *The Foundations of American Citizenship: Liberalism, the Constitution, and Civic Virtue* (New York: Oxford University Press, 1992), 96.

8. Brutus, writing to the citizens of New York, in Herbert J. Storing, ed., *The Anti-Federalist: An Abridgment, by Murray Dry, of the Complete Anti-Federalist* (Chicago: University of Chicago Press, 1985), 118.

9. *Federalist* # 51, 163.

10. Adam Smith, *An Inquiry into the Nature and Causes of the Wealth of Nations,* R. H. Campbell and A. S. Skinner, eds. (Oxford: Oxford University Press, 1976), V.i.b.1, 708.

11. Werhane, *Adam Smith and His Legacy,* 80.

12. Stephen Holmes, *Passions and Constraint: On the Theory of Liberal Democracy* (Chicago: University of Chicago Press, 1995), 244.

13. Editors, in Adam Smith, *The Theory of Moral Sentiments,* 6th ed., D. D. Raphael and A. L. Macfie, eds. (Oxford: Oxford University Press, 1976), *20.*

14. Serge-Cristophe Kolm, "Altruism and Efficiency," *Ethics* 94 (October 1983): 22 and 62.

15. Editors, in Smith, *Theory of Moral Sentiments, 20.*

16. Editors, in Smith, *Theory of Moral Sentiments, 24.*

17. Editors, in Smith, *Wealth of Nations, 2* and *4.*

18. Smith, *Wealth of Nations,* IV.ix.51, 687.

19. Athol Fitzgibbons, *Adam Smith's System of Liberty, Wealth and Virtue* (Oxford: Clarendon Press, 1995), 5. For further discussion of the "Adam Smith Problem," see Robert L. Heilbroner, "The Socialization of the Individual in Adam Smith," *History of Political Economy* 14 (# 3, 1982): 427-28 and passim, on the integral connection of Smith's two books. See also Charles L. Griswold, Jr., *Adam Smith and the Virtues of Enlightenment* (New York: Cambridge University Press,

1999), 368, footnote 7; Stephen Copley and Kathryn Sutherland, eds., *Adam Smith's Wealth of Nations: New Interdisciplinary Essays* (Manchester: Manchester University Press, 1995), 4-5; Andrew Stewart Skinner, *A System of Social Science: Papers Relating to Adam Smith,* 2d ed. (Oxford: Clarendon Press, 1996), 2-3 and 45. But the issue is still debated; for example, Peter Minowitz, *Profits, Priests, and Princes: Adam Smith's Emancipation of Economics from Politics and Religion* (Stanford: Stanford University Press, 1993), 140, is critical of those who deny the existence of an "Adam Smith Problem," and Michael J. Shapiro, *Reading "Adam Smith": Desire, History and Value* (Newbury Park, Cal.: Sage Publications, 1993), 76-77, is ambivalent about the question.

20. Werhane, *Adam Smith and His Legacy,* 14-15.

21. "Much of the moral thrust of Smith's political economy lies in its claim to better the lot of the ordinary person" (Griswold, *Smith and Enlightenment,* 13).

22. Smith, *Theory of Moral Sentiments,* II.ii.2.1, 83.

23. Werhane, *Adam Smith and His Legacy,* 31; see also Griswold, *Smith and Enlightenment,* 264.

24. That was how Manning described himself in the title to his 1799 pamphlet, "The Key of Liberty."

25. Michael Merrill and Sean Wilentz, eds., *The Key of Liberty: The Life and Democratic Writings of William Manning, "A Laborer," 1747-1814* (Cambridge: Harvard University Press, 1993), 128.

26. Merrill and Wilentz, eds., *Key of Liberty,* 154.

27. Richard Hofstadter, "The Founding Fathers: An Age of Realism," in *The Moral Foundations of the American Republic,* 3d ed., Robert H. Horwitz, ed. (Charlottesville: University of Virginia Press, 1986), 62 and 64.

28. Gordon S. Wood, *The Radicalism of the American Revolution* (New York: Alfred A. Knopf, 1992), 12.

29. John Adams started an autobiography but did not complete it. What he wrote is available in Butterfield's edited version of the Adams's papers; L. H. Butterfield, ed., *The Adams Papers: Diary and Autobiography of John Adams,* 3 (New York: Atheneum, 1964), originally published by Harvard University Press, 1961.

30. John Adams, Autobiography, in Butterfield, ed., *Diary and Autobiography,* 3, 326.

31. Robert L. Heilbroner, *The Worldly Philosophers,* rev. ed. (New York: Simon and Schuster, Inc., 1961), 53.

32. Smith, *Wealth of Nations,* IV.ix.51, 687-88.

33. Smith, *Wealth of Nations,* I.xi.b.5, 163, IV.i.c.2, and IV.i.d.1, 723-24.

34. Jerry Z. Muller, *Adam Smith: In His Time and Ours* (Princeton: Princeton University Press, 1993), 85.

35. Smith, *Wealth of Nations,* II.ii.94 and 106, 324 and 329, V.i.e.30, 754, IV.v.a.39, 523, IV.i.f.57, 786 and V.ii.k.6-7, 871-72.

36. Muller, *Adam Smith,* 125.

37. John Jay, *Federalist,* #2, 31.

38. John P. Diggins, *The Lost Soul of American Politics: Virtue, Self-Interest, and the Foundations of Liberalism* (Chicago: University of Chicago Press, 1984), 57.

39. John Adams, diary entry, undated, in Butterfield, ed., *Diary and Autobiography,* 1, 221-22.

40. John Adams, in Butterfield, ed., *Diary and Autobiography*, 2, 59. This maxim is also inscribed on a statue of John Adams in Quincy, Massachusetts.

41. Lester J. Cappon, ed., *The Adams-Jefferson Letters: The Complete Correspondence between Thomas Jefferson and Abigail and John Adams,* 2 (Chapel Hill: University of North Carolina Press, for the Institute of Early American History and Culture, 1959), 456.

42. Clinton Rossiter, "The Legacy of John Adams," *Yale Review* 46 (1957): 541, states that, in contrast to Paine's perspective that government was "'a necessary evil,'" Adams believed that government was natural, reasonable and that the common good depended "'entirely on the constitutions of government.'"

43. Cotton Tufts, letter to John Adams, August 10, 1785, in Richard Alan Ryerson, et al., eds., *Adams Family Correspondence,* 6 (Cambridge: Belknap Press of Harvard University Press, 1993), 256-57.

44. John Adams, letter to Cotton Tufts, September 10, 1783, in Ryerson, ed., *Adams Family Correspondence*, 5, 241.

45. John Quincy Adams and Charles Francis Adams, *John Adams* (New York: Chelsea House, 1980), 2, 110.

46. John Adams, letter to William Gordon, April 8, 1777, in Robert J. Taylor, ed., *Papers of John Adams,* 5 (Cambridge: Belknap Press of Harvard University Press, 1983), 149.

47. Colleen A. Sheehan and Gary L. McDowell, eds., *Friends of the Constitution; Writings of the "Other" Federalists, 1787-1788* (Indianapolis: Liberty Fund, 1998), 21.

48. Charles Edward Merriam, *A History of American Political Theories* (New York: Augustus M. Kelley, 1969), 63; see also Pangle, *Spirit of Modern Republicanism*, 94-95.

49. Pangle, *Spirit of Modern Republicanism*, 262.

50. Writing in 1913, Walter Lippmann argued that we must balance two quite different truths: a Jeffersonian distrust of police helps protect us from tyrannical collectivism but, on the other hand, "without a vivid sense of the possibilities of the state we abandon the supreme instrument of civilization." Just as it is "true that that government is best which governs least" so also it is "true that that government is best which provides most" (in Clinton Rossiter and James Lare, eds., *The Essential Lippmann: A Political Philosophy for Liberal Democracy* [Cambridge: Harvard University Press, 1982], 323).

51. Frank Bourgin, *The Great Challenge: The Myth of Laissez-Faire in the Early Republic* (New York: George Braziller, 1989), 108-09.

52. Peterson, ed., *Portable Jefferson*, 416-17.

53. Pauline Maier, *From Resistance to Revolution: Colonial Radicals and the Development of American Opposition to Britain, 1765-1776* (New York: Random House, 1972), 24-28 and 40.

54. John R. Nelson, Jr., *Liberty and Property: Political Economy and Policymaking in the New Nation, 1789-1812* (Baltimore: Johns Hopkins University Press, 1987), 12-13.

55. Nelson, *Liberty and Property*, 14. Among the problems the Constitution was intended to attack was "the ability of the legislatures to nullify contracts and absolve debtors from their obligations under them" (Editors' footnote in Sheehan and McDowell, *Friends of the Constitution*, 332).

56. Hamilton, *Federalist*, #70, 210.

57. Wood, *Radicalism of the American Revolution*, 262.

58. Bourgin, *Great Challenge*, 37-38.

59. Herbert J. Storing, "Introduction," in Sheehan and McDowell, eds., *Friends of the Constitution*, xxxiii.

60. Editors, in Sheehan and McDowell, *Friends of the Constitution*, xv and 163; "A Pennsylvania Farmer," 23; James Wilson, 84 and 238; John Dickinson, 222; Tench Coxe, 260; and Oliver Ellsworth, 288-89 and 294. Also, see Jaspar Yeates as reported by Sinopoli, *Foundations of American Citizenship*, 125.

61. Sheehan and McDowell, eds., *Friends of the Constitution*, 339. Holmes, *Passions and Constraint*, 22, contrasts the American framers and the Paris Constituent Assembly. Unlike the French, the American framers had been frustrated by their experience of a weak central government. Virtually absent from Paris, Holmes states, was "devotion to governmental energy and effectiveness," prime concerns of the Americans.

62. Ralph Lerner, *The Thinking Revolutionary: Principle and Practice in the New Republic* (Ithaca, N.Y.: Cornell University Press, 1979), 100.

63. John Ferling, *John Adams: A Life* (Knoxville: University of Tennessee Press, 1992), 314-15.

64. Wood, *Radicalism of the American Revolution*, 189.

65. Madison, *Federalist*, #10, 49-50.

66. Cappon, ed., *Adams-Jefferson Letters*, 1, 213-14.

67. George A. Peek, Jr., ed., *The Political Writings of John Adams: Representative Selections* (Indianapolis: Bobbs-Merrill Co., Inc., 1954), 114-15 and 117.

68. Peek, ed., *Political Writings of Adams*, 352.

69. Peek, ed., *Political Writings of Adams*, 397-98.

70. Peek, ed., *Political Writings of Adams*, 147.

71. John R. Howe, Jr., *The Changing Political Thought of John Adams* (Princeton: Princeton University Press, 1966), 194.

72. John Adams, letter to Abigail Adams, July 6, 1774, in L. H. Butterfield, ed., *Adams Family Correspondence*, 1 (Cambridge: Belknap Press of Harvard University Press, 1963), 127.

73. John Adams, letter to the *Boston Gazette*, August 29, 1763, in Taylor, ed., *Papers*, 1, 77.

74. Cappon, ed., *Adams-Jefferson Letters*, 2, 351.

75. John Adams, letter to Joseph Hawley, August 25, 1776, in Taylor, ed., *Papers*, 4, 496.

76. Adrienne Koch and William Peden, eds., *The Selected Writings of John and John Quincy Adams* (New York: Alfred A. Knopf, 1946), 148-49.

77. John Adams, letter to James Warren, May 12, 1766, in Taylor, ed., *Papers*, 4, 183; John Adams, letter to Jonathan Jackson, October 2, 1780, in Gregg L. Lint, et al., eds., *Papers of John Adams,* 10 (Cambridge: Belknap Press of Harvard University Press, 1996), 192.

78. Peter McNamara, *Political Economy and Statesmanship: Smith, Hamilton, and the Foundation of the Commercial Republic* (DeKalb: Northern Illinois University Press, 1998), 111.

79. See Ralph Adams Brown, *The Presidency of John Adams* (Lawrence: University Press of Kansas, 1975), passim.

80. Robert J. Morgan, "Madison's Analysis of the Sources of Political Authority," *American Political Science Review* 75 (September 1981): 615. See Noah Webster, in Sheehan and McDowell, eds., *Friends of the Constitution,* 194, for another Federalist's criticism of faction: "No form of government can preserve a nation which can't control the party rage of its own citizens." George Washington also criticized faction in his Farewell Address, in Daniel J. Boorstin, ed., *An American Primer* (New York: Penguin Books, 1966, 219.

81. Storing, ed., *Anti-Federalist*, 16, 19, 37, 125-26, and 340.

82. Merriam, *American Political Theories*, 60 and 75.

83. The religious community was not unaware of the dangers of political factionalism. Samuel McClintock, preaching in New Hampshire in 1784, warned that faction could "overturn the foundations of government and throw all things into confusion" (McClintock, "A Sermon on Occasion of the Commencement of the New Hampshire Constitution," in Ellis Sandoz, ed., *Political Sermons of the American Founding Era, 1730-1805* [Indianapolis: Liberty Press, 1991], 811-12).

84. Bernard Bailyn, *The Origins of American Politics* (New York: Alfred A. Knopf, 1970), 36-37.

85. Smith, *Theory of Moral Sentiments,* III.3.43, 155-56.

86. Smith, *Wealth of Nations*, V.iii.90, 944-45.

87. Smith, *Wealth of Nations*, I.x.c.61, 157.

88. Smith, *Wealth of Nations*, IV.ii.43, 471.

89. Smith, *Wealth of Nations*, IV.viii.30, 654.

90. For criticisms of the factional power of business in general, see Smith's fears of the bad effects of chambers of commerce and manufacturing in his letter to Le Duc De La Rochefoucauld, November 1, 1785, in Ernest Campbell Mossner and Ian Simpson Ross, eds., *The Correspondence of Adam Smith* (Oxford: Oxford University Press, 1987), 286; also, see *Wealth of Nations,* IV.iii.c.10, 493-94. A sarcastic comment on the British nation of shopkeepers and the influence of that faction in

maintaining an empire and fighting against the thirteen colonies' independence is in *Wealth of Nations*, IV.vii.c.63, 613. For additional comments critical of woolen manufacturers, see *Wealth of Nations*, IV.viii.17, 647-48. Specific industries which Smith criticized, in addition to wool, included linen "which is carried on for the benefit of the rich and the powerful" (*Wealth of Nations*, IV.viii.4, 644), and leather (*Wealth of Nations*, IV.viii.34, 655). And see *Theory of Moral Sentiments*, VI. ii.3.3, 235 for his statement that "private interest should be sacrificed to the public interest." Inferior interests should be sacrificed to universal interests.

91. *Federalist*, #51, 163.

92. *Federalist*, #10, Madison, 51, italics in the original.

93. Wood, *Radicalism of the American Revolution*, 259.

94. Two contemporary analysts speak to this issue. Benjamin R. Barber, *Strong Democracy: Participatory Politics for a New Age* (Berkeley: University of California Press, 1984), 207, sees divisions among the people as a rebuke; in seeking to create a common future, he looks not to majority rule but to mutualism. Amitai Etzioni, *The Moral Dimension, Toward a New Economics* (New York: Free Press, 1988), 215, argues that "pluralism requires a countervailing factor of unity, a community or nation-wide We, to balance the multiple particular interests"; he sees both as legitimate.

95. *Statistical Abstract of the United States, 1998,* 473. David L. Norton, *Democracy and Moral Development* (Berkeley: University of California Press, 1991), 123, states that, in the United States, the top fifth of families owns almost eighty percent of the wealth, while the bottom fifth owns only two-tenths of a percent.

96. Michael Novak, *Free Persons and the Common Good* (New York: Madison Books, 1989), 153.

97. Robert N. Bellah, et al., eds., *Habits of the Heart: Individualism and Commitment in American Life* (New York: Harper and Row, 1985), 38.

98. Michel Crozier, *The Trouble with America: Why the System Is Breaking Down* (Berkeley: University of California Press, 1984), 85.

99. Crozier, *Trouble with America*, 97.

100. Jane J. Mansbridge, ed. *Beyond Self-Interest* (Chicago: University of Chicago Press, 1990), xii, writes that self-interest probably outweighs the public good in liberal democracies, "especially in the United States." She calls for a balance of "techniques and institutions that assume self-interest and those that assume public spirit."

101. Paul Tillich, *The Socialist Decision*, 52-53.

Chapter Six

Self-Interest and the Economy

Individuality and free markets can both be valuable concepts, if implemented in a *yin-yang* style. However, when one moves away from *yin-yang* to a dialectical application, these otherwise valuable concepts cause problems for society. And that has happened in the United States. This is not to deny that self-interest and free markets are factors which help explain the economic development of the United States. Adam Smith did indeed write that actions motivated by self-interest could support the common good, but many good ideas are distorted when taken to an absurd extreme. The economic excesses of the 1980s, which were a rerun of the economic excesses of the 1920s, which were a rerun of similar periods of economic excess in the nineteenth century, illustrate individualistic capitalism taken to an extreme. Government had a very definite role in the excesses of the 1980s. The federal government emphasized self-interested economic behavior and thus reinforced avarice, the greed of the Milkins and Boeskys and thousands of other operators.

Instead, government could have played a *yin-yang* role of tempering acquisitiveness within a social context, of moderating individualism by insisting that individual economic acts respect the community. Such a role for government would have allowed both civil society and economic development, both the public good and individuality within communities. In short, a government concerned for the common good would attempt to encourage virtue in its citizens. Self-interest must be tempered by civic virtue; both are necessary for an economically flourishing yet civil society. Adam Smith and many of our founders expected individuals to act in their own interest, but they also expected them to act with an awareness of social context. Individuality in this sense is demonstrated by people who are industrious and show initiative but are careful not to self-aggrandize by oppressing others. However, as argued in a previous chapter, government encouragement of virtue is not to be taken to an extreme.

Government can support the development of virtuous citizens, but it cannot command individual virtue. Other (non-governmental) community organizations must play a crucial role in such values development. However, this chapter analyzes individual self-interest and its implications for government's role in the economy.

Since I believe that the United States' political economy is not currently balanced between private and public interests, much of this chapter (and the following chapter, "Property and Democracy") will be somewhat critical in tone. Yet, because many Americans are proud of our economic successes and sensitive to criticisms of capitalism, a word of explanation is, perhaps, warranted. McWil-liams writes about a tension between the idea of a liberal free market and more traditional American ideas: "Our political history has involved a conflict between modern, dominantly liberal ideas and those derived from religion and traditional philosophies and cultures, and that 'check' to exchange relations and modern ideas has been the source of much of our political resilience."[1] This quotation alludes to all three of the strands in American revolutionary thinking. When McWilliams uses "liberal" in this quotation, he is referring to its philosophic meaning of freedom and individual rights. Many writers connect such liberalism with the free market economy. However, the liberal strand, when taken to an individualistic extreme, conflicts with the civic republican and religious strands. Thus, while Americans should be proud of the many accomplishments stemming from liberal freedom, I believe our society and economy would be even stronger if we achieved a better balance among liberalism, civic republicanism, and religion.

Moreover, while the competitive free market system has produced economic wonders, a basic assumption of this chapter is that the circumstances which supported such wondrous free market economic growth in the United States were unique and have passed forever. It is unlikely that the United States will ever again be a sparsely settled country and we can never start anew in developing an unexploited continent rich in natural resources. The growth of American capitalism in the eighteenth and nineteenth centuries owes much to these unique circumstances. Our economy is now part of an interdependent world economy, and thus is very different from the eighteenth-century American economy. In addition, to a much greater degree than individualists would like to believe, two major community factors account for much of America's spectacular economic growth: government programs to support the economy and individuals working together cooperatively.

In spite of the unique factors and the community contributions, many people seem to assume that ruggedly independent economic individualism is efficient in the modern world. So, the religious and philosophical "check" McWilliams mentions is important; to preserve the essence of free markets and to restore democracy, the excesses of extreme economic individualism must be eliminated. Failure to modify American capitalism will be doubly disastrous; our economic standard of living will suffer and our democracy will deteriorate.

One could argue that the New Deal is a good model here. Franklin D. Roosevelt's policies modified American capitalism and thereby strengthened both our capitalist system and our democracy. (The connection to democracy is considered in chapter 7.) This chapter is written, then, in the spirit of that continuing debate among liberal individualism and its civic republican and religious critics. The chapter aims for a balance of self-interest tempered by the public good. To continue this debate we will first examine the nature of American economic individualism in the revolutionary era.

Economic Individualism

After the Revolutionary War most Americans emphasized individual economic concerns. This is not surprising, even though it contrasts with the founders' emphasis on public service and political activism. After any war, participants have a natural tendency to want to get their own personal lives in order. Galston argues that seventeenth- and eighteenth-century thinkers believed that republican government could best be secured by liberating the acquisitive interests of the middle class.[2] After the war for independence, there were advocates of such liberated acquisitiveness, people who argued that self-interested action, replacing civic virtue, would promote the common good. In an essay entitled "Of the Mode of Education Proper in a Republic," Benjamin Rush wrote that "'study and business'" should be the "'principal pursuits in life'" for the citizen of the young republic. A good citizen should "'love life, and endeavour to acquire as many of its conveniences as possible by industry and economy.'"[3] Benjamin Rush's essay is one example of a widely held view. However, ten years after this essay, Rush reconsidered. In an 1808 letter to John Adams, he was rueful of his support for the cause of liberty, even wishing that he could erase his name from the Declaration of Independence. Why? America had become a "bedollared nation."[4]

John Adams thought that republican values had been replaced by a venal concern for personal gain as early as the autumn of 1776. That some public servants were returning to their private careers and some workmen were taking advantage of the war-induced labor shortage to demand higher wages was, for Adams, evidence of corruption; this indicated to him that the idealism of the early stages of the struggle had been replaced by self-interest.[5] Adams was also concerned about the increase in wealth that would come with rapid commercial expansion in the republic; he feared that such wealth would corrupt the republic by dividing society into politically antagonistic economic classes.[6]

Early in the nineteenth century, both Jeffersonian-Republicans and Federalists thought that self-interest was perhaps the only common bond among Americans. Just as republican virtue had been acclaimed during the early phases of the struggle against Great Britain, making money was now praised. According to

Wood, Americans were no longer restrained by appeals to virtue. "Americans govern themselves . . . because it was in their interest to do so. The desire to make money and get ahead helped them to develop habits of self-control."[7] While there is disagreement on when this phenomenon began, it is clear that individuals motivated by self-interest were the norm in the early republic.

However, the self-interest advocated by some of the founders and observed in the 1830s by Tocqueville, was not the dialectical extreme which many Americans practice today. Lerner presents Tocqueville's understanding of a balance between public interest and private passions:

> The generalized expression of the commercial republican view of man and of human association was what Tocqueville called "the doctrine of self-interest properly understood," the fusing of public interest and private profit to the point where "a sort of selfishness makes [the individual] care for the state." The result was a kind of patriotism in no way to be confused with the ardent love of the ancient citizen for his city; it was less a public passion than a private conviction, a conviction arising out of private passions. Each individual would come to recognize his need for involvement with others; he might even learn to temper his selfishness. Whatever else might be said of this frame of mind, there was no denying that it sustained and was sustained by commercial activity.[8]

Self-interest was a balanced concept. However, as the United States developed during the nineteenth century, the balance was lost.

By the early nineteenth century, Americans became aware of Adam Smith's *Wealth of Nations*,[9] but not many actually read that work. Ironically, many Americans learned economics from texts which had been written by clergy; many of these texts distorted both Smith's moral theory and his economics. These texts emphasized laissez-faire, a word Smith did not use, and competitive individualism, at the cost of the benevolence and justice which Smith emphasized.[10] Before the Revolution, well-educated Americans had been familiar with Smith, the moral philosopher, but his influence increased enormously after the Revolution because he was often perceived to be a supporter of extreme individualism. According to Hirschman, "The main impact of *The Wealth of Nations* was to establish a powerful *economic* justification for the untrammeled pursuit of individual self-interest."[11] Werhane states an important implication of such self-interested action: "as some students of the *WN* conclude, Smith means to imply that the harmony of these individual pursuits will, autonomously and unintended by the actors, often produce economic good."[12] The subtler, balanced self-interest of the revolutionary era was replaced by extreme economic individualism. Many twentieth-century Americans operate in that mode; ignoring the common good, they approach the pole of pure greed.

Critique of Pure Greed

Extreme economic individualism fulfilled the worst fears of our founders. The founders did not trust commerce and feared the corrupting influence of luxury (see "Property, or the Pursuit of Happiness," in chapter 2). To refresh your memory of John Adams's thoughts on luxury, here is one more example; he wrote to Mercy Warren in April 1776 that New Englanders well understood trade and as passionately loved it as any other people; but this did not mean that he was uncritical of its effects. He continued: "The Spirit of Commerce, Madam, which . . . corrupts the Morals of Families as well as destroys their Happiness, it is much to be feared is incompatible with that purity of Heart, and Greatness of soul which is necessary for an happy Republic."[13] The religious community supported the founders on this. During the late 1770s, several ministers inveighed against selfishness, greed, avarice, oppression, and monopoly, and equated exploitation with the scheming of satan.[14]

Storing states that a "powerful argument" of the Anti-Federalists was that "the aggregate selfishness encouraged by the great commercial republic will destroy those qualities of moderation and public spiritedness on which republican government depends."[15] Storing writes that many Federalists did not respond to this criticism, but Madison's comments below are a clear response. Madison also feared that people would pursue their own self-interest at the expense of the public good. "But the mild voice of reason, pleading the cause of an enlarged and permanent interest, is but too often drowned, before public bodies as well as individuals, by the clamours of an impatient avidity for immediate and immoderate gain."[16]

Jefferson provides one final example that the type of economic system the founders envisioned was not the self-interested system which developed. Jefferson's view of invention rights, for instance, illustrates his different view of individual economic enterprise:

> Jefferson did not consider invention an *original* act. . . . Each new gadget just re-exemplifies the great Newtonian laws. . . . This explains Jefferson's opposition to long or rigorous patent rights. No one can truly "own" the "invention" of things that work, since no one can own Nature, and all things work by the laws of Nature and of Nature's God. Jefferson was opposed to the individualist vision of private enterprise. All enterprise is public, is common. Not only does the earth belong to the living. So do all the forces driving the earth.[17]

How could Jefferson argue that "All enterprise is public" when most enterprise was privately owned at the time he was writing, as is still the case today in the United States? He was not arguing for public ownership, but for private trusteeship of the public good. Whether businesses were privately or publicly owned would not matter if all businesses respected the common good. Jefferson's view, like similar statements in previous chapters, clearly shows that the founders hoped for a more balanced economy than that which has developed in this country. But what was the source of this imbalance? In addition to factors explaining the decline in public spirit presented in chapter 4, a major cause of the imbalance was that many Americans held and still hold distorted views of the ideas of Adam Smith.

Misinterpreting Adam Smith

Various commentators have construed the works of Adam Smith as supporting an unbalanced version of capitalism. Extreme individualists often cite Smith as an authority for their position; as noted above, some see this as the prevailing view of Smith's meaning. However, other scholars consider this to be a gross distortion of Smith. Fitzgibbons, for example, insists that Smith believed society should be based on a balance of self-love and the virtues; moreover, "the foundation of society was *justice*."[18]

This societal context of Smith's thought can be illustrated by numerous parts of his writing. Griswold states that, for Smith, the prudent person had "moral ties to others, including those of benevolence and justice."[19] Werhane emphasizes Smith's conclusion "that no economy can exist without a strong foundation of justice buttressed by other social and political institutions that provide a background of law, order, and continuity of religious tradition and morality."[20] She reminds us to interpret Smith's ideas within the context of his century; he was, she writes, "firmly rooted in the eighteenth century."[21] That century was much more oriented toward religion than the current century, and Adam Smith was firmly a part of that religious orientation. In short, the religious agnosticism of many contemporary Americans may blind them to important implications of Smith's thought;[22] ironically, some contemporary people of religion seem blind to Smith's ideas about social virtue.

In his first book, referring to Christianity and the precept of loving one's neighbor as oneself, Smith wrote "that to feel much for others and little for ourselves, that to restrain our selfish, and to indulge our benevolent affections, constitutes the perfection of human nature; and can alone produce among mankind that harmony of sentiments and passions in which consists their whole grace and propriety."[23] Thus I argue here and in chapter 4 that the Smith of *Theory of Moral Sentiments* simply cannot be drafted into the army of extreme individualists. The community orientation of his thinking is equally clear in his more famous book. As Fitzgibbons, considering both of Smith's books, puts it, individualism and self-love were at the bottom of the moral ladder for Smith, who "implied that moral considerations were superior to economic ones."[24]

Early in *Wealth of Nations*, he discusses the general diffusion of plenty to all socioeconomic classes: "It is the great multiplication of the productions of all the different arts, in consequence of the division of labour, which occasions, in a well-governed society, that universal opulence which extends itself to the lowest ranks of the people."[25] In short, in a balanced system, high worker productivity provides widely diffused economic well-being, even for the poor. This aspect of *Wealth of Nations* led Heilbroner to characterize the work as a revolutionary one. For Smith, wealth "consists of the goods which *all* the people of society consume; note *all*—this is a democratic, and hence radical, philosophy of wealth."[26] Smith's concern was with melding societal and individual interests to attain a just system for everyone in society.

Commenting on wages, Smith shows his concern for the laborer who is so often forgotten by extreme individualists.

> Is this improvement in the circumstances of the lower ranks of the people to be regarded as an advantage or as an inconveniency to the society? The answer seems at first sight abundantly plain. Servants, labourers and workmen of different kinds, make up the far greater part of every great political society. But what improves the circumstances of the greater part can never be regarded as an inconveniency to the whole. No society can surely be flourishing and happy, of which the far greater part of the members are poor and miserable. It is but equity, besides, that they who feed, cloath and lodge the whole body of the people, should have such a share of the produce of their own labour as to be themselves tolerably well-fed, cloathed and lodged.[27]

Similarly, he later argued that good wages are an important "cause of the greatest publick prosperity" and that such wages had important motivational benefits for industry:

> The liberal reward of labour, as it encourages the propagation, so it increases the industry of the common people. The wages of labour are the encouragement of industry, which, like every other human quality, improves in proportion to the encouragement it receives. A plentiful subsistence increases the bodily strength of the labourer, and the comfortable hope of bettering his condition, and of ending his days perhaps in ease and plenty, animates him to exert that strength to the utmost.[28]

If workers are well paid, they will be more productive, and the population of the nation will also grow.[29] As Holmes puts it, "Smith justified high wages by invoking the well being of the majority." But he did so "because of a prior commitment to distributive justice."[30] Also, in an undated letter to Sir John Sinclair of Ulbster, Smith wrote of his concern for oppression of the poor in the following terms: "I dislike all taxes that may affect the necessary expenses of the poor."[31]

In addition, Smith knew that, because of political power disparities, the laws favored the employers against the workers. While he criticized the violence and tumult of combinations of workers disputing wages (in other words, unions), he also wrote that because the number of bosses, masters, was smaller than the number of workers, it was easier for the masters to collude; "and the law, besides, authorises, or at least does not prohibit their combinations, while it prohibits those of the workmen. We have no acts of parliament against combining to lower the price of work; but many against combining to raise it."[32]

Smith was aware that working conditions could be harmful to the health of the laborers. Masters should not speed up the work rate. "It will be found, I believe, in every sort of trade, that the man who works so moderately, as to be able to work constantly, not only preserves his health the longest, but, in the course of the year, executes the greatest quantity of work."[33] The range of Smith's concerns for the laboring man helps explain why many scholars have seen *Wealth of Nations* as a "working-man's tract," one of the best ever written.[34] His concerns are hardly consistent with the class warfare against the working and poor classes practiced by both government and business in the United States in the last decades of the twentieth century. One suspects that advocates of such policies have not read *Wealth* with much care, if at all.

Businessmen, Smith warns, will be aware of their interests and willing to take harsh actions to improve their profit margins at the expense of the public.

> The interests of the dealers, however, in any particular branch of trade or manufactures, is always in some respects different from, and even opposite to, that of the public. To widen the market and to narrow the competition, is always the interest of the dealers. To widen the market may frequently be agreeable enough to the interest of the publick; but to narrow the competition must always be against it, and can serve only to enable the dealers, by raising their profits above what they naturally would be, to levy, for their own benefit, an absurd tax upon the rest of their fellow-citizens. The proposal of any new law or regulation of commerce which comes from this order, ought always to be listened to with great precaution, and ought never to be adopted till after having been long and carefully examined, not only with the most scrupulous, but with the most suspicious attention. It comes from an order of men, whose interest is never exactly the same with that of the publick, who have generally an interest to deceive and even to oppress the publick, and who accordingly have, upon many occasions, both deceived and oppressed it.[35]

Labeling such tactics "an absurd tax" is consistent with other comments by Smith on excess profits. He is very clear in his defense of profits as one of the components of prices, a rental for the use of stock, as it were, or, in more modern parlance, a return on investment.[36] But he is also very clear in his criticism of excess profits, even characterizing high profits of merchants and manufacturers as having pernicious effects.[37]

He made similar comments about the mercantilist arrangements for trade with the thirteen American colonies, labeling them monopolistic and "a very grievous tax upon the colonies" that raised the profits of some people in Great Britain, but diminished the revenue "of the great body of the people."[38] And he argued that high profits were equal to or perhaps a greater factor than high wages in raising the prices of British goods with the effect that Britain lost those markets in which it did not have a monopoly.[39]

Smith had no faith that businessmen believed in the free market. "People of the same trade seldom meet together, even for merriment and diversion, but the conversation ends in a conspiracy against the publick, or in some contrivance to raise prices." *Wealth of Nations* contains repeated criticisms of "the wretched spirit of monopoly."[40] Very early in that work he shows clearly that he is concerned with much more than a legalistic definition of monopoly: "The exclusive privileges of corporations, statutes of apprenticeship, and all those laws which restrain, in particular employments, the competition to a smaller number than might otherwise go into them, have the same tendency, though in a less degree. They are a sort of enlarged monopolies."[41]

What is the source of the range of human failings that Adam Smith saw in capitalist behavior? According to Werhane, "Smith admits that we are often greedy, indolent, or shortsighted." Actions against the public interest, "weaknesses of free enterprise, can be traced to a lack of vision, imprudence in economic affairs, parochialism, collusion, an unequal distribution of advantages, or simply a failure of justice in the system itself."[42]

If these comments are grating to modern sensibilities, the discomfort is an indication of how much of Adam Smith has been lost to common understanding. His first biographer, Dugald Stewart, noted that Smith's comments about commerce "were expressed in a tone of indignation, which he seldom assumes in his political writing."[43] To put the strength of Smith's critique in more modern terms, Heilbroner wrote that Smith "was more avowedly hostile to the motives of businessmen than most New Deal economists."[44]

In other words, "self-interest" interpretations of Smith seriously distort his writings by placing heavy emphasis on self-interest passages, to the virtual exclusion of the justice context and the societal passages.[45] Smith did indeed write: "It is not from the benevolence of the butcher, the brewer, or the baker, that we expect our dinner, but from their regard to their own interest. We address ourselves, not to their humanity but to their self-love and never talk to them of our own necessities but of their advantages."[46] He was realistic about the human drive for self-preservation. But, in contrast to more simplistic commentators on human nature and economics, he understood that individuals exist in a social context. This is especially clear in his discussion of patriotism, which, he stated, consists of respect for the government and constitution and a desire to make "our fellow citizens as safe, respectable, and happy as we can." He emphasized this point by writing: "he is certainly not a good citizen who does not wish to promote, by every means in his power, the welfare of the whole society of his fellow-citizens."[47] Humans truck, barter, and exchange out of self-interest but should do so while promoting the happiness of the whole society.

In short, Smith advocated a more balanced position than the extremist individualism which is sometimes attributed to him. He advocated free market competition because of its benefits but also knew that the weakness of human nature restricted these benefits. He was a strong critic of pure greed.

Other Critics

Roger Williams, driven out of Massachusetts Bay Colony by religious intolerance, caustically criticized the individualism he observed in New England economic development. Williams said that many New Englanders demonstrated

> "a depraved appetite after the great vanities, dreams and shadows of this vanishing life, great portions of land, land in this wilderness, as if men were in as great necessity and danger for want of great portions of land, as poor, hungry, thirsty seamen have, after a sick and stormy, a long and starving passage. This is one of the gods of New England, which the living and most high Eternal will destroy and famish."[48]

Williams feared that the younger generation had a new trinity of profit, preferment, and pleasure; even worse, they had a new god—land, as great a god for them as gold had been for the Spaniards.[49] Community-oriented New Englanders, working within a mercantilist colonial system, were, according to Williams's damning critique, becoming crass materialists.

By the middle of the nineteenth century, some Americans were seriously concerned about the nature of American society and the human impact of the economic system. For instance, Henry David Thoreau wrote of wealth as "an illusion in pursuit of a phantom." Diggins notes that Thoreau denounced an obsession with wealth and the "commercial spirit" for undermining the purity of village life in America. In addition, "Trade, credit, speculation, commerce, investment, supply and demand—all such activities Thoreau dismissed as a polite form of gambling where the risk taker wages the present against the future."[50] One wonders what Thoreau would say about the practices of late-twentieth-century American capitalism.

At the end of the nineteenth century, Theodore Roosevelt was contemptuous of American materialists. He stated that there was "not in the world a more ignoble character than the mere money-getting American, insensible to every duty, regardless of every principle, bent only on amassing a fortune, and putting his fortune only to the basest uses." And he specifically attacked speculating in stocks. He feared that America lacked martial virtues, but he also thought that commerce alone would not deal with the "terrible social problems" the world faced.[51] Twelve years later, in 1909, Herbert Croly wrote that American economic individualism "inflicts the most serious damage on American individuality." He thought that our system contributed to individual impoverishment in politics, science and the arts. In contrast to prevailing perceptions, he argued that "popular enjoyment of practically unrestricted economic opportunities is precisely the condition which makes for individual bondage."[52]

Writing in 1934, Walter Lippmann advocated a "method of free collectivism," which would be neither laissez-faire, nor communism, nor fascism, but would be a product of American experience. It would be "collectivist because it acknowledges the obligation of the state for the standard of life and the operation of the economic order *as a whole.*" It would be "free because it preserves within very wide limits the liberty of private transactions." And he called on government to "redress the balance of private transactions" where necessary, to protect the weak against the strong.[53]

One of the ironies of extreme economic individualism is that religion has been used to support this vice. On the one hand, both Christian and classical Greek traditions saw commerce and the pursuit of gain as "inimical to the pursuit of virtue."[54] On the other hand, Pangle notes that Calvinism contributed to extreme economic individualism. Yet this was a corrupted Calvinism; Calvin was not a partisan "of the capitalist spirit, or of worldly self-interest and the accumulation of wealth without limit."[55] In its crude form, this distorted form of Calvinism argued that wealth was a sign of God's grace. Obviously, this begs the question of how one's wealth was obtained. To put this in contemporary terms, is it a sign of God's grace when a druglord "earns" millions of dollars? However, for those who accepted this interpretation, capitalist enterprise could be seen as a road to salvation. (Note that this is a distortion of Calvinism; I assume that ordinary people, nontheologians, made a logical leap from "a sign of God's grace" to "a road to salvation.") Even if such a businessperson were highly ethical and followed business practices which were all perfectly legal, such a doctrine completely denies the Christian doctrine of salvation through faith, not works. That this interpretation of Calvinism is a travesty, indeed reverses the relation between religion and capitalism, was emphatically stated early in the twentieth century, by Walter Rauschenbusch, who argued, in *Christianity and the Social Crisis*, that capitalism weakened religion "by encouraging envy, rivalry, pride, indulgence, and other sins of the flesh. 'Competitive commerce exalts selfishness to the dignity of a moral principle.'"[56] Rauschenbusch was not praising selfishness.

Contemporary Critics

More recently, an American historian harshly criticized the policies implemented by the settlers of the Western Hemisphere and related these policies to economic individualism. Zinn questioned whether the brutality toward the Indians, all the bloodshed and deceit, from Columbus to Cortes, from Pizarro to the Puritans, was a necessary price of progress.[57]

The extreme economic individualism practiced by so many Americans has produced aggregate growth statistics which indicate that the rich are doing well, but this growth has undermined the economic potential of the country and has neglected millions of Americans who are under- or unemployed, poorly fed, poorly housed, poorly clothed, undereducated and/or lacking health insurance. As Barber states, factors which once made such inequality acceptable have changed dramatically:

> Diversity and private interest were the necessary conditions of capitalist expansion in America; but now, in the late stages of capitalist development, in which speculation and entrepreneurship are no longer virtues and in which pointless consumption becomes more salient than expanding production, privatism nourishes alienation and despair, feeding only that scourge faction—the dark side of pluralism so dreaded by the founders.[58]

I am not sure we can know that capitalism is in the late stages of its development and I disagree with his statement that entrepreneurship is no longer a virtue. Still, I believe that Barber states some important points for our analysis of contemporary America. Note well his argument that economic inequality is feeding alienation and note also the comment about faction. Factionalism and alienation are major forces undermining American democracy. (For their impact on democracy, see chapter 7.)

In addition, I emphatically agree with Barber's classification of speculation as a vice; in fact, I probably go further than he because I do not think speculation has ever been a virtue. Perhaps I am drawing too fine a line between speculation and risk-taking entrepreneurship. But note that Adam Smith was also critical of speculative ventures, whether in "agriculture, mines, fisheries, trade, or manufactures," because they must result in "some diminution in what would otherwise have been the productive funds of the society."[59] Speculation reduces the wealth of the nation.

Conservatives often defend free market capitalism as the most efficient of economic systems. Such a free market argument, however, requires critical analysis. Robert E. Lane notes an argument that "the market rewards people as much on the basis of luck and chance as on the basis of performance" and questions whether advocates of free markets give due credit to historical factors which have contributed to current production: "To accept the market's criteria of 'contribution to production' is to ignore history, the history of the many previous contributions to productivity that make possible the current high level of payments to members of affluent societies."[60] By reminding us that current individual productivity is possible only because society has developed, over decades and centuries, infrastructure and education systems, among other things, Lane destroys much of the extreme individualist argument. Further, Etzioni reminds us that a market economy is a subsystem of a more encompassing society, that competition is dependent on its "societal 'capsule.'"[61] So capitalism depends on historical and contemporary connections; free market success stories are really about communities. Economic stories are often written as if one hero, a Horatio

Alger, conquered all, but in reality that "hero" required a supporting cast of thousands.

To summarize, extreme economic individualism was feared by our founders; moreover, various commentators both before and since American independence have criticized such extremism. Atomistic individualism is a distortion of the capitalism Adam Smith advocated. Individualism weakens the American economy because the quest for immediate profits mortgages the future of both the company and the country. Finally, the extreme version actively impedes the role government could play in supporting economic justice for all.

Government and Economy

In the previous chapter, I argued that the Constitution was instituted because of a perceived need for strong government. In this section I argue that the founders assumed that a strong government would have a major role in strengthening the economy. I label this "activist government," meaning that government would have an important supportive role in the economy. However, this role would be limited in two ways: government would not be allowed to impinge on fundamental individual freedoms; and government activism would have to be in the common interest, not for the benefit of any faction. Such activist government would be neither laissez-faire, nor dictatorial. Before we look at the founders' views, note that many businessmen supported revision of the Articles of Confederation and note that the founders had strong philosophical support for the concept of activist government.

Business Support

Soon after the Revolution, businessmen realized that the weakness of government under the Articles of Confederation was stunting the growth of their enterprises. Jameson argued that businessmen provided major support in the drive for a new constitution because they believed that the weak national government, established by the Articles, was impeding commercial development. He also wrote: "This furnishes the explanation of the fact that, in all the efforts which statesmen were making in these years from 1783 to 1789 to erect a stronger federal government, they found their best helpers among the commercial classes."[62] Lienesch makes the same point when he argues that the rising group of manufacturers in the middle states saw the need for a stronger central government in order to strengthen the economy. They wanted "an early 'American system' that would rely on the inland rivers and overland routes to create a national trading union."[63]

Hofstadter writes the following about the founders: "Although they did not believe in impeding trade unnecessarily, they felt that failure to regulate it was one of the central weaknesses of the Articles of Confederation, and they stood closer to the mercantilists than to Adam Smith."[64] That should not be surprising; the founders had lived, for most of their lives, under a mercantilist system and Smith's *Wealth of Nations* was too recent to be widely known in the new republic. Politicians and businessmen had positive experiences with activist government during the colonial period and were in agreement on the need for such a government in the new republic.[65] They had a sophisticated ability to differentiate between, on the one hand, the evils of British mercantilist restrictions on their (external) trade and, on the other hand, the beneficial support of government for development of the colonial economies (internally).

Philosophical Support

The founders not only saw a connection between activist government and a strong economy, but also had support from philosophers on this point. John Locke, a precursor of Adam Smith, is often seen as an advocate of protection of property. But, according to Pangle, "Locke in his political economy evinces repeatedly an acute awareness of the need for governmental 'regulation,' including, in some cases, governmental ownership." Locke insisted that property rights were not absolute but were "justified on the basis of the good or the common good" and that property rights pointed "toward, not away from, government regulation in the name of 'the common benefit of each.'"[66] The United States today lacks "an acute awareness of the need for governmental 'regulation'"; indeed conservatives positively abhor the idea. The same could be said of property rights "justified on the basis of . . . the common good." This ethical perspective on property has largely disappeared from contemporary America.

Adam Smith is usually seen as an advocate of pure laissez-faire, but this is a misinterpretation. Tribe argues that Smith's advocacy of free trade has been transmuted into support for laissez-faire but that was not "part of Smith's original intention." Smith wanted laissez-passer, free trade, not a government which stayed rigidly separated from the economy.[67] In fact, Smith argued that a wide range of government regulation was sometimes necessary. In the context of an argument in favor of banking regulation he wrote: "But those exertions of the natural liberty of a few individuals, which might endanger the security of the whole society, are, and ought to be, restrained by the laws of all governments; of the most free, as well as of the most despotical."[68] While he was a staunch defender of free trade, even this was not an absolute principle; Smith did call for restraints on foreign imports in certain cases. Specifically, humane concern for one's fellow man might "require that the freedom of trade should be restored only by slow gradations, and with a good deal of reserve and circumspection"; such action would be appropriate when many people had been employed in a domestic industry protected by duties and other prohibitions against foreign competition. Otherwise, cheap foreign goods might flood the domestic markets, throwing thousands of people into unemployment, resulting in "considerable" disorder.[69] This is a good example of Smith's balanced approach; he was for free trade, but aware that government might have to regulate it in some instances. Note also that, while individual actions are often based on self-interest, a flourishing society requires more than individual self-interest; governments must sometimes enact policies for the common good.

Policies responding to the needs of the people probably required, for Adam Smith, a more activist government than many Americans would think. Skinner presents a wide range of government activities advocated by Smith, and the principles he presented in justifying them. Further, he thinks that Smith and John Maynard Keynes would have agreed on many of the principles guiding management of an economy.[70] For example, in an extensive discussion of government's responsibility for education, Smith analyzed the impact of repetitive motion types of work. He thought that a man who worked all his life in a job requiring repetitive operations might develop great skill in his trade while becoming "as stupid and ignorant as it is possible for a human creature to become." He became incapable of judgment in political issues and unable to defend his country if there were a war. This situation, so incompatible with civic virtue, was "the state into which the labouring poor, that is, the great body of the people, must necessarily fall, unless government takes some pains to prevent it."[71] Note Smith's argument that a free market economy causes deterioration in social and intellectual skills, but does not take any steps to prevent or alleviate the deterioration. Furthermore, such problems weaken democracy and the government's ability to protect the nation.

Smith was not alone. Other thinkers in England and the United States also saw a major role for government in the economy, attempting to prevent the corrupting excesses of exorbitant wealth through sumptuary laws (which restricted certain luxuries) and laws against concentration of property. Some wanted laws against dramatic presentations "and extravagant expenses in dress, diet, and the like." In addition, for some people, "it was the duty of a republic to control 'the selfishness of mankind. . .; for liberty consists not in the permission to distress fellow citizens, by extorting extravagant advantages from them, in matters of commerce or otherwise.'"[72] Wood also points out that Pennsylvania considered legislation in 1776 to prevent concentration of property ownership. And he states that America has struggled with finding a solution to the dilemma "of controlling the amassing and expenditure of men's wealth without doing violence to their freedom."[73] Leveling legislation, such as that considered in Pennsylvania, was not adopted in the United States as a whole. The governmental control inherent in such legislation was seen as fundamentally in conflict with liberty, the prime value for most Americans.

Founders' Views on Activist Government

Both philosophers and members of the business community supported a more energetic government. Also, even though the national government was weak under the Articles of Confederation, it had an activist policy in some economic areas. Bourgin states that Congress, under the Articles, was normally loath to act, but that it sometimes did act to improve the economy, for instance by planning carefully for the development of the Northwest Territories. In addition, because of the founders' mercantilist background, government was expected to play a positive role, but not to control all commerce. The men who drafted the Constitution shared a belief that government should exert all possible efforts to aid private enterprise.[74] In short, our founders still had mercantilist goals but their thinking about government's role in the economy was more balanced than the extremes of total government control on the one hand or of individualist capitalism on the other; it was more akin to the capitalism of Japan and Germany with their "industrial policies."

John Adams consistently supported an activist role for government. In the Continental Congress, on March 21, 1776, Adams proposed two resolutions which today might be called part of an industrial policy:

> "Resolved that it be recommended to the said Assemblies &c. that they take the earliest measures for erecting and establishing in each and every Colony, a Society for the Improvement of Agriculture, Arts, Manufactures and commerce, and to maintain a Correspondence between such Societies, that the rich and numerous natural Advantages of this Country for supporting its Inhabitants may not be neglected."

> "Resolved that it be recommended to the said Assemblies &c. that they forthwith consider of Ways and means of introducing the Manufactures of Duck, Sail Cloth and Steel, where they are not now understood, and of encouraging, encreasing and improving them, where they are."[75]

That manufacturing such products was important for the war effort does not weaken the point; Adams argued that the Continental Congress should encourage the states to provide government support for industry. As an editor of the *Papers of John Adams* points out, he had made similar recommendations as early as 1763 in a variety of newspaper articles.[76]

He pushed Massachusetts for similar government activism. In between tours of diplomatic duty in Europe, he wrote much of the Massachusetts Constitution. Late in October 1779 he inserted in Chapter VI, Section II, a paragraph for the support of literature, the university at Cambridge (Harvard), and schools in the towns; also the state was to provide "rewards and immunities, for the promotion of agriculture, arts, sciences, commerce, trades, manufactures, and a natural history of the country."[77] Years later he wrote Benjamin Waterhouse that he expected this section to be attacked on grounds of "Affectation, Pedantry, Hypocrisy, and above all Oeconomy," but it was readily accepted, and he considered it to be one of his greatest accomplishments.[78]

Adams maintained this belief in activist government into his presidency. His inaugural address contained his whole creed, according to Charles Francis Adams:

"a wish to patronize every rational effort to encourage schools, colleges, universities, academies, and every institution for propagating knowledge, virtue, and religion among all classes of the people, not only for their benign influence on the happiness of life in all its stages and classes, and of society in all its forms, but as the only means of preserving our constitution from its natural enemies, the spirit of sophistry, the spirit of party, the spirit of intrigue, profligacy, and corruption, and the pestilence of foreign influence, which is the angel of destruction to elective governments; . . . a love of equal laws, of justice and humanity in the interior administration, . . . an inclination to improve agriculture, commerce, and manufactures for necessity, convenience, and defence."[79]

Government's role in education has long been accepted by Americans; but the last sentence of the quotation, with the exception of defense, goes far beyond what Americans usually accept as within the legitimate scope of government action. His other reasons, "necessity" and "convenience," imply a major government role in the economy. Further, Adams even wrote his revolutionary compatriot Benjamin Rush on June 20, 1808, that he wished "that ambition and avarice may be restrained by law and be subservient to liberty."[80] For the ordinarily realistic Adams, ever wary of the potential for abuse of power, to make such a suggestion indicates the depth of his concern for the dearth of virtue in the young republic. However, none of these suggestions for activist government mean that Adams advocated an intrusive government role in the economy. He had a subtle appreciation for what government could and could not accomplish. For instance, in an April 6, 1777, letter to his wife, he questioned the efficacy of a Massachusetts trade embargo: "The Act, my dear, that you were so fond of will do no good. Legislatures cannot effect Impossibilities. I detest all Embargoes, and all other Restraints upon Trade."[81]

His strong support for free trade is even clearer in a Revolutionary War propaganda pamphlet he wrote during his second diplomatic tour of duty in Europe. Former colonial governor Thomas Pownall had written a pamphlet on relations between the old and the new worlds in 1780. This pamphlet was heavily influenced by Adam Smith's *Wealth of Nations*. Adams revised it for clarity and conciseness.[82] While Adams freely admitted his authorship and distributed his revision widely in the Netherlands, at the time it was attributed to others, including Benjamin Franklin.[83] The revision was a crucial catalyst for Adams's thinking. In his version he formed, according to the editors, "a coherent and unified theory regarding the proper course for the foreign policy of the United States, that, with few exceptions, he adhered to for the rest of his life."[84] A major aspect of that foreign policy was free trade, as is illustrated by the number of pages in the document devoted to free trade and commerce.[85] Other propaganda pieces that Adams wrote while in the Netherlands attempting to gain Dutch support for the American war effort also emphasized free trade; his letters responding to questions from Dutch politicians who were potential allies in the struggle to gain Dutch recognition and assistance provide many examples.[86] In short, Adams and Smith both advocated free trade (laissez-passer) *and* activist government.

One might argue that James Madison was also an early advocate of industrial policy. He wrote that government should be ready to accommodate changes in the economy by supporting American manufactured goods with bounties; in addition, government should not discourage industry with export duties.[87] In contemporary terms, he advocated government subsidies to industry. Governmental flexibility in support of the growth of industry is consistent with Madison's concern for the "solid happiness of the people" and his insistence that "the public good, the real welfare of the great body of the people, is the supreme object to be pursued" by government.[88] Other Federalists also advocated a strong government role in the economy. Oliver Ellsworth (later to become Chief Justice of the Supreme Court from 1796 to 1800) called for a government with the power to "protect commerce, encourage business, and create a ready demand for the productions of . . . farms."[89]

So, what specific government actions in the economy did the founders assume would be legitimate? Bourgin provides the following conjecture: "during the early period of affirmative government, it seems to have been assumed by a number of persons in high political authority that powers such as those over roads and canals, granting charters of incorporation, encouraging agriculture and manufactures, and establishing seminaries and schools were well within the scope of federal authority."[90] Alexander Hamilton's hopes were even more activist; he foresaw development of the United States as an industrialized country with the government "assisting private enterprise by means of large-scale, continuous programs of national planning."[91] Hamilton wrote that, for new manufactures to be successful, "it is evident that the interference and aid of their own governments are indispensable."[92]

In his plans for industrial policy, Hamilton was quite detailed. His "Report on Manufactures"[93] has often been interpreted as a protectionist document, but it was much more than that. Hamilton was aware of the many techniques used by other countries to support industry[94] and he wanted the United States to adopt similar policies.

> Hamilton presented the criteria by which industries to be encouraged would be selected. As an initial exercise in planning, it was a practical beginning. He also listed the separate industries and products of which the United States stood especially in need. He showed that the record of these industries justified a belief in their continued progress. In each case, he analyzed what should be done and the method that should be employed. The

Report on Manufactures was only a preliminary stage of industrial plan-ning. No production goals were stated and no date fixed for their ultimate realization. The important fact is that industrial planning was based not on hope but on proven production trends.[95]

As Secretary of the Treasury, Hamilton foresaw a fiscal surplus for the fed-eral government. As proposed in his "Report on Manufactures," one use for this surplus would be the establishment of a board of at least three commissioners, to provide subsidies for manufactures and otherwise to stimulate industry:

> Let those commissioners be empowered to apply the fund confided to them
> to defray the expenses of the emigration of artists, and manufacturers in par-
> ticular branches of extraordinary importance; to induce the prosecution and
> introduction of useful discoveries, inventions, and improvements, by pro-
> portionate rewards, judiciously held out and applied; to encourage by pre-
> miums both honorable and lucrative, the exertions of individuals and
> classes, in relation to the several objects they are charged with promot-
> ing.[96]

He also advocated "Judicious regulations for the inspection of manufactured commodities," arguing that such was "not among the least important of the means by which the prosperity of manufactures may be promoted."[97] Hamilton's plans went for naught, however, because agricultural interests dominated the country and considered his plans to be a form of special privilege which would be paid for at their expense.[98]

Resistance to Hamilton's plans also came from the "laborer," William Manning, who thought that national prosperity would result from maximizing the income of the laborers. In contrast to Hamilton's restricted commerce, na-tional bank, and tightly controlled money supply, he wanted free commerce, lo-cal banks, and a large money supply, "not because they expanded the number of opportunities for a few, very enterprising men to get rich, but because they helped to raise the price of labor and its produce, thus to ensure a decent return to the vast majority of laboring people who expected no more than to live by their labor."[99]

People like Manning could advocate active government and still not like Hamilton's means of providing government support for the economy because of a belief that Hamilton's plans would concentrate wealth. Hamilton insisted that his plans "were not designed to benefit any particular groups or sections at the expense of others," even though the immediate impact was on creditors, in-vestors, and manufacturers and even though northern businessmen reaped imme-diate profits. Hamilton argued that a large industrial-commercial sector would increase the demand for agricultural products.[100] But this early version of the trickle-down theory was unacceptable to both John Adams and the Jeffersonian-Republicans. Adams's complaints were very similar to Manning's: the national bank enriched a few at the expense of the many. A few people got rich "out of the pocketts of the poor and the middle Class of People."[101] This does not mean that Adams opposed all banking; he abhorred the Hamiltonian system but understood that funding systems were "absolutely and indispensably necessary in the present state of the world."[102]

Jeffersonian-Republican leaders were interested in activist government. But they wanted to go beyond Hamilton's merchants to a broadly inclusive economic support policy. While James Madison had been a prime architect of the Constitution and, with Hamilton, a successful advocate for its adoption, Madison became concerned that, because of Hamilton's policies, government had become a tool used by the few to oppress the many. So, Madison and Jefferson opposed Hamilton not out of general opposition to commerce and manufacturing but because of "politicization of the debt, rampant speculation, and economic stagnation." The Republicans were unhappy with Hamilton's insistence on free trade because it resulted in British domination of the American market. To counter this, Jefferson proposed massive federal aid plus aid from state governments; Hamilton's plan had omitted state aid to manufacturing.[103]

Nelson argues that Jeffersonian-Republican leaders had a "sophisticated interpretation of economic liberalism" in contrast to pure laissez-faire.[104] But this certainly represents evolution of Jefferson's policy after his first inaugural address, which aimed to keep the federal government small.[105] In his second inaugural address, Jefferson indicated what he proposed to do with federal revenues once the Revolutionary War debt was retired: "'Redemption once effected, the revenues thereby liberated may, by a just repartition among the States, and a corresponding amendment to the Constitution, be applied, in times of peace, to rivers, canals, roads, arts, manufactures, education and other great objects within each State.'"[106] Also, Jefferson planned for the government to work mines and establish factories, among other economic activities designed to develop the Louisiana Purchase territories.[107] Note that Jefferson advocated an active role for government in peacetime. The historical record shows an expansive government during war emergencies; that wartime role has not been controversial. Jefferson's advocacy of activist government in peacetime would be rejected by many contemporary conservatives, but it was accepted across the political spectrum in his time. That Jeffersonian-Republicans disagreed with Hamilton on the specific application of this principle does not detract from the agreement on the principle. So, let us now examine some examples of how this disagreement over implementation of an agreed principle worked out in practice.

Activist Government: Historical Examples

Political and business leaders not only talked and wrote about activist government, but government also actually had a large role in the economy in the early years of the new republic. This statement is a necessary correction of the common misperception that laissez-faire dominated this country from its first days. Arthur A. Schlesinger, Jr., has noted that, early in the twentieth century, "the economic historian Guy Stevens Callender had brilliantly delineated the role of governments, both state and national, in guiding American economic development. But Callender's work was not known at all to political scientists and had even been forgotten by historians."[108] That some scholars at the turn of the twentieth century understood the important economic role of the governments in the early republic does not make that common knowledge. The common misperception, not the reality seen by a few scholars, shapes popular attitudes against a strong government role in the economy.

As noted above, Jeffersonian-Republican support for economic growth was based on a subtle interpretation of economic liberalism, a view which supported governmental activism. But such activism was not simply on the initiative of government leaders. Manufacturers repeatedly petitioned Congress for aid; they complained of foreign competition (especially from Great Britain) and requested protective tariffs, relaxation of duties on raw materials, and federal loans.[109] Under the Jeffersonian-Republicans, Federal government expenditures in support of economic development were greater than any aid Hamilton ever provided.[110] Such aid reached a peak during the presidency of John Quincy Adams, with more expenditures on canal and road building than during all the preceding presidencies.[111] Extreme capitalists would be appalled to know that his administration also intervened in capital markets by buying stock; the federal government invested over $1 million in the stock of several canal companies.[112]

At the state level, there was, if anything, even more governmental involvement in the economy. Hartz documents extensive economic activity by the government of Pennsylvania. The state guaranteed interest on corporate loans, made loans to farmers and entrepreneurs, and owned stock in more than 150 corporations, including banks, bridges, canals, and railroads. Bank dividends were a major source of revenue for the state in the 1820s. In certain sectors, such as railroads, state involvement increased into the 1850s.[113]

State governments were activist in the economy longer than the federal government. But note that, until extreme laissez-faire attitudes took hold with the presidency of Andrew Jackson, the federal government had played an active role in the economy.[114] The election of Jackson produced a sharp break in the practice of activist government. His policy could reasonably claim support from Jeffersonian-Republican thinkers who wanted the new nation to separate public from private interest; they "tended to view with suspicion the traditional monarchical practice of enlisting private wealth and energy for public purposes by issuing corporate privileges and licenses to private persons. In a republic no person should be allowed to exploit the public's authority for private gain."[115] This Jeffersonian-Republican attitude was interpreted by Jacksonians as requiring laissez-faire. However, it has been impossible to attain their dialectical goal of keeping the government out of the economy, just as it has been impossible to make a clear distinction between public and private interest.

The Jacksonian approach did not survive the Civil War. Abraham Lincoln favored federal government financing of and subsidies to the states for canals and highways. In his view, benevolent government had greater responsibilities than merely protecting property; he felt that government should "'do for a community of people whatever they need to have done, but cannot do at all, or cannot do so well for themselves, in their separate and individual capacities.'"[116]

There is no denying that there were enormous economic and human implications in the government's disposition of property confiscated during the Civil War. Congress and President Lincoln agreed that the property would be returned to the heirs of the Confederate owners.[117] It is interesting to speculate whether this nation would be more just and racially harmonious if all or some portion of that property had been used to establish the freed slaves on some economically stable base. Certainly, the economic inequality which still persists has been a major factor weakening our democracy. Such speculation assumes, however, acceptance of the argument in the next chapter that widespread ownership of property is necessary for democracy.

Federal support of individual and corporate enterprise became quite significant again during the Civil War. With the withdrawal from Congress of southern Democrats who had previously blocked such legislation, Republican economic legislation dealing with national banking and land-grant colleges, among other things, was passed.[118] For another example, the Homestead Act provided free land for anyone willing to settle on the land and farm it for a minimum number of years. Fifty million acres were granted under the Homestead Act. But twice that amount was given by the federal government to railroads; this was in addition to 25 million acres of state government grants to railroads during the 1850s. In order to finance the transcontinental railroads, the federal government granted corporations ten percent of federal lands, plus $51 million in government loans. There were also land grants to promote western irrigation projects.[119] Loans and land grants represented a major role for the government and obviously were not laissez-faire. Note that the aid was not aberrant government behavior; throughout American history, up to the present, both federal and state governments have played major roles developing and maintaining various modes of transportation.

When the railroads abused the privilege granted them by government, by granting rebates to preferred customers while gouging the ordinary farmer, outraged consumers demanded regulation of freight rates. President Grover Cleveland spoke of the need for regulation in his 1887 state of the union address: "'Opportunity for safe, careful, and deliberate reform is now offered; and none of us should be unmindful of a time when an abused and irritated people . . . may insist upon a radical and sweeping rectification of their wrongs.'"[120] Zinn goes on to argue (on the same page) that the Interstate Commerce Commission (ICC), established by the Interstate Commerce Act of 1887, was then co-opted by the railroads. But whether or not the railroads co-opted the ICC, this is still an example of government economic activism compelled by popular pressure.

(This and myriad other examples of government regulation seem to make a very important point: unethical business activity elicits government intervention or, put more positively, ethical businesses may avoid governmental regulation.)

Allow me to finish with two more examples: the New Deal,[121] which probably saved capitalism in America, and the Interstate Highway system, started during the administration of Dwight D. Eisenhower. Without this and all sorts of additional government aid for transportation by ship, plane, and train, plus aid to communications, such as government development of the Internet, plus support for science and technology, business today could not function with any degree of efficiency. All of these examples of energetic government are intended to give you a taste of American economic history. The government role in the economy has often been very activist.

Conclusion

Given that the founders wanted an energetic, active government, and given that many Presidents since then have agreed with the founders, why is the American government relatively uninvolved today? A partial answer to that question is that government activism has varied over time, depending on circumstances, such as whether the nation was at war or peace, or economically depressed or prosperous. Political parties and ideologies obviously have also been important variables. In the latter part of the twentieth century, the United States has been in a less activist phase because the presidency has been controlled since 1968, with only two exceptions, by the Republican Party. And during those short time periods when Democrats have controlled the presidency, action has often been prevented by Republican majorities in the Senate and/or the House of Representatives. Split government is a recipe for stalemate, not activism.

But even in less activist times, government's impact on the economy is real. Etzioni states that much economic analysis disregards the use of government by powerful economic actors. He lists several types of government aid which can contribute to excess profits while charging market rates for one's product.

> These include gaining capital at below the market interest rates, for instance via industrial development bonds; tax exemptions or tax credits that are tailored to a particular firm or industry; cheap labor via government financed 'work-study,' training, and other such programs; and exemptions from laws or regulations such as those concerning the minimum wage or immigration; out-right subsidies; rights to benefit commercially from government financed R&D; purchase of government assets at fire-sale prices, and accelerated depreciation schedules which favor some industries over others.[122]

Such profits are less visible, but can in no way be considered the result of free market competition. Businessmen obviously have a sophisticated view of the positive uses of government. Nevertheless, such actions are not laissez-faire.

In contrast to this subtle business view, ordinary Americans often distrust government because they tend to assume that markets are fair, while the government is not.[123] Lane explains some of the implications of such assumptions: people may sympathize with those who are unemployed or handicapped, but "will regard these non-productive others as externalities, for in the market they are undeserving. People tend to prefer somewhat more egalitarian outcomes than the market provides, but their love of market methods inhibits them from advocating any solutions that seem to frustrate these methods."[124]

Another implication of the American preference for allowing the free market to attempt to solve problems is that many Americans are wary of government planning. One example of such a bias is provided by Novak, who wrote that late-eighteenth-century liberals "came to the insight that free persons could not be expected to agree in advance about common intentions, aims, or purposes. A society respectful of the freedom and dignity of persons would have to forebear any direct and conscious assault upon the common good."[125] Yet, surely, one can accept the premise that no human is omniscient and come to other conclusions about planning for the common good. While I am well aware of the abysmal performance of the centrally planned economies of the communist states, planning does not have to be absolutist. Planning can take the form of suggestions; direction and suggestion are not synonyms for compulsion. A democracy can respect individual liberty and still act, as Japan and Germany have shown with their planned but capitalist economic successes. Japan's economic difficulties in the 1990s do not invalidate this point. Planning and a strong governmental role in the economy did bring Japan rapid development. When the causes of Japan's troubles are fully analyzed, it is quite possible that a large part of the problem will be attributed to the weakness of Japan's government in the 1990s, and consequently that government's inability to play an effective and active role in the economy at a time when most analysts argued for such activism.

Therefore, I believe that our government could have an activist role in the economy, that such a role would be consistent with much of American history, that the budget costs of such a role would be justified because our economy would be healthier, and that an active government which aims at the happiness of all would have an egalitarian impact which would be good for our democracy. That last statement requires careful explanation. Let us now analyze relationships of economics and democracy.

Notes

1. Wilson Carey McWilliams, "On Equality as the Moral Foundation for Community," in *The Moral Foundations of the American Republic*, 3d ed., Robert H. Horwitz, ed. (Charlottesville: University of Virginia Press, 1986), 311.

2. William A. Galston, "Liberal Virtues," *American Political Science Review* 82 (December 1988): 1278.

3. Quoted in Michael Lienesch, *New Order of the Ages: Time, the Constitution, and the Making of Modern American Political Thought* (Princeton: Princeton University Press, 1988), 172-73.

4. John A. Schutz and Douglass Adair, eds., *The Spur of Fame: Dialogues of John Adams and Benjamin Rush, 1805-1813* (San Marino, Calif.: Huntington Library, 1966), 109.

5. John Ferling, *John Adams: A Life* (Knoxville: University of Tennessee Press, 1992), 165-66. Adams was well aware of the importance of interest in motivating individual action. But at the same time, he believed in the common good and that the state had an identity and interest of its own; see Oscar Handlin and Mary Flug Handlin, *Commonwealth: A Study of the Role of Government in the American Economy, Massachusetts, 1774-1861*, rev. ed. (Cambridge: Belknap Press of Harvard University Press, 1969), 28-29.

6. John R. Howe, Jr., *The Changing Political Thought of John Adams* (Princeton: Princeton University Press, 1966), 102 and 136.

7. Gordon S. Wood, *The Radicalism of the American Revolution* (New York: Alfred A. Knopf, 1992), 336-37.

8. Ralph Lerner, *The Thinking Revolutionary: Principle and Practice in the New Republic* (Ithaca, N.Y.: Cornell University Press, 1979), 206-07.

9. Joyce Appleby, *Liberalism and Republicanism in the Historical Imagination* (Cambridge: Harvard University Press, 1992), 40, states that Smith's *Wealth of Nations* was not influential in the United States until early in the nineteenth century when economics entered the college curriculum. But, as noted earlier, a few of the political elite, such as Jefferson and Hamilton, were familiar with it in the 1780s and 1790s.

10. Henry F. May, *The Enlightenment in America* (New York: Oxford University Press, 1976), 349. See below, "Misinterpreting Adam Smith," and the previous chapter, on justice, for discussion of these points.

11. Albert O. Hirschman, *The Passions and the Interests: Political Arguments for Capitalism before Its Triumph*, 20th anniv. ed. (Princeton: Princeton University Press, 1997), 100.

12. Patricia H. Werhane, *Adam Smith and His Legacy for Modern Capitalism* (New York: Oxford University Press, 1991), 5.

13. John Adams, letter to Mercy Otis Warren, April 16, 1776, in Robert J. Taylor, ed., *Papers of John Adams*, 4 (Cambridge: Belknap Press of Harvard University Press, 1979), 124-25. Adams remained critical of luxury throughout his

life; note what he wrote Jefferson on December 21, 1819: "Will you tell me how to prevent riches from producing luxury? Will you tell me how to prevent luxury from producing effeminacy intoxication extravagance Vice and folly?" Lester J. Cappon, ed., *The Adams-Jefferson Letters: The Complete Correspondence between Thomas Jefferson and Abigail and John Adams*, 2 (Chapel Hill: University of North Carolina Press, for the Institute of Early American History and Culture, 1959), 551.

14. Ruth Bloch, *Visionary Republic: Millennial Themes in American Thought, 1756-1800* (Cambridge: Cambridge University Press, 1985), 98.

15. Colleen A. Sheehan and Gary L. McDowell, eds., *Friends of the Constitution; Writings of the "Other" Federalists, 1787-1788* (Indianapolis: Liberty Fund, 1998), xlvii.

16. Madison, *Federalist*, #42, 138. Madison's concerns seem especially appropriate today; many critics have pointed to the short-term orientation of many American capitalists as a major impediment to international competitiveness. The quest for immediate gain has often been at the cost of long-term corporate health. In addition, the search for immoderate gains characterized the 1980s. Often the long-term result was that previously sound corporations went bankrupt, but only after various investment bankers and bankruptcy lawyers had parasitically sucked millions of dollars out of the companies; see Donald L. Bartlett and James B. Steele, *America: What Went Wrong?* (Kansas City: Andrews and McMeel, 1992), passim, for examples.

17. Garry Wills, *Inventing America: Jefferson's Declaration of Independence* (New York: Random House, 1978), 365-66.

18. Athol Fitzgibbons, *Adam Smith's System of Liberty, Wealth and Virtue* (Oxford: Clarendon Press, 1995), 140, italics in the original; he criticizes modern classical economists for a major misunderstanding: "Smith regarded society as a fundamentally moral enterprise, and the classical school does not" (190). Ian Simpson Ross, *The Life of Adam Smith* (Oxford: Oxford University Press, 1995), 420, agrees, writing that Smith aimed to "help us aspire to virtue rather than wealth, and so become members of a truly civil society."

19. Charles L. Griswold, Jr., *Adam Smith and the Virtues of Enlightenment* (New York: Cambridge University Press, 1999), 206.

20. Werhane, *Smith and His Legacy*, 166.

21. Werhane, *Smith and His Legacy*, 166.

22. Michael J. Shapiro, *Reading "Adam Smith": Desire, History and Value* (Newbury Park, Calif.: Sage Publications, 1993), 103, argues that *Wealth of Nations* had a "secularizing impulse," but that Smith was "ultimately ambivalent" on this secularizing. I wonder if Adam Smith was ambivalent. Perhaps, instead, Shapiro is too much a twentieth-century rationalist to understand Smith's eighteenth-century religious context.

23. Adam Smith, *The Theory of Moral Sentiments*, 6th ed., D. D. Raphael and A. L. Macfie, eds. (Oxford: Oxford University Press, 1976), I.i.5.5, 25.

24. Fitzgibbons, *Smith's System of Liberty*, 69.

25. Adam Smith, *An Inquiry into the Nature and Causes of the Wealth of Nations*, R. H. Campbell and A. S. Skinner, eds. (Oxford: Oxford University Press, 1976), I.i.10, 22.

26. Robert L. Heilbroner, *The Worldly Philosophers*, rev. ed. (New York: Simon and Schuster, Inc., 1961), 38, italics in the original.

27. Smith, *Wealth of Nations*, I.viii.36, 96.

28. Smith, *Wealth of Nations*, I.viii.42 and I.viii.44, 99.

29. Fitzgibbons, *Smith's System of Liberty*, 175, indicates that Smith was caustic on this point. He saw the commercial system as a "perverse and paradoxical system of power" and the very opposite of "a true value system." Among other failings, the commercial system aimed for low wages when high wages were the only sensible goal.

30. Stephen Holmes, *Passions and Constraint: On the Theory of Liberal Democracy* (Chicago: University of Chicago Press, 1995), 253.

31. Adam Smith, *The Correspondence of Adam Smith*, Ernest Campbell Mossner and Ian Simpson Ross, eds., (Oxford: Oxford University Press, 1977), 327.

32. Smith, *Wealth of Nations*, I.viii.12, 83-84.

33. Smith, *Wealth of Nations*, I.viii.44, 100. Shapiro, *Reading "Adam Smith,"* xxxi, states that Smith "overcame a silence surrounding working conditions" and helped to enfranchise the "working poor, and to draw them into a new conversation on problems of inequity, a conversation that could not be held within the old, mercantilist conversation on value." Griswold, *Smith and Enlightenment*, 13, agrees.

34. Griswold, *Smith and Enlightenment*, 261. According to Jerry Z. Muller, *Adam Smith: In His Time and Ours* (Princeton: Princeton University Press, 1993), 8, Smith was more concerned with the material and moral welfare of "the vast majority of society" than with the welfare of the elite.

35. Smith, *Wealth of Nations*, I.xi.p.10, 266-67.

36. Smith, *Wealth of Nations*, I.vi.5, 65-66, and I.vi.7, 9-10, 67-68.

37. Smith, *Wealth of Nations*, I.ix.24, 114-15.

38. Smith, *Wealth of Nations*, IV.vii.c.67, 618.

39. Smith, *Wealth of Nations*, IV.vii.c.29-30, 599.

40. Smith, *Wealth of Nations*, I.x.c.27, 145 and IV.ii.21, 461.

41. Smith, *Wealth of Nations*, I.vii.28, 79. Lerner notes Smith's awareness of negative aspects of the "commercial spirit." Smith saw the result of commercialism "as bringing about a narrowing and demeaning of souls, with the 'heroic spirit' being 'almost entirely extinguished.' . . . Smith recognized the need that civilized society had for civilized men and women . . . [which capitalism] . . . normally would not nurture" (Lerner, *Thinking Revolutionary*, 216).

42. Werhane, *Adam Smith and His Legacy*, 173. Similarly, Fitzgibbons, *Smith's System of Liberty*, 94, argues that Smith wanted a society where "the pursuit of virtue in active life" led to impartiality in culture and laws.

43. Dugald Stewart, "Account of the Life and Writings of Adam Smith, LL.D.," in Adam Smith, *Essays on Philosophical Subjects*, W. P. D. Wightman and J. C. Bryce, eds. (Oxford: Oxford University Press, 1980), 316.

44. Heilbroner, *Worldly Philosophers*, 54.

45. Many more references to Smith's works could be given, such as his *Essays on Philosophical Subjects*, 136, and numerous other places in both *Theory of Moral Sentiments* and *Wealth of Nations*. Many other scholars could be cited to reinforce the argument that, for Smith, self-interest was within a societal context; see, for examples, Karl Polanyi, *The Great Transformation: The Political and Economic Origins of Our Time* (Boston: Beacon Press, 1957), 111-12, and Shapiro, *Reading "Adam Smith,"* xxxi. It is of some historical interest that Henry C. Carey, writing in 1858, understood the societal context of Smith's *Wealth of Nations*; Carey criticized political economists for their limited view and for taking a position opposite to Smith; see Carey, "Of Wealth," in *The American Intellectual Tradition, A Sourcebook*, 2d ed., 1, David A. Hollinger and Charles Capper, eds. (New York: Oxford University Press, 1993), 268-69.

46. Smith, *Wealth of Nations*, I.ii.2, 26-27.

47. Smith, *Theory of Moral Sentiments*, VI.ii.2.11, 231.

48. Quoted in Howard Zinn, *A People's History of the United States* (New York: Harper and Row, 1980), 16-17.

49. Lawrence W. Towner, in Daniel J. Boorstin, ed., *An American Primer* (New York: Penguin Books, 1966), 41.

50. John P. Diggins, *The Lost Soul of American Politics: Virtue, Self-Interest, and the Foundations of Liberalism* (Chicago: University of Chicago Press, 1984), 207.

51. Theodore Roosevelt, *American Ideals and Other Essays, Social and Political* (New York: G. P. Putnam's Sons, 1897), 9-11.

52. Herbert Croly, *The Promise of American Life* (New Brunswick, N.J.: Transaction Publishers, 1993), 409.

53. Clinton Rossiter and James Lare, eds., *The Essential Lippmann: A Political Philosophy for Liberal Democracy* (Cambridge: Harvard University Press, 1982), 331-34, italics in original.

54. Muller, *Adam Smith*, 39-41.

55. Thomas L. Pangle, *The Spirit of Modern Republicanism: The Moral Vision of the American Founders and the Philosophy of Locke* (Chicago: University of Chicago Press, 1988), 16-17.

56. Diggins, *Lost Soul of American Politics*, 336-37.

57. Zinn, *People's History*, 16-17, states an extremely important ethical principle in this context: "If there *are* necessary sacrifices to be made for human progress, is it not essential to hold to the principle that those to be sacrificed must make the decision themselves? We can all decide to give up something of ours, but do we have the right to throw into the pyre the children of others?"

58. Benjamin R. Barber, "The Compromised Republic: Public Purposelessness in America," in *Moral Foundations*, Horwitz, ed., 54.

59. Smith, *Wealth of Nations*, II.iii.26, 341.

60. Robert E. Lane, "Market Justice, Political Justice," *American Political Science Review* 80 (June 1986): 399-400.

61. Amitai Etzioni, *The Moral Dimension, Toward a New Economics* (New York: Free Press, 1988), 199.

62. J. Franklin Jameson, *The American Revolution Considered as a Social Movement* (Boston: Beacon Press, 1956), 71.

63. Lienesch, *New Order of the Ages*, 111.

64. Richard Hofstadter, "The Founding Fathers: An Age of Realism," in *Moral Foundations*, Horwitz, ed., 69.

65. For example, see Bernard Bailyn, *The Origins of American Politics* (New York: Alfred A. Knopf, 1970), 103, footnote 37, on South Carolina and Massachusetts. Alan Tully, *William Penn's Legacy: Politics and Social Structure in Provincial Pennsylvania, 1726-1755* (Baltimore: Johns Hopkins University Press, 1977), 121, provides examples from Lancaster, Pennsylvania, of diverse economic regulations which to him "illustrate that in the early eighteenth century immigrants brought social ideas and a sense of responsibility that were not wholly those of 'liberalism' and 'privatism.'"

66. Pangle, *Spirit of Modern Republicanism*, 169.

67. Keith Tribe, "Natural Liberty and *laissez faire:* How Adam Smith Became a Free Trade Ideologue," in *Adam Smith's Wealth of Nations: New Interdisciplinary Essays*, Stephen Copley and Kathryn Sutherland, eds. (Manchester: Manchester University Press, 1995), 41.

68. Smith, *Wealth of Nations*, II.ii.94, 324.

69. Smith, *Wealth of Nations*, IV.ii.40, 468-69.

70. Andrew Stewart Skinner, *A System of Social Science: Papers Relating to Adam Smith*, 2d ed. (Oxford: Clarendon Press, 1996), 186-205.

71. Smith, *Wealth of Nations*, V.i.f.50, 782.

72. Gordon S. Wood, *The Creation of the American Republic 1776-1787* (Chapel Hill: University of North Carolina Press, for the Institute of Early American History and Culture, 1969), 64.

73. Wood, *Creation of American Republic*, 64-65 and 89.

74. Frank Bourgin, *The Great Challenge: The Myth of Laissez-Faire in the Early Republic* (New York: George Braziller, 1989), 38-39. John E. Crowley, *The Privileges of Independence: Neomercantilism and the American Revolution* (Baltimore: Johns Hopkins University Press, 1993), 117, agrees, and states that *The Federalist* is explicit in its mercantilism. Further, he argues that Anti-Federalists shared mercantilist analysis of the American economy (121). Joyce Appleby, *Capitalism and a New Social Order: The Republican Vision of the 1790s* (New York: New York University Press, 1984), 22-23, argues that the Constitution provided the political framework for the modern notion of liberty undergirding the free market system. Appleby is not necessarily contradicting Bourgin and Crowley. The free market system has indeed developed under this Constitution. I believe this was an unintended effect of the framers' work.

Frank Bourgin's 1989 work is a slightly revised version of a doctoral dissertation which was rejected in the early days of the Great Depression. It seems that the rejection was not connected to the quality of his scholarship, since the University of Chicago reversed itself and awarded him the Ph.D. degree in 1988. Given these circumstances, the bibliographic citation is misleading; his work is actually about sixty years old.

75. John Adams, Autobiography, in L. H. Butterfield, ed., *The Adams Papers: Diary and Autobiography of John Adams*, 3 (New York: Atheneum, 1964), 372-73.

76. Editor's note in Taylor, ed., *Papers*, 4, 4.

77. John Adams, draft of a constitution for Massachusetts, about October 28-31, 1779, in Gregg L. Lint, et al., eds., *Papers of John Adams*, 8 (Cambridge: Belknap Press of Harvard University Press, 1989), 260. The Massachussetts Constitution was ratified in 1780.

78. John Adams, letter to Benjamin Waterhouse, August 7, 1805, cited in editor's note in L. H. Butterfield and Marc Friedlaender, eds. *Adams Family Correspondence*, 3 (Cambridge: Belknap Press of Harvard University Press, 1973), 226. For detailed analysis of the implementation of this clause in the Massachusetts Constitution, see Handlin and Handlin, *Commonwealth*, passim.

79. John Adams, "Inaugural Address," in Adrienne Koch and William Peden, eds., *The Selected Writings of John and John Quincy Adams* (New York: Alfred A. Knopf, 1946), 142-43.

80. Schutz and Adair, eds., *Spur of Fame*, 110-11.

81. John Adams, letters to Abigail Adams, April 6, 1777, and May 28, 1777, in L. H. Butterfield, ed., *Adams Family Correspondence*, 2 (Cambridge: Belknap Press of Harvard University Press, 1963), 201 and 250.

82. Gregg L. Lint, one of the editors of the *Papers of John Adams*, said, in a private conversation, that there is no indication that John Adams ever read Smith's *Wealth of Nations*. But the Pownall revision shows that Adams was indirectly aware of the work. Pownall's pamphlet had been heavily influenced by *Wealth of Nations*; Adams thoroughly revised the pamphlet. However, Adams's free trade views were the result of his experiences as a patriot, one of many Americans chafing at British mercantilist restrictions on the colonies' trade. His free trade views paralleled Smith's, but he owed no intellectual debt to Smith for these ideas.

83. Editorial note on Thomas Pownall's *Memorial*, in Lint, et al., eds., *Papers*, 9, 163.

84. Editorial note on Thomas Pownall's *Memorial*, in Lint, et al., eds., *Papers*, 9, 157-58.

85. John Adams, "Translation of Thomas Pownall's *Memorial* . . . into common Sense and intelligible English," in Lint, et al., eds., *Papers*, 9, 209-16.

86. John Adams, "Letters from a Distinguished American," in Lint, et al., eds., *Papers*, 9, 545-46, 567, and 574-77.

87. Madison, *Federalist*, #41, 135.

88. Madison, *Federalist*, #45, 148.

89. In Sheehan and McDowell, eds., *Friends of the Constitution*, 294. For another example, in 1802, William Emerson, a minister (and father of Ralph Waldo Emerson), celebrated the federal constitution for, inter alia, its economic role. "It patronized genius and learning, gave stimulus to enterprize, and reward to labor. It encouraged agriculture and manufactures" (William Emerson, "An Oration in Commemoration of the Anniversary of American Independence," in *Political Sermons of the American Founding Era, 1730-1805*, Ellis Sandoz, ed. [Indianapolis: Liberty Press, 1991], 1564).

90. Bourgin, *Great Challenge*, 45.

91. Bourgin, *Great Challenge*, 68.

92. Boorstin, ed., *American Primer*, 201.

93. Thomas C. Cochran (in Boorstin, ed., *American Primer*, 196-97) indicates that, while the report was Hamilton's, others, such as Tenche Coxe, contributed to it; further, it represented an important school of thought on policy for national economic development. And Crowley, *Privileges of Independence*, 153, indicates that Hamilton closely paralleled parts of *Wealth of Nations*, but that while Hamilton saw Smith as authoritative he presented his Report as an exception to a Smithian liberal political economy.

94. See Boorstin, ed., *American Primer*, 200-209.

95. Bourgin, *Great Challenge*, 102-03.

96. Boorstin, ed., *American Primer*, 208-09.

97. Boorstin, ed., *American Primer*, 206-08.

98. Bourgin, *Great Challenge*, 106.

99. Michael Merrill and Sean Wilentz, eds., *The Key of Liberty: The Life and Democratic Writings of William Manning, "A Laborer," 1747-1814* (Cambridge: Harvard University Press, 1993), 205.

100. Bruce Miroff, *Icons of Democracy: American Leaders as Heroes, Aristocrats, Dissenters, and Democrats* (New York: Basic Books, 1993), 37.

101. Cappon, ed., *Adams-Jefferson Letters*, 2, 401-02.

102. Schutz and Adair, eds., *Spur of Fame*, 193-94.

103. John R. Nelson, Jr., *Liberty and Property: Political Economy and Policymaking in the New Nation, 1789-1812* (Baltimore: Johns Hopkins University Press, 1987), 71-75.

104. Nelson, *Liberty and Property*, 117-18.

105. Dumas Malone's commentary on Thomas Jefferson's first inaugural address (in Boorstin, ed., *American Primer*, 236-37) is clear on this, and also that Jefferson's policy was in contrast to Federalist preferences. But then Malone states that Jefferson would have been the first person to understand that "To follow that policy under the conditions of a much later time would be manifestly impossible." That Jefferson's economic policy emphasized the "unimpeded exertions of individuals" is clear to Appleby, *Liberalism and Republicanism*, 275; but she also states that such exertions were to be "protected and facilitated by government."

106. Bourgin, *Great Challenge*, 128.

107. Bourgin, *Great Challenge*, 130-31.

108. Arthur Schlesinger, Jr., Foreword to Bourgin, *Great Challenge*, xii.

109. Nelson, *Liberty and Property*, 151.

110. Nelson, *Liberty and Property*, 156-57.

111. Bourgin, *Great Challenge*, 153-54. Diggins, *Lost Soul of American Politics*, 150, disagrees with Bourgin, stating that national programs for roads, canals, and scientific observatories were repeatedly defeated in Congress during the John Quincy Adams administration. But I think that Diggins's point is compatible with Bourgin. The John Quincy Adams administration preceded Andrew Jackson's, which was a watershed in government involvement in the economy. Under John Quincy Adams, the aid could well have peaked, followed by Congressional rejection of new initiatives. Jurgen Gebhardt, *Americanism: Revolutionary Order and Societal Self-Interpretation in the American Republic*, Ruth Hein, trans. (Baton Rouge: Louisiana State University Press, 1993), 160, seems to support this interpretation; he states that the John Quincy Adams administration spent almost as much on internal improvements in four years as in the previous administrations' twenty-four years combined, and that the federal government was the largest entrepreneur in the country. The federal government role in the economy was "sharply contested" in the 1820s and 1830s, according to Michael Kammen, *A Machine That Would Go of Itself: The Constitution in American Culture* (New York: Alfred A. Knopf, 1987), 61.

112. Bourgin, *Great Challenge*, 171.

113. Louis Hartz, *Economic Policy and Democratic Thought: Pennsylvania, 1776-1860* (Cambridge: Harvard University Press, 1948), 82-86, 90, and 290.

114. Bourgin, *Great Challenge*, 22.

115. Wood, *Radicalism of the American Revolution*, 187.

116. Diggins, *Lost Soul of American Politics*, 322.

117. Zinn, *People's History*, 192.

118. James M. McPherson, *Abraham Lincoln and the Second American Revolution* (New York: Oxford University Press, 1990), 12.

119. Howard Zinn, *Declarations of Independence: Cross-Examining American Ideology* (New York: HarperCollins, 1990), 153-54 and 233; Jonathan Hughes, "Do Americans Want Big Government?" in *Second Thoughts: Myths and Morals of U.S. Economic History*, Donald N. McCloskey, ed. (New York: Oxford University Press, 1993), 117, and Patrick G. Marshall, "Transportation: America's 'Quiet Crisis,'" *Editorial Research Reports* 2 (August 11, 1989): 458.

120. Quoted by Zinn, *People's History*, 253.

121. Given Franklin D. Roosevelt's proposal for an economic bill of rights (in his 1944 state of the union address) it is interesting to speculate on what the American political economy would look like today had FDR been able to complete his fourth term. Among other things, he called for rights to a job, medical care, a good education as well as rights for all businessmen to be free from domination and monopolies (Kammen, *Constitution in American Culture*, 342).

122. Etzioni, *Moral Dimension*, 220.

123. Lane, "Market Justice," 385.

124. Lane, "Market Justice," 397.

125. Michael Novak, *Free Persons and the Common Good* (New York: Madison Books, 1989), 92.

Chapter Seven

Property and Democracy

John Jay's favorite maxim was: "'The people who own the country ought to govern it.'"[1] If everyone owned property, Jay's maxim would not be problematic for democracy, but the reality is that many Americans own no property. Further, for those who do, the range of holdings is wide and the concentration of ownership is enormous. Wealth brings political power. Thus, Jay's statement applied to contemporary America is economically elitist and destructive to democracy. I am not saying that Jay intended to be anti-democratic (even though the founders' fears of the masses led to the Electoral College and other constitutional impediments to democracy); instead, I maintain that gross inequities in property ownership, inequities which have accelerated in the last century, give his maxim implications which undermine democracy. Since propertyless Americans today have voting rights, in contrast to the revolutionary era, I am arguing that what counts in a democracy are the loci of power, not simply a facade of popular rule, such as elections.

To support this contention, note how Nutter connects democracy, property, and power. Power is needed if one is really to be free; individual power comes from property ownership. "Broadly dispersed and predominately private" property supports democracy. But, in addition, "there must always be collective property embodied in the power of even the freest state and accumulated through the instrument of taxation, itself an inherent property right of every state."[2] Nutter's statement is firmly within the American tradition; the founders were convinced that concentration of property in a few hands would endanger democracy. Nutter worries about ownership by the state; but, when property ownership is concentrated, it does not matter whether the state or a few citizens hold the title because it is the concentration that endangers democracy. The Philippines and many Latin American countries are examples of such political domination resulting from large amounts of property in the hands of a relatively small number of families. Democracy has been a facade, at best, in those areas. Communist countries show the danger from concentrated state ownership. But it appears that non-concentrated state ownership is not a problem for democracy; the governments of the United States, Sweden, and the United Kingdom have varying degrees of ownership of productive facilities, such as in the transportation sector, but all three countries are generally considered to be democratic. Of course, in each of those nations an enormous proportion of property is privately owned. Note that Nutter also assumes some state ownership of property ("collective property") but, to be fair, he and I probably disagree on what proportion and types of state ownership would be legitimate.

In the United States, power and property ownership have been closely related. Lindblom criticizes his political science colleagues for ignoring the reality that the market affects democracy, for example, the impact of income inequalities on political campaigns. In addition, he argues that business has a privileged position in politics and that the market impact on democracy has also led to "a degeneration of political discourse that greatly weakens popular control over elites."[3]

Concentrated economic power is a threat to the competitive market system as well as to the political system. Political power that is gained by economic interests can be used to reinforce anticompetitive practices.[4] But this chapter does not look at the use of such political power to undermine free markets; instead, it focuses on the negative effects of concentrated economic power on democracy. In addition to the atomistic individualism of modern capitalism which I have criticized throughout this work, note the two factors which, according to Barber, "jeopardize strong democracy": economic determinism and "the giantism of the modern, monopolistic multinational corporation."[5] Economic determinism, crudely put, assumes that all of life (society, polity, even religion) is caused by the material factors of existence. Barber states that economists both on the left and on the right have adhered to materialist beliefs. Of course, a huge irony here is that capitalist Americans have been very anti-communist, but at the same time have been oblivious to the fact that they share with Marxism the philosophical assumption of materialism.

While I certainly do not believe that economics is the universal causative factor, there is a connection between economic and political power, a relationship which democrats ignore at their peril. So, let us analyze the founders' view that most Americans should own property so that the people would have power, or, in other words, so that the country could be democratic. (Barber's concern for giant corporations does not become a factor until the nineteenth and twentieth centuries, and, thus, is considered later in the chapter.)

Views on Property and Democracy

Throughout the new republic, there was a belief that propertyless people, politically dependent on patrons, were not qualified to vote in a democracy. Generally, in both ancient and modern republics, the propertyless included women, children, tenants, slaves, and wage laborers; it was assumed that all of these lacked virtue, individuality, and autonomy, the qualities of a citizen. According to James Wilson, one of the framers of the Constitution, it was improper for poor people to vote because they were "subject to the undue influence of their superiors."[6] Similarly a convention in Essex County, Massachusetts, in 1778, stated that propertyless dependents (in this case, women and young men) could not vote because "'they were so situated as to have no wills of their own.'"[7]

John Adams

Two years before the Essex convention John Adams wrote about the issue of property in terms similar to the convention statement: "Such is the Frailty of the human Heart, that very few Men, who have no Property, have any Judgment of their own. They talk and vote as they are directed by Some Man of Property, who has attached their minds to his interest."[8] Adams, as indicated in earlier chapters, was concerned about anything with potential to corrupt the new republic. Dependence was only one such factor; economic inequalities were another: "Property monopolized or in the Possession of a few is a Curse to Mankind. We should preserve not an Absolute Equality.—this is unnecessary, but preserve all from extreme Poverty, and all others from extravagant Riches."[9]

In a 1776 letter he argued that balanced power required widely dispersed property ownership and suggested a way to accomplish this: "The only possible Way then of preserving the Ballance of Power on the side of equal Liberty and public Virtue, is to make the Acquisition of Land easy to every Member of Society." He suggested that property be divided into small plots, so that many people could own property because "If the Multitude is possessed of the Ballance of real Estate, the Multitude will have the Ballance of Power, and in that Case the Multitude will take Care of the Liberty, Virtue, and Interest of the Multitude, in all Acts of Government."[10] America already differed from the Old World in that many of the people owned land,[11] but Adams suggested that even more people should be owners.

Adams's desire to disperse property ownership in order to balance power came from a life-long belief that each economic class would abuse power, if not checked. As early as 1763 he wrote of his concern that all types of governmental systems can be corrupted by power; if any one of the economic classes held unchecked power, that class would tyrannize the powerless classes. Monarchy would become despotism. Aristocracy would become oligarchy. Democracy would become anarchy, "such an Anarchy that every Man will do what is right in his own Eyes, and no Mans life or Property or Reputation or Liberty will be secure."[12] In 1766, while still a loyal subject of the King, he praised the British constitution for balancing monarchy, aristocracy and democracy so that "each of these powers may have a controul both in legislation and execution, over the other two, for preservation of the subjects liberty." In the same letter to the *Boston Gazette*, he wrote that the purpose of the British constitution was equality for even "the meanest and lowest of the people."[13]

Much of his life he would struggle to find means to balance power, so that the multitude would have equality. He wanted "to protect simplemen against powerful party leaders surreptitiously representing wealth and privilege."[14] There were a few people who appreciated what his critics did not understand: the democratic purpose behind Adams's analysis of aristocracy. But he was roundly criticized, even vilified for his views, even by supporters of the supposed party of the common people, the Jeffersonian-Republicans. For instance, Tunis Wortman, in an 1800 presidential campaign pamphlet in defense of Jefferson, wrote the following about John Adams:

> I hold it to be a maxim essential to our safety, that the government of the United States should only be administered by a republican. Whatever may be the virtues or religion, whatever the talents of Mr. Adams, his principles are not republican, his sentiments are not congenial with the spirit of the constitution, he has published and proclaimed his opinions, they stand as an everlasting record and monument against him; his religion and his piety may possibly be sincere, but they cannot atone for the destruction of the constitution, and the slavery of the people; Mr. Adams is the advocate of privileged orders and distinctions in society, he would willingly engraft the armorial trappings and insignia of aristocracy upon the simple majesty of republican institutions. Mr. Adams would destroy the essential nature and character of a republic; his principles would wrest the government from the hands of the people, and vest its dominion and prerogatives in the distinguished and "wellborn few"—Mr. Adams is the advocate of hereditary power, and hereditary privileges.[15]

Perhaps the only correct item in Wortman's diatribe is that Adams had published his opinions.

Wortman's pamphlet was only one small part of a firestorm of criticism elicited by Adams's 1787 publication of *A Defence of the Constitutions of Government of the United States of America*, which contained his analysis of aristocracy. In that work, John Adams used the classical categories of the one, the few, and the many. He argued that these orders of people were facts of human nature. His work was not a forerunner of Marxian class analysis. While he was aware of economic inequality, he believed, based on his exhaustive reading of history, that all societies throughout time had had conflicting socioeconomic classes. Adams's perspective was consistent with Adam Smith's understanding that "a central fact of economic life" was the existence of different classes. In addition, "class interest does not necessarily coincide with . . . the interest of the society as a whole."[16] Adams argued that the many often deferred to people of distinction, and that one important source of distinction was wealth. The group which worried him the most was the natural aristocracy, which included the wealthy but was also based, in his opinion, on inequalities of beauty, birth, genius, and virtue.[17] He believed that all should have power; no one person or group should have the power to be tyrannical.[18] Even though most people did not comprehend what Adams was doing, he was attacking a real problem, one that could have destroyed democracy in the new republic.

At least one "laborer," who quite possibly was among those criticizing Adams, understood the problem Adams aimed to solve. Manning wrote: "But the Few cannot bear to be on a level with their fellow creatures, or submit to the determination of a legislature where (as they say) the swinish multitude are fairly represented." Manning also thought that, even though their numbers were small, "by their arts, combinations, and schemes they [the few] have always made out to destroy free government sooner or later."[19] In addition, the Anti-Federalist George Mason feared that the new Constitution would produce either a monarchy or an aristocracy.[20] Federalists, of course, attacked such Anti-Federalist arguments. For instance, John Dickinson argued that every branch of the new government would be popular.[21] In contrast, Noah Webster, writing a pamphlet on the French Revolution, understood Adams's viewpoint and defended him in 1794. He saw that Adams, rather than advocating aristocracy, recognized its existence and suggested ways to guard "against its pernicious effects in government."[22]

There were historical roots for Adams's perspective. In his 1630 "modell of Christian Charity," John Winthrop was concerned about moderating and restraining the wicked "soe that the riche and mighty should not eate vpp the poore, nor the poore, and dispised rise vpp against theire superiours."[23] Unfortunately for John Adams, no matter how many historical antecedents there were for his analysis and no matter who shared his understanding of the reality of classes and political power, his opinions were not appreciated by the majority; the popular misconception prevailed. He was seen as an apostate who had abandoned democracy, and thus he was not reelected president.

Most certainly, Adams had been wronged. Ellis states that criticism of Adams's ideas for a strong executive and aristocratic senate amounted to "libelous attacks."[24] One also wonders about Jefferson's role in all this. No presidential candidate can control every supporter, but the widespread nature of

Jeffersonian-Republican attacks is disturbing in that Thomas Jefferson shared John Adams's disapproval of aristocratic oppression of the poor. Jefferson wrote from Paris: "It seems to be the law of our general nature, in spite of individual exceptions; and experience declares that man is the only animal which devours his own kind; for I can apply no milder term to the governments of Europe, and to the general prey of the rich on the poor."[25] Similarly, Appleby argues that Jefferson's ideas about agricultural development "fueled his hopes that ordinary man might escape the tyranny of their social superiors both as employers and magistrates."[26] An irony in this is that Adams was simply applying to economic classes the general American distrust of unlimited power. He continued to argue against unlimited power, wherever it reared its ugly head.

Adams is still misunderstood today. In a generally fine biography, Ferling criticizes Adams, not only for his emphasis on a strong executive, but also because "he had clearly raised the specter of aristocratic domination, never an inherent feature of political life in America." Ferling also argues that, had Adams waited until returning to America from diplomatic duty, he might have gotten in touch with "intellectual currents abroad in his homeland" and might not have written about such "concepts alien to an America about to enter the final decade of the eighteenth century."[27] For Ferling to argue that aristocracy has never been part of American politics is historically wrong, as Ferling himself must realize, given what he wrote later in the biography. He states that Adams "Knew that powerful families had made 'monstrous fortunes' through the institutions that Washington and Hamilton had erected; in some states, power and wealth were becoming increasingly concentrated in fewer and fewer hands."[28] To imply that Adams advocated elite domination ignores the written record; in *Defence of the Constitutions* Adams clearly argues against an American nobility, and for the control of elite power in order to preserve the commonwealth and protect "the public liberty."[29] It would seem that Ferling has confused what Adams intended as description of human nature for political prescription, which Thompson indicates is a common error in reading Adams.[30]

In addition, Ferling fundamentally misconceives who John Adams was. Implying that he was importing alien concepts goes much too far. One of Adams's revolutionary era friends, Benjamin Rush, wrote to Adams on August 14, 1805, to report that James Madison had been in Philadelphia and had spoken highly of Adams; Madison had agreed that Adams never had "unfriendly designs . . . upon the present form of our American governments."[31] In short, a leader of the Jeffersonian-Republican opposition to Adams recognized that his intention had been to serve, not destroy, the new American republic. As Thompson shows, *Defence of the Constitutions* was well received in both the United States and Europe. Adams's political thought was within the American mainstream. He may even have found some Federalists insufficiently appreciative of the capacity of Americans for self-rule.[32] Most important, Thompson states that many historians agree that the principles and forms of the new federal government, "a written constitution; the idea of constituent and ratifying conventions; equality of representation; separation of powers among legislative, executive, and judicial branches; a bicameral legislature with checks and balances; an independent and unified executive with a legislative veto," were very similar to the Massachusetts Constitution and to what Adams suggested in his *Defence*.[33] (Remember that John Adams had written the Massachusetts Constitution.)

The problem is part perception and part terminology. Adams's use of the term, aristocracy, blinded people to the real situation he was attacking. He saw that economic elites did have political advantages and were using the political system for their benefit. Also, he was convinced that pretending there was no aristocracy guaranteed domination by that oligarchy.[34] Such ideas, however, were not widely understood and, in fact, were so contrary to the prevailing ideology of a classless, egalitarian America that people, focusing on the term aristocracy, assumed Adams had renounced his democratic beliefs. It is easy to understand why Americans, who had so recently fought and won their independence from monarchical-aristocratic Great Britain, would be upset by his use of the word aristocracy.[35]

However, the perceptual problem was complicated by the problem of communicating to the two very different audiences for which *Defence* was written. Today we know he wrote *Defence* for a European audience as well as for America.[36] In Europe, the word aristocracy would be understood; had he used a different term, his European audience might have been confused. *Defence* was an argument against Turgot's belief in unicameral legislatures with severely restricted executive power, based on the theory that egalitarian nations did not need artificial "orders" for the sake of balance.[37] But Turgot did not appreciate two things that Adams knew. All power must be checked, not just executive power. Second, a reality of human nature is that differentials in human qualities will produce an elite. Adams was not interested in establishing any artificial "orders"; he wanted to structure the government so that all classes would have equal power.

Finally, Ferling's comment about being in touch with American intellectual currents misses several fundamental points. John Adams was never shy about criticizing ideas, no matter how "current" or "intellectual," if he felt they were wrong. Moreover, had Adams waited until his return, his opinion would not have changed, because he would learn little that he did not already know. While he was in Europe, especially while he was Ambassador in England, Adams carried on a prodigious correspondence with American friends and relatives, who kept him well informed about the American scene (wartime correspondence, also amazing in quantity, was a bit restricted by the uncertainties of naval engagements). His *Defence* was intended, among other things, to warn his countrymen of a danger that the "intellectual currents" missed.

Although John Adams's observations of European politics and society certainly affected what he wrote, he was not the type of person who would change his beliefs, or misrepresent his beliefs in writing, to pander to American tastes. Modern politicians use spin doctors, but Adams wrote without guile. Ellis states that he was psychologically unable to appear to support faddish or fashionable political ideas.[38] His fears of aristocracy long predated his European experiences and they survived long after his return to the United States. In fact, the more he observed the new republic, the more he was convinced of the dangers of a new, American aristocracy. Instead of criticizing him for warning his compatriots of something which was un-American (which is the way many saw his fears of aristocracy), we should be praising him as a political analyst well ahead of his time. Long before Robert Michels formulated his "Iron Law of Oligarchy," Adams saw it functioning in the new republic.

Note, however, that Adams's arguments against aristocracy cannot be taken as an indication of a desire to destroy the rights of the rich. In the very work which stirred up such a storm about Adams's supposed aristocratic proclivities *(Defence of the Constitutions),* Adams emphasized that the rich are also people, that they have rights, including a right to property, "that oppression to them is as possible and as wicked as to others; that stealing, robbing, cheating are the same crimes and sins, whether committed against them or others"; and he argued that both rich and poor deserved protection.[39] Conkin, understood Adams's argument. He states that Adams knew that "the richman is both as selfish and as reasonable as the poor," and that each must be protected against the other. A good government protects all ranks of people, preventing any class from exploiting another. The rich and the poor must both have freedom, but not a monopoly of power or, for that matter, dominance short of monopoly. "The poor must be protected in their small and vulnerable property (Adams's analysis does not encompass a large class of non-propertied people) and in their opportunity for advancement, yet denied the full control of society that seems, on superficial analysis, to be their due as a numerical majority."[40] One reason he fought so vociferously against Turgot's idea of a unicameral legislature was that he believed such systems had proven very ineffective, falling prey either to aristocratic manipulation or majority tyranny.[41] Under such a simplistic system, one class or another would certainly be oppressed.

Adams's letter to Benjamin Rush on April 18, 1808, demonstrates the balance in his approach:

> An aristocracy of wealth, without any check but a democracy of licentious-
> ness, is our curse. I wish that aristocracy was in a hole, guarded by
> Hercules with his club on one side and an honest people with their million

hands on the other. The eternal intrigues of our monied and landed and *slaved* aristocracy are and will be our ruin. I will be neither aristocrat nor democrat without a mediator between the two. With such a mediator I will be both.[42]

A strong executive was Adams's suggestion for that necessary mediator. And that was basically the role Adams played when he was President: an impartial intermediary, not involved in factious party politics.[43] Adams acted on his perception of the common good, but he was perceived by many to be undemocratic because he assumed, based on his reading of history, that America had economic classes as did all other countries; but his view was in conflict with the prevailing ideology of classless equality.

His family biographers wrote: "The true aim of government, in his idea, was to establish, upon the firmest footing, the rights of all who live under it, giving to no one interest power enough to become aggressive upon the rest, and yet not denying to each a share sufficient for its own protection."[44] Adams understood what is still a fundamental dilemma of pluralist democracy: allowing interests enough power for self-protection while limiting the power of those interests to infringe on the rights of others. The problem becomes even more difficult when many citizens own little or no property.

Jefferson and Others

While Adams's fears of aristocracy were controversial, many founders agreed with him on the necessity of widespread property ownership. Thomas Jefferson is famous for his paeans of praise for the independent proprietor, working his own land, sending his surplus production to market.[45] For example he wrote in his *Notes on Virginia*: "'Those who labour in the earth are the chosen people of God. . . . Corruption of morals in the mass of cultivators is a phaenomenon of which no age nor nation has furnished an example.'"[46] Jefferson's ideas were widely shared throughout Virginia; Wood explains the political significance of such thinking; property would make men "equally free and independent," according to the Virginia declaration of rights. But, in that era, property had a traditional meaning. It was thought of as "a source of personal authority or independence." Rather than being simply something men possessed, it was "an attribute of a man's personality that defined him and protected him from outside pressure." Jefferson feared the urban rabble because they lacked such property and were therefore dependent. His fear that propertyless men would be easily manipulated by the ambitious, led him to propose that Virginia grant fifty acres of land to any man who did not already own that many acres.[47]

Jefferson did realize that complete equality of property was impossible. Nonetheless, he believed in strong government action to assure relative equality.

In a letter from France on October 28, 1785, he wrote James Madison advocating legislative creativity to limit concentrated property ownership and thus to move toward equality: "legislators cannot invent too many devices for subdividing property." An example of the creativity he suggested included equal inheritance for all children. Contemporary readers might miss the significance of his suggestion that all the children should share equally in an inheritance. Jefferson was living in a time when the feudal practice of primogeniture was still the rule, so he was suggesting a radical change. He continued:

> Another means of silently lessening the inequality of property is to exempt all from taxation below a certain point, and to tax the higher portions of property in geometrical progression as they rise. Whenever there is in any country, uncultivated lands and unemployed poor, it is clear that the laws of property have been so far extended as to violate natural right. The earth is given as a common stock for man to labour and live on. If, for the encouragement of industry we allow it to be appropriated, we must take care that other employment be furnished to those excluded from the appropriation. If we do not the fundamental right to labour the earth returns to the unemployed. It is too soon yet in our country to say that every man who cannot find employment but who can find uncultivated land, shall be at liberty to cultivate it, paying a moderate rent. But it is not too soon to provide by every possible means that as few as possible shall be without a little portion of land. The small landholders are the most precious part of a state.[48]

Note his suggestion of progressive taxation and note that he believed that natural justice required that everyone have employment. If that is true, and if free market mechanisms do not provide employment for everyone, should the government be the employer of last resort?

The progressive taxation which he advocated was implemented only in the twentieth century through an income tax. However, myriad loopholes and recent tax reform have eliminated any real progressiveness in that tax. All of this goes against Adam Smith's first of four maxims on taxes: "The subjects of every state ought to contribute toward the support of the government, as nearly as possible, in proportion to their respective abilities; that is, in proportion to the revenue which they respectively enjoy under the protection of the state."[49] He also wrote: "It is not very unreasonable that the rich should contribute to the publick expence, not only in proportion to their revenue, but something more than in that proportion."[50] Adams also agreed on this. He wrote his wife in 1780: "As to Taxes, the more they tax me, provided they tax others in Proportion, the happier I am. It is our best Policy and I fear our only Resource."[51] A few months later, in a letter to a Dutch supporter of America, he approvingly reported that taxes were "heaviest upon the rich and the higher Classes of People."[52]

When he became president in 1801, Jefferson appointed Albert Gallatin as his Secretary of the Treasury. Gallatin was a strong advocate of the ideas in Adam Smith's *Wealth of Nations*. And the most important goal of Secretary of the Treasury Gallatin was equal access for all citizens to property ownership. He believed that property ownership open to all would have significant political benefits, promoting political cohesion and stability; indeed, it was essential to the maintenance of a democratic republic.[53]

Note that the views of Jefferson and other founders on wide dispersal of property ownership assumed agrarian virtue, a tenet from the ancient republican tradition, going back to Aristotle, of the yeoman farmer as the guardian of liberty. Such views were shared by many thinkers after the Greeks: "Throughout the eighteenth century, leading republicans had cited Machiavelli, Montesquieu, and the English libertarians like Harrington and Sidney to the effect that independent landowners were the foundation on which all true republics would stand."[54]

Adam Smith also provides support for this argument, but in a slightly different context. He argued that independence in the common people was an effective way to reduce crime. Dependency increased crime:

> In Glasgow, where almost no body has more than one servant, there are fewer capital crimes than in Edinburgh. In Glasgow there is not one in several years, but not a year passes in Edinburgh without some such disorders. Upon this principle, therefore, it is not so much the police that prevents the commission of crimes as the having as few persons as possible to live upon others. Nothing tends so much to corrupt mankind as dependencey, while independencey still encreases the honesty of the people.[55]

Smith continued by arguing that no one would be mad enough to lead a life of crime if he could make better wages honestly. While his argument assumed employment at good wages in commerce and manufactures, in contrast to the agrarian emphasis of Jefferson, he and Jefferson both agreed on the principle that dependency is abhorrent because of the problems it causes.

The founders had also had their own experiences with monarchy to warn them of the problems of dependency. They did not want any patrons controlling enormous blocs of votes. In order to avoid such dependency, they did not advocate the extreme of absolute equality, even though some radicals suggested laws to limit concentration of property ownership.[56]

Pangle points out that such ideas were not a monopoly of the Jeffersonians; Federalist thinkers also wanted to avoid concentration of capital: "Inheritance and taxation laws are to insure that the accumulation of property will proceed in tandem with its being rendered mobile or widely diffused and available to as many as possible, within the limits of respect for individual effort and rights."[57] Federalists shared with Anti-Federalists the founders' fears of the corrupting influence of commerce on the yeoman's virtues. Both Federalists and Anti-Federalists worried that commerce was a threat to the independent farmer's agrarian life.[58] At least one Anti-Federalist also agreed with Federalists that rough equality of property was needed for free government to exist.[59]

Noah Webster, an important intellectual force in the early republic, argued in his 1787 Federalist essay, *An Examination into the Leading Principles of the Federal Constitution*, that equality of property ownership was essential, "the very soul of a republic." He stated that *"property* is the basis of *power"* and that national freedom and civic virtue depended on a *"general and tolerably equal distribution of landed property."*[60] Agricultural states with relatively equal land distribution were the most free and stable, because they lacked an oppressive aristocracy to oppress and the people, lacking grievances, were not rebellious.[61] Webster's wise observation that widespread ownership of property reduces grievances is, too often, forgotten.[62]

The founders' concern about concentrated wealth was shared by Adam Smith, who discussed the economic benefits of avoidance of concentrated economic power. The market functions best, is fairest, when competition is among relatively equal parties. Werhane states that Smith repeatedly praised competition in markets composed of approximately equal actors; such markets were efficient, fair, and advantageous to producers, workers, and customers.[63] Moreover, Smith thought such competition would produce a "useful inequality in . . . fortunes . . . which naturally and necessarily arises from the various degrees of capacity, industry, and diligence in the different individuals." But inequality in wealth did not mean concentration; great wealth would be advantageous to the nation only when there was "a gradual descent of fortunes betwixt these great ones and others of the least and lowest fortune. For it will be shewn hereafter that one who leaps over the heads of all his country men is of real detriment to the community."[64]

These examples of views on property ownership in relation to democracy are intended to show that dispersing property ownership widely (avoiding concentrated property ownership) was generally seen as important to the success of the new country's democratic experiment. But this view was not universally shared. Alexander Hamilton, as Secretary of the Treasury for President Washington, believed concentrated political-economic power was inevitable, and actively promoted such inequality; further, his policies "weakened honest and accountable government" by "fostering the power of a small and unrepresentative elite."[65]

Rough equality was not enshrined as a principle within the text of the Constitution. Sadly, the only aspect of property in the new Constitution was the infamous three-fifths compromise, whereby slave states were allowed to count every five slaves as three persons for purposes of apportioning seats in the House of Representatives. Of course, no slave was given the right to vote. Anti-Federalists were very critical of this part of the Constitution. Brutus, writing to the citizens of New York, caustically analyzed the compromise:

> But it has never been alledged that those who are not free agents, can, upon any rational principle, have any thing to do in government, either by themselves or others. If they have no share in government, why is the number of members in the assembly, to be increased on their account? Is it because in some of the states, a considerable part of the property of the inhabitants consists in a number of their fellow men, who are held in bondage, in defiance of every idea of benevolence, justice, and religion, and contrary to all the principles of liberty, which have been publickly avowed in the late glorious revolution? If this be a just ground for representation, the horses in some of the states, and the oxen in others, ought to be represented—for a great share of property in some of them, consists in these animals; and they have as much controul over their own actions, as these poor unhappy creatures, who are intended to be described in the above recited clause, by the words, "all other persons."[66]

Melancton Smith also criticized this aspect of the Constitution at the New York ratifying convention.[67]

While the belief in widely dispersed property ownership was not enshrined in the Constitution, neither was it prohibited. Even though some founders disagreed with this idea, it was shared by so many that the principle still merits our consideration. Finally, because property is not a right we are born with (it is a right which is determined by society),[68] the American people could consider political-economic modifications to disperse property more widely.

Nineteenth Century

The relationship of property and democracy was also an issue for political thinkers after the founding generation. There is a certain delicious irony in changes which developed in Jeffersonian-Republican views. Eight years after Adams and Jefferson died, William Leggett, editor of the leading New York City Jeffersonian newspaper, the *Evening Post,* was scathingly critical of the "cupidity of the rich," injuring the poor, and of the "power of monopoly" and corporate privilege. He felt that the people were menaced again by avarice and ambition. And he warned that the tyrant now came in the form of "a mighty civil gentleman . . . mincing and bowing to the people," but the tyrant represented a "CONCENTRATED MONEY POWER," and was "a usurper in the disguise of a benefactor, an agent exercising privileges which his principal never possessed."[69] The Jeffersonians finally realized that Adams's analysis of aristocracy was real. America had not escaped human nature.[70]

Political analysts in the nineteenth century continued to fear that economic concentration was destroying democracy. In the 1830s, Alexis de Tocqueville observed two factors which undermined democratic structures: slavery, which degraded whites as well as blacks, and the industrial system. Bellah notes that the Civil War destroyed slavery but "enormously furthered the growth of the industrial structures"; he also writes of Tocqueville's concern about the relationship between the owners of increasingly concentrated industries and the dependent workers, often women and immigrants: "Tocqueville feared the rise of a new form of aristocracy that would make owners and managers into petty despots and reduce workers to mechanically organized, dependent operatives, a condition incompatible with full democratic citizenship."[71] The founders believed that no dependent person was capable of fulfilling the responsibilities of citizenship. Tocqueville believed that the industrial system was reducing independent artisans into such dependent people and thus was weakening democracy.

However, by the middle of the twentieth century, the political effects of this loss of independence for many artisans was somewhat mitigated by the growth of unions. Note that unionization thrived only after a long, grueling struggle and only after the federal government reversed positions (the National Labor Relations Act supported unionization efforts, in contrast to the previous government policy of using federal soldiers to thwart unions). By the time that unionization was protected by law, the concentrated wealth gained by industrialists profiting from cheap, unprotected labor, had distorted American democracy because unions, although at times politically powerful, have not generally been able to counter the political power of money. Long-term decline in union membership in the late twentieth century further exacerbates the problem, and thus, concentrated wealth continues to distort American democracy. One result of this distortion is that many Americans are cynical of politics, believing that it has been corrupted by interest group power.

That contemporary perspective sounds remarkably similar to a view shared by Henry Adams and his brother Charles Francis Adams, Jr. In the 1860s and 1870s, they wrote several studies exposing the corruption of American politics by capitalism; Diggins reports that Henry Adams was disturbed by the thought "that the American constitutional system was powerless to prevent the purchase of influence and power by money," and that "in the face of corporate wealth," the Constitution seemed useless.[72] Bellah states that, in the age of the robber barons, the unconstrained pursuit of wealth, while ignoring social justice, "was destroying the fabric of a democratic society."[73] Reforming authors like Henry George, Jacob Riis, Josiah Strong, and Henry Demarest Lloyd, writing in the late nineteenth century, "agreed that industrial America had strayed dangerously from both republican principles and Christian ethics. Unless social justice was speedily granted, they warned their readers, the oppressed might seek redress of their own through violent revolution."[74]

Twentieth Century

By the twentieth century, industrialization and urbanization had destroyed the yeoman base of American democracy. Americans had historically distrusted the evils of Europe, which they connected to the corrupting effects of European cities. The American antidote had been the "autonomy and equality of the virtuous yeoman farmer."[75] But the United States also became a nation of teeming cities and very few farmers. Farming became a capital intensive industry, often within a corporate agribusiness structure.

Merriam, at the beginning of the twentieth century, wrote that concentrated wealth was destroying the economic basis of democracy; the masses were losing power. "The forms of power . . . cannot long remain in conflict with the actual forces and facts, and as the organization of industry has become undemocratic, the organization of government must soon follow in the same direction."[76] Beard also saw the dominance of economic power and thought that "the long-feared threat of 'commerce' had in fact extinguished the precious ideal of 'virtue.'"[77] Merriam and Beard were not alone.[78]

Replacement of the small, family-operated farm by the business corporation as the most important organization in the American economy has had dramatic effects on our democracy, as Dahl explains: "Through a highly successful case of ideological transfer, the Lockean defense of private property, which in the agrarian order made good sense morally and politically, was shifted over intact to corporate enterprise." He sees this type of political-economic management affecting democracy in two ways: "First, the new order generated much greater differences than the old in political resources, skills, and incentives within the demos itself." And second, the hierarchical nature of corporations means that most people spend most of their lives working in a despotic system, instead of a democracy.[79] This quotation is not intended to condemn all corporations. Such thinking would be too dialectical. Also, I certainly do not advocate returning to pre-corporate America.[80] What I do argue is that we must analyze the impact on democracy of changes in the economic system. And Dahl's quotation leads to three questions. Does the constitutional system established for an agrarian country allow democracy when the economy has changed so dramatically? Can we be democratic when there is great inequality in political resources? And how is democracy affected when most of us spend so much of our lives within authoritarian workplaces?

Changes in the economic system have also undermined one of the founders central virtues: the public good, or public spirit. Bellah fears that we have lost a concept important to our history, that the role of the citizen has been destroyed by economic man. "The tension between private interest and the public good is never completely resolved in any society. But in a free republic, it is the task of the citizen, whether ruler or ruled, to cultivate civic virtue in order to mitigate the tension and render it manageable."[81] Our individualism is often expressed in the economic realm, which is fine in and of itself, except that economic individualism, for many people, completely replaces citizenship. When that happens, the very concept of democracy is vitiated.

Before we turn to solutions, allow me one final quotation to support my argument that the system is broken. The following is a list of "benchmarks" of areas where further progress is needed if America is to prosper in the increasingly interdependent world economy:

> What is the condition of the poor and the disabled? What is being done for the elderly and for children? What about foreign laborers, migrants, and illegal immigrants? Is the level of employment what it ought to be? Interest rates, foreign debt, and trade policy? What about Third World debts, the openness of markets to Third World goods, and competition from foreign goods? Then there are the "externalities": do damages to the environment outweigh environmental improvements (such as irrigation, erosion control, forest management, the development of new sources of clean water, and the like)? These represent only a small fraction of the claims of perfection upon today's worldly economies. All such claims represent legitimate benchmarks. Altogether, they can be pressed as utopian claims demanding paradise on earth. One by one, though, each such benchmark has its own validity. Critical intelligence properly ferrets out the shortcomings of the present.[82]

Novak, as a conservative defender of free markets but as one who also assumes that markets function within a set of moral standards, sees these items as goals for perfecting the system. I see them somewhat differently as a fundamental indictment of system failure. However, I agree with Novak that it would be dangerous to infer from such a list a need for utopian solutions; these problems will not be solved overnight, but we can make more rapid progress in resolving them than we have in recent decades.

In short, economic inequality not only results in political inequality, but could lead to a revolutionary end of our democratic republic. Wise conservatives have usually known this. Economic inequality is undemocratic for two reasons: (1) it deprives large numbers of citizens (the poor and the middle classes) of equal political power, and (2) if inequality is too extreme, it can lead to revolutionary attempts to replace a democratic system with a "perfect" system. The tragedy of such utopian attempts to establish just societies is that they so often produce dictatorships, such as the Stalinism that resulted from the Bolshevik Revolution.

The corruption that the Adams brothers observed in the 1860s and 1870s may be less blatant today but it is nonetheless destroying our democracy. Even when anti-corruption laws are not broken, the power of interest groups, or the power of one individual to become a Presidential candidate solely by virtue of a pledge to spend $100 million of his own personal wealth, destroys democracy. Corruption as legally defined has not disappeared from our system and is obviously a danger for democracy. But a graver danger for American democracy comes from the powerful, subtle, legal use of money to buy influence.

It is precisely this vitiation of political equality which destroys Francis Fukuyama's argument in his *End of History*. It is certainly true that the failed communist systems merit much criticism; however, that does not mean that liberal democracy is the goal of history.[83] Marx and his followers erred in basing political economy on what man should be, not on what man is. Had they appreciated Adams and Smith, they would not have made such a tragic mistake. But Fukuyama also errs. While he rightly criticizes failings of communism, he idealizes liberal democracy, instead of analyzing what really exists in the United States. His *End of History* is counterrational in its speculation; he cannot know that liberal democracy is the goal of history. Both Adams and Smith were against such "philosophizing," emphasizing instead reality-based reasoning. Given that individuals and groups continually struggle for power, how can we be sure there will not be some better approach to protecting the rights of all? Fukuyama does not resolve the contradiction in liberal democracy; economic inequality, the result of the liberal part of the term, undermines the democratic part of the term. Liberal democracy has existed for about two centuries. Who can deny the possibility that liberal democracy could be replaced by a society which is economically just (as Smith advocated) and democratically balanced (which John Adams advocated) within another two hundred years?

In his June 3, 1776, letter to Patrick Henry (quoted in chapter 2) John Adams trumpeted that "a more equal liberty" than ever before "must be established in America." Implementing that proud announcement must be placed at the top of the American agenda. Liberty should no longer trump equality. We must, as a nation, rejoin the perennial struggle to achieve a *yin-yang* reconciliation of these seemingly contradictory values of equality and liberty so that twenty-first century America may be known as the nation of equal democratic liberty!

Conclusion

Ultimately, the solution is within us. But therein lies a problem, one which Henry David Thoreau examined. He saw Americans as conformist materialists. Thoreau believed in individuality and self-reliance, but he was also critical of an American illusion: "the illusion of political freedom and the reality of moral slavery to economic passions and interests."[84] One can never be a free individual, even in a supposedly democratic state, when one is subject to materialist conformity pressures. Remember that Tocqueville, in his classic *Democracy in America*, emphasized the conformity pressures he observed in Jacksonian America, pressures which still exist to this day. Such pressures come very close to what a contemporary conservative warns are deadly foes of liberty: "relativism, decadence, hedonism, and nihilism."[85] However, I assume Novak would not agree with my contention that all four of these deadly foes are caused by extremist capitalism. It is time to return to our values, to have a moral, but not moralistic nation. This is not a new idea; writing at the height of the Cold War, Walter Lippmann argued that our strength in the struggle with communism was not in "cloak and dagger business" but in "being true to ourselves" and taking "our own principles seriously."[86]

Two nineteenth-century thinkers also suggest a reordering of our priorities; for Abraham Lincoln and Herman Melville, politics should not be "merely the crass 'pursuit of happiness.' Instead, it must offer the possibility of moral striving, of educating the soul and opening up the heart to 'pity.'"[87] The balance inherent in this view is consistent with the founders' preference for balancing public spirit and the pursuit of happiness.

So economic concentration makes economies less efficient and weakens democracy. Can the economically and politically debilitating effects of concentrated wealth be reversed? What can we do to achieve wider and more equal distribution of property, which our founders advocated? What should our priorities be? Let us now examine some solutions.

Notes

1.   Richard Hofstadter, "The Founding Fathers: An Age of Realism," in *The Moral Foundations of the American Republic*, 3d ed., Robert H. Horwitz, ed. (Charlottesville: University of Virginia Press, 1986), 73.

2.   G. Warren Nutter, "Freedom in a Revolutionary Economy," in *The American Revolution: Three Views*, Irving Kristol, et al. (New York: American Brands, Inc., 1975), 117.

3.   Charles E. Lindblom, "Market and Democracy—Obliquely," *PS: Political Science & Politics* (December 1995): 686. Similarly, Richard Ashcraft, "Class

Conflict and Constitutionalism in J. S. Mill's Thought," in *Liberalism and the Moral Life,* Nancy L. Rosenblum, ed. (Cambridge: Harvard University Press, 1989), 125-26, criticizes modern liberals for demonstrating "little interest in exposing and criticizing the fundamental defects and injustices" of political economic institutions.

4. Amitai Etzioni, *The Moral Dimension, Toward a New Economics* (New York: Free Press, 1988), 182-83.

5. Benjamin R. Barber, *Strong Democracy: Participatory Politics for a New Age* (Berkeley: University of California Press, 1984), 253 and 255.

6. Barry A. Shain, *The Myth of American Individualism: The Protestant Origins of American Political Thought* (Princeton: Princeton University Press, 1994), 182-83; John R. Nelson, Jr., *Liberty and Property: Political Economy and Policymaking in the New Nation, 1789-1812* (Baltimore: Johns Hopkins University Press, 1987), 9; Paul K. Longmore, *The Invention of George Washington* (Berkeley: University of California Press, 1988), 4-5; Lorraine Smith Pangle and Thomas L. Pangle, *The Learning of Liberty: The Educational Ideas of the American Founders* (Lawrence: University Press of Kansas, 1993), 118. This belief was generally accepted throughout the eighteenth century. Shain, *Myth of American Individualism,* 301, points out the religious dimension of the aversion to dependency.

7. Gordon S. Wood, *The Radicalism of the American Revolution* (New York: Alfred A. Knopf, 1992), 178-79.

8. John Adams, letter to James Sullivan, May 26, 1776, in Robert J. Taylor, ed., *Papers of John Adams,* 4 (Cambridge: Belknap Press of Harvard University Press, 1979), 210.

9. John Adams, Fragmentary notes for "A Dissertation on the Canon and the Feudal Law" [May-August, 1765], in Robert J. Taylor, ed., *Papers,* 1, 106.

10. John Adams, letter to James Sullivan, May 26, 1776, in Taylor, ed., *Papers,* 4, 210.

11. C. Bradley Thompson, *John Adams and the Spirit of Liberty* (Lawrence: University Press of Kansas, 1998), 247.

12. John Adams, "An Essay on Man's Lust for Power" [post August 29, 1763], in Taylor, ed., *Papers,* 1, 83.

13. John Adams [*Boston Gazette* letters], in Taylor, ed., *Papers,* 1, 167-69.

14. Paul K. Conkin, *Puritans and Pragmatists: Eight Eminent American Thinkers* (New York: Dodd, Mead and Company, 1968), 146.

15. Tunis Wortman, "A Solemn Address to Christians and Patriots," in *Political Sermons of the American Founding Era, 1730-1805,* Ellis Sandoz, ed. (Indianapolis: Liberty Press, 1991), 1519.

16. Clinton Rossiter, "The Legacy of John Adams," *Yale Review* 46 (1957): 537; Heinz Lubasz, "Adam Smith and the 'Free Market,'" in *Adam Smith's Wealth of Nations: New Interdisciplinary Essays,* Stephen Copley and Kathryn Sutherland, eds. (Manchester: Manchester University Press, 1995), 57.

17. Thompson, *Adams and the Spirit of Liberty,* 312.

18. Writing about the French Revolution in 1794, Noah Webster, "The Revolution in France," in *Political Sermons,* Sandoz, ed., 1279-80, argued that America would be saved from civil strife or dictatorship either by a majority discouraging factions or by laws destroying factions and securing equal rights and equal influence for each individual. He and Adams agreed on equality of rights for individuals.

19. Michael Merrill and Sean Wilentz, eds., *The Key of Liberty: The Life and Democratic Writings of William Manning, "A Laborer," 1747-1814* (Cambridge: Harvard University Press, 1993), 138.

20. George Mason, "Objections to the Constitution of Government Formed by the Convention," in *The American Intellectual Tradition, A Sourcebook,* 2d ed., 1, David A. Hollinger and Charles Capper, eds. (New York: Oxford University Press, 1993), 136.

21. Colleen A. Sheehan and Gary L. McDowell, eds., *Friends of the Constitution; Writings of the "Other" Federalists, 1787-1788* (Indianapolis: Liberty Fund, 1998), 226-27; see also the positively Adamsian arguments of Atticus in *Friends of the Constitution,* 336-41; Richard Vetterli and Gary Bryner, *In Search of the Republic: Public Virtue and the Roots of American Government,* rev. ed. (Lanham, Md.: Rowman and Littlefield Publishers, Inc., 1996), 175, argue that all educated statesmen, including Hamilton, Madison, and Jefferson in addition to Adams, knew that class struggle "had eventually destroyed every republican state in history."

22. Noah Webster, "Revolution in France," in *Political Sermons,* Sandoz, ed., 1288-89.

23. Daniel J. Boorstin, ed., *An American Primer* (New York: Penguin Books, 1966), 28. Ruth Bloch, *Visionary Republic: Millennial Themes in American Thought, 1756-1800* (Cambridge: Cambridge University Press,1985), 98, indicates that various religious figures in the 1780s supported economic equality, such as the English minister Richard Price, "widely read in America," who wrote of the need to preserve a hardy yeomanry and to avoid economic disparities. See also 179-81 for her description of religious criticism of indigenous elitism in the 1790s.

24. Joseph J. Ellis, *Passionate Sage: The Character and Legacy of John Adams* (New York: W. W. Norton and Company, 1993), 73.

25. Pangle and Pangle, *Learning of Liberty,* 111.

26. Joyce Appleby, *Liberalism and Republicanism in the Historical Imagination* (Cambridge: Harvard University Press, 1992), 269.

27. John Ferling, *John Adams: A Life* (Knoxville: University of Tennessee Press, 1992), 290.

28. Ferling, *John Adams,* 373.

29. George A. Peek, Jr., ed., *The Political Writings of John Adams: Representative Selections* (Indianapolis: Bobbs-Merrill Co., Inc., 1954), 136-37 and 139-40.

30. Thompson, *Adams and the Spirit of Liberty,* 172.

31. John A. Schutz and Douglass Adair, eds., *The Spur of Fame: Dialogues of John Adams and Benjamin Rush, 1805-1813* (San Marino, Cal.: Huntington Library, 1966), 33.

32. Thompson, *Adams and the Spirit of Liberty*, 252-53, 256-57, and 264.

33. Thompson, *Adams and the Spirit of Liberty*, 260.

34. Ellis, *Passionate Sage*, 160-61.

35. Joyce Appleby, *Capitalism and a New Social Order: The Republican Vision of the 1790s* (New York: New York University Press, 1984), 75, states that Adams's analysis was so upsetting to Jeffersonian-Republicans because he insisted that inequality was part of human nature. In other words, Adams was attacking the American principle of equality. He still believed in equality, but did not believe in the absolute version held by some Americans, nor did he believe that America had escaped the laws of human nature.

36. Thompson, *Adams and the Spirit of Liberty*, 106 and 259, argues that *Defence* was "a new and positive contribution to a transatlantic debate over the science of politics in revolutionary societies" and was similar to Aristotle's *Politics* and Montesquieu's *Spirit of the Laws* in that it was designed to teach the fundamental principles of political architecture.

37. Thompson, *Adams and the Spirit of Liberty*, 128-29.

38. Ellis, *Passionate Sage*, 131.

39. Peek, ed., *Political Writings of Adams*, 156.

40. Conkin, *Puritans and Pragmatists*, 142-43 and passim; for more information on the "aristocracy" issue, one can do no better than the relatively available series of papers of John Adams. In addition, several scholars have excellent analyses of the issue: Thompson, *Adams and the Spirit of Liberty*, 91-106, 166-85, 202-65, and passim; Ellis, *Passionate Sage*, passim; and Rossiter, "Legacy of John Adams," 537-48.

41. Thompson, *Adams and the Spirit of Liberty*, 185.

42. Schutz and Adair, eds., *Spur of Fame*, 108.

43. See Bernard Bailyn, *The Origins of American Politics* (New York: Alfred A. Knopf, 1970), 20-23, for the English model of a mixed government, theoretically protecting the rights of the one, the few, and the many. From 1770-1772, John Witherspoon taught James Madison (and other pupils at the College of New Jersey) the mixed and balanced British form of government; see Ellis Sandoz, *A Government of Laws: Political Theory, Religion, and the American Founding* (Baton Rouge: Louisiana State University Press, 1990), 184-85. Adam Smith believed that Great Britain, in his era, had a mixed and balanced government; Athol Fitzgibbons, *Adam Smith's System of Liberty, Wealth and Virtue* (Oxford: Clarendon Press, 1995), 117-20.

44. John Quincy Adams and Charles Francis Adams, *John Adams*, 1 (New York: Chelsea House, 1980), 405-06.

45. Note that I do not refer, at this point, to the yeoman farmer. According to Appleby, *Liberalism and Republicanism*, 258-59, that word was rarely used in revolutionary America and never, to her knowledge, by Jefferson.

46. Quoted in Michael Lienesch, *New Order of the Ages: Time, the Constitution, and the Making of Modern American Political Thought* (Princeton: Princeton University Press, 1988), 87.

47. Wood, *Radicalism of the American Revolution*, 178-79.

48. Merrill D. Peterson, ed., *The Portable Thomas Jefferson* (New York: Penguin Books, 1975), 396-97.

49. Adam Smith, *An Inquiry into the Nature and Causes of the Wealth of Nations*, R. H. Campbell and A. S. Skinner, eds. (Oxford: Oxford University Press, 1976), V.ii.b.3, 825.

50. Smith, *Wealth of Nations*, V.ii.e.6, 842. Stephen Holmes, *Passions and Constraint: On the Theory of Liberal Democracy* (Chicago: University of Chicago Press, 1995), 252, argues that Smith justified progressive taxation based on a "belief that the rich got rich with the implicit or explicit *cooperation* of the poor" (italics in original).

51. John Adams, letter to Abigail Adams, May 12, 1780, in L. H. Butterfield and Marc Friedlaender, eds., *Adams Family Correspondence*, 3 (Cambridge: Belknap Press of Harvard University Press, 1973), 339.

52. John Adams, letter to Hendrik Calkoen, October 26, 1780, in Gregg L. Lint, et al., eds. *Papers of John Adams*, 10 (Cambridge: Belknap Press of Harvard University Press, 1996), 243.

53. Nelson, *Liberty and Property*, 122, 139, and 206.

54. Lienesch, *New Order of the Ages*, 87.

55. Adam Smith, *Lectures on Jurisprudence*, R. L. Meek, D. D. Raphael, and P. G. Stein, eds. (Oxford: Oxford University Press, 1978), [B] 204, 486-87.

56. Wood, *Radicalism of the American Revolution*, 234. Howard Zinn, *A People's History of the United States* (New York: Harper and Row, 1980), 62, discusses a statement from a Pennsylvania group which inveighed against the dangers of "'an enormous proportion of property vested in a few individuals'" as "'destructive of the common happiness.'"

57. Thomas L. Pangle, *The Spirit of Modern Republicanism: The Moral Vision of the American Founders and the Philosophy of Locke* (Chicago: University of Chicago Press, 1988), 97.

58. Pangle, *Spirit of Modern Republicanism*, 34.

59. Centinel, in Herbert J. Storing, ed., *The Anti-Federalist: An Abridgment, by Murray Dry, of the Complete Anti-Federalist* (Chicago: University of Chicago Press, 1985), 16.

60. Sheehan and McDowell, eds., *Friends of the Constitution*, 400-01 (emphasis in original).

61. Lienesch, *New Order of the Ages*, 93.

62. Pangle and Pangle, *Learning of Liberty,* 131-32, point out that Webster also saw education as an additional support for freedom. This is clear in the Sheehan and McDowell collection, *Friends of the Constitution,* 402, which reprints Webster's pamphlet.

63. Patricia H. Werhane, *Adam Smith and His Legacy for Modern Capitalism* (New York: Oxford University Press, 1991), 105-06.

64. Smith, *Lectures on Jurisprudence* [A], vi.19, 338 and iii.139, 196.

65. Bruce Miroff, *Icons of Democracy: American Leaders as Heroes, Aristocrats, Dissenters, and Democrats* (New York: Basic Books, 1993), 48 and 42.

66. Brutus, in Storing, ed., *Anti-Federalist:* 123-24.

67. Melancton Smith, in Storing, ed., *Anti-Federalist,* 336.

68. This point is documented in the next chapter.

69. William Leggett, "Selection from *Political Writings,*" from the *Evening Post,* December 6, 1834, in *American Intellectual Tradition,* 1, Hollinger and Capper, eds., 232-33, emphasis in the original.

70. See Lawrence Frederick Kohl, *The Politics of Individualism: Parties and the American Character in the Jacksonian Era* (New York: Oxford University Press, 1989), 25, for discussion of Jacksonian fears of an emergent aristocracy with a resulting tendency to increase dependency. Ronald Takaki, *Iron Cages: Race and Culture in 19th-Century America* (New York: Oxford University Press, 1990), 70-71, reports a study indicating that, in the Jacksonian era, the wealthiest one percent of Americans increased their ownership of the nation's wealth from roughly one-quarter to one-half, but most people still believed America was an egalitarian society.

71. Robert N. Bellah, et al., *Habits of the Heart: Individualism and Commitment in American Life* (New York: Harper and Row, 1985), 41-42.

72. John P. Diggins, *The Lost Soul of American Politics: Virtue, Self-Interest, and the Foundations of Liberalism* (Chicago: University of Chicago Press, 1984), 257.

73. Bellah, *Habits of the Heart,* 43.

74. John F. Kasson, *Civilizing the Machine: Technology and Republican Values in America, 1776-1900* (New York: Penguin Books, 1976), 186-87; Takaki, *Iron Cages,* 260, quotes Strong's 1885 criticism of capitalists and monopolists as representatives of a modern feudalism which threatened republican society and liberty.

75. Lienesch, *New Order of the Ages,* 89.

76. Charles Edward Merriam, *A History of American Political Theories* (New York: Augustus M. Kelley, 1969), 343.

77. Diggins, *Lost Soul of American Politics,* 129.

78. Herbert Croly, a Progressive era political thinker, advocated a "national democracy" which would include a social balance, "the amelioration of social conflict through national governmental policy." Political leaders would have to be responsible to the electorate as a whole, not just to economic elites; see Herbert

Croly, *The Promise of American Life* (New Brunswick, N.J.: Transaction Publishers, 1993), xxiii and xxx.

79. Robert A. Dahl, "On Removing Certain Impediments to Democracy in the United States," in *Moral Foundations,* Horwitz, ed., 237-39.

80. Gordon Wood's comments about gentility and labor indicate what we have escaped. Working to make a living had been considered, in England, as servile and low status (Wood, *Radicalism of the American Revolution,* 37-38). American capitalism has been much more dynamic than it would have been if our culture had continued the colonial practice of valuing gentility and demeaning honest labor.

81. Bellah, *Habits of the Heart,* 270-71.

82. Michael Novak, *Free Persons and the Common Good* (New York: Madison Books, 1989), 139-40.

83. Francis Fukuyama, *The End of History and the Last Man* (New York: Avon Books, 1992). The destruction of political equality inherent in economic inequality is shortsighted, to say the least. Holmes, *Passions and Constraint,* 93-94, points out Hobbes's appreciation of "the self-defeating character of unconstrained authority." Further, "authority is excessive when it is self-defeating, when it undermines itself by alienating potential cooperators." This is not a perfect analogy to the United States because power is not unconstrained, yet. But the political emasculation of a large portion of the population indicates that power is moving in the direction of such excess. Many "potential cooperators" are alienated.

84. Diggins, *Lost Soul of American Politics,* 20 and 217.

85. Novak, *Free Persons,* 119.

86. Clinton Rossiter and James Lare, eds., *The Essential Lippmann: A Political Philosophy for Liberal Democracy* (Cambridge: Harvard University Press, 1982), 81.

87. Diggins, *Lost Soul of American Politics,* 332.

Chapter Eight

Democracy: Political Equality and Justice for All

In the spirit of John Adams and Adam Smith, this has been a didactic work, but it cannot be a prescriptive work. Boorstin warns of the danger of hearing "not what dead men wanted to say, but what the living want to hear."[1] But the problem is greater than that; the societal context is so different today that it would be extremely unwise to bring policy prescriptions from the eighteenth into the twenty-first century. Several scholars have warned of the dangers of transporting Smith's suggestions into the twentieth century. Skinner, for example, states that this would be "quite inconsistent with Smith's own teaching."[2] We simply cannot know what Adams or Smith would prescribe were either alive today. Thus, I present herein suggestions to improve liberal democracy with the intention of faithfulness to the principles of Adams and Smith but I do not argue that Adams and/or Smith would have advocated any of these specific ideas. The solutions, therefore, must be judged in terms of their efficacy in delivering political equality and justice for all.

Adams and Smith died long ago, but their analyses of human social interaction are still pertinent today, especially their shared advocacy of justice; and delivering justice for all leads us to several other values and virtues. Even though values change over time, several of the founders' values assumptions and civic virtues would help us develop a more just society. Their basic values, "Nature's God," the pursuit of happiness, equality, and liberty, have not yet been perfected; the same is true for moderation, tolerance, and disinterested public concern for the common good. These eighteenth-century values and virtues are still needed in the new millennium; renewed attention to them would result in a more perfect union, a more just society.

These values and virtues imply, for me, the universalism which was also a prime virtue of the founders. Moreover, we must now be truly universal; the racial, gender, and other exclusions of eighteenth-century society have no justification in a new millennium. Equal political power will give all the people the opportunity to pursue happiness, which should result in widely dispersed economic well-being. In short, consistent with the three major strands of the thinking of the revolutionary generation, including the religious strand, our goal should be to have a free people, all the people, known for civic virtue. Skeptics might be concerned about the implications of the religious strand for tolerance and moderation, so let us begin there.

Tolerance

We must remember the founders' wisdom on the importance of religion for virtue education, as a support for the stability of the state. This is not to be taken in a Hamiltonian manipulative sense, but in a Smithian "invisible hand" sense—free religion, as religion, conduces to good citizenship. Religious leaders, in return for the benefit inherent in the right to practice religion free of state interference, must understand that they play a major role in politics, whether or not they want to do so. The most important political role they play is as teachers of tolerance, since we all know that, throughout history, some individuals have taken religious disagreements as a license to kill. The founders understood the dangers of enthusiasm as well as the bloodiness of religious intolerance. They had fresher memories than we today have of the devastating religious wars fought in Europe. When some people of religion make claims which seem to be exclusive, rationalists and people of other religions rightfully become alarmed. (I am alluding to various statements by members of the Christian Coalition criticizing some very fine people who happen to be on different sides of political issues. These statements sometimes seem to exclude some Christians from God's grace—to say nothing of the implications for people of other faiths—forgetting the biblical injunction not to judge for that is the Lord's job. The most egregious of such statements is the "Christian nation" statement, which has been made by representatives of the Christian right as well as by at least one politician.[3] For all the qualifying phrases which are often attached to such statements, they exclude both non-Christians and also, implicitly, many Christians who disagree with the religious and/or political ideas of these groups.)

Exclusive claims for religion have caused me some trepidation in writing a book advocating a renewed attention to values. After all, values clashes have been so lethal. Think of the multitudes of innocent victims in the recent turmoil in the former Yugoslavia, the horrors of Cambodia's killing fields, the gas ovens of the holocaust, the long misery of centuries of slavery and its aftermath in the United States. But what makes values potentially so pernicious is the combination of a presumption of knowledge of values with a paucity of intellectual humility.

Such hubris ignores the wisdom of a deeply religious Indian, Mohandas Gandhi, who taught that one must always be open to the truth that the other side holds. Living his life as a constant search for truth proved to be immensely powerful, eventually winning support from so many Indians that Britain peacefully acquiesced to Indian independence. That some of Gandhi's Muslim compatriots did not see things Gandhi's way is a warning to us. If the saintly Gandhi could not gain the trust of some Indian Muslims (to say nothing of some Hindus—his assassin was an extremist Hindu), how can we be sure that a particular religious approach to politics will not have similarly disastrous results in the United States?[4]

We must strengthen values in this new millennium, but that imperative comes with a crucial caveat: the values must be within a context of tolerant truth-seeking. We must all search for the truth, but with a certainty of the high probability that another, any other person, may have even more of the truth than we ourselves have. Human beings, Americans especially, often want quick, easy solutions. But tolerant truth-seekers, intellectually humble believers in strong values as the basis for a just society, cannot provide such simplistic solutions. Moreover, religions will be major participants (sometimes positively, but unfortunately sometimes negatively) in this humble search for true values.

Religion and politics will always be interrelated. At the same time, separation of church and state is imperative. But our First Amendment, which is commonly understood to mandate "separation of church and state," requires instead no establishment of religion; it does not, indeed cannot, require the separation of politics and religion. To expect rigid separation of religion and politics is to expect the impossible because religious people would then either have to be schizoid (this is the Sabbath, so we can be religious; this is election day so we can be political) or they would have to abjure politics altogether if they insisted on living religiously whole lives. (Note that such lives would not be whole, because the political part of life would have been amputated.)

Assuming continued interaction of religion and politics, religious leaders have a heavy responsibility to be humble Gandhian truth-seekers.[5] This is imperative in order to avoid the dangers of religious actions which deprive others of their rights. Freedom of religion, after all, means freedom of religious belief, but does not extend to actions which violate the rights of others. Even more difficult, religious leaders must have the humility and the nerve to enjoin their followers, repeatedly, to exercise skeptical democratic discernment of political positions taken by religious leaders, especially their own positions. A collateral requirement, somewhat easier, is to make similar entreaties about the religious positions taken by political leaders.[6]

Tolerance also places requirements on rationalists. They must learn tolerance of religion (just as people of religion must tolerate them). More difficult, they must abandon their overweening pride in reason; a little intellectual humility would sometimes be wonderful. Macedo may be correct in arguing that humility is not among the liberal virtues;[7] but it is certainly true that its antonym, arrogance, is a civic vice. And many rationalists seem arrogant when discussing religion.[8] This is not to deny that there is enormous power in human reason, but is to suggest that there are other ways of knowing.[9] Religious believers may have another way: non-rational knowledge, which, however, does not justify irrationality. John Adams's insistence on applying reason to religion speaks to us here.[10] Indeed, this is what much of theology is about today. The founders understood that revelation must be tested by reason. Does that destroy revelation? I think not. I believe that what it does is to protect fallible persons from human perversions of religious truths. Man's thought mediates God's revelation. Unless done with great humility and great love, this mediation can produce (and throughout history has produced) cataclysmic horrors. By the same token people of religion, of all varieties, must also not fall into the trap of pride, relative to other religions, and relative to rationalists. The other, any other, might know part or all of the truth.

Even if religion played a respectable and respected role in education for virtue, we would still have much to do to attain a country of civic virtue. Virtue education may develop increased citizen virtue, but there must also be a restoration of civic virtue in the leaders. To that end, what Hamilton wrote about laws applies to civic virtues as well:

> Wise politicians will be cautious about fettering the government with restrictions that cannot be observed, because they know that every breach of the fundamental laws, though dictated by necessity, impairs that sacred reverence which ought to be maintained in the breast of rulers towards the constitution of a country, and forms a precedent for other breaches where the same plea of necessity does not exist at all, or is less urgent and palpable.[11]

Hamilton was not a soft-hearted idealist; his political views were as realistic and power-oriented as any politician today. John Adams, and probably other contemporaries of Hamilton as well, would have questioned whether Hamilton lived up to the ideal inherent in that quote. Nevertheless, we must restore a sense that the strengthening of the system is more important than any short-term gain which might be obtained by cutting corners. Massive distrust of government today can be directly traced to a "win at all costs" attitude, an attitude which has subverted the Constitution and the laws of the land in foreign and domestic policy (for example, Vietnam and Watergate) and which has had ethically dubious results in elections due to the manipulation of public opinion with crass, demagogic appeals.

Justice

Even if education for virtue were significantly improved, it would be important to attack structural impediments to democracy, especially given our founders' certainty that religion was not a sufficient check against vice. In particular, given the two intractable realities of factionalism and self-interest, how can we develop a more democratic government, which is to say a more just government that is responsible to all the people? (I define democracy as a government which is responsible to the sovereign people, with majority rule and minority rights, in contrast to the oligarchy we now have, with its rule by factions.) Let us now look at some suggestions for improving democracy. But note that these ideas do not provide quick and easy solutions. Improving democracy will require hard work over a period of years; there is no quick fix.

Education

It is obvious from the low rate of eligible voter participation in United States elections that one way to improve democracy must be increased citizen participation in government; the founders also were concerned about this issue. John Adams, for instance, writing in "A Dissertation on the Canon and Feudal Law," sought "to rouse Americans out of their 'habits of reserve, and a cautious diffidence of asserting their opinions publickly.'" But he knew that the liberty to assert American rights was not an unqualified good. It would be "little better than a brutal rage" if the people were without knowledge.[12] In his balanced approach, citizens must be active, but their action must be based on understanding, knowledge. Education was very important to Adams because he saw a direct relationship between the educational level of the citizens and the form of government: the more education, the more free and self-governing were the citizens.[13] Promotion of enlightened public opinion was one of George Washington's recommendations in his Farewell Address.[14] Noah Webster emphasized education as an auxiliary support for freedom; as indicated above, he believed property was the main support of freedom, but the people's knowledge of their rights was also important.[15] Other founders concerned about the need for education in civic virtue include Jefferson, Benjamin Rush, and James Wilson.[16] Webster's linkage of education and freedom, with property as the main defense, brings us to the economic implications of education. Good education promotes both the wealth of individuals (and nations) and the civic virtue of the people.

Political apathy is widespread in this country; so citizens, opting not to participate, leave a vacuum which factions are all too willing to fill. Adams still calls us to develop our understanding of issues and then to speak out, to participate actively, as citizens. Bellah argues that we need political imagination and vision to resolve our problems.[17] We need to analyze the problems and determine whether the system can be reformed (or, if it cannot be reformed, whether to take Jefferson's ultimate step of rebellion). Ironically, governmental resources can help analyze the problems, but citizens must take the initiative; public virtue requires that in a democracy.

When a college professor advocates education as one step in improving our democracy, that sounds like special pleading. When one adds to that John

Adams's first career, the schoolteacher in Worcester, Massachusetts, one might think this argument can be discounted completely because of the self-interest of the proponents. Nevertheless, I assert the primacy of this aspect of the solution, because so many others have, without the supposed taint of self-interest, argued for the same solution. Both Adams and Smith advocated education for all.[18] Adams was especially strong in his arguments that, if the people were to be sovereign, they must be educated.

Impediments to Citizen Sovereignty

An educated citizenry is only part of the answer. One reason for apathy is that many citizens feel that no one in government is listening. But if government is to listen to all the people, not just a few of the people, one must eliminate structural impediments to democracy. One of America's leading political scientists, Dahl, has criticized our Constitution for increasing the power of minorities against the majority, with consequences that appear "arbitrary and quite lacking in a principled justification." He also states that, because the founders "succeeded in designing a system that makes it easier for privileged minorities to prevent changes they dislike than for majorities to bring about the changes they want, it is strongly tilted in favor of the status quo and against reform."[19] The constitutional system supports factional politics at the expense of democracy, the power of the few at the expense of the power of the many. The institutions our founders designed have worked well enough to survive for two centuries; but, as circumstances have changed, the system has lost a critical component: democratic responsibility.

One reason our system lacks responsibility to the people is our founders' fear of power. Earlier I quoted, in full, John Adams's maxim: "trust no man living with power to endanger the public liberty." There is a lot of wisdom in that maxim. But how to implement it is crucial, as John Adams himself recognized. His ideas of balanced government have been misunderstood. He wanted to prevent any one class from dominating; neither the one, nor the few, nor the many should be in control. Each should balance the others. In contrast, our governmental checks and balances have, for many years, unbalanced the system in favor of powerful interest groups, at the expense of society as a whole. This is exactly what John Adams wanted to prevent. So, our founders' suspicion of power has resulted in an unbalanced system which is beyond popular control.

If, as Adams argued, the people are sovereign, then the people should be able to counterbalance the powerful interest groups. But such a balancing role assumes clear lines of responsibility, which do not exist in our current system. Our intricate checks and balances have produced split governments for most of this century (the administrations of Franklin D. Roosevelt and Lyndon B. Johnson are exceptions) and thus have produced irresponsible governments. When Patrick Henry asked where the responsibility was in the new constitution, he was concerned about excessive executive power. Presidential power has grown during the twentieth century, but the problem goes beyond the president to encompass the entire system. Whom should the people hold responsible for government action or inaction: congress? the president? When both congress and the president can reasonably argue that the other branch prevented action or forced unwise action, the people cannot easily determine who did what. And without that knowledge, the people cannot guard the guardians, cannot control their representatives. That problem does not exist in a two-party parliamentary system, but to accept such a system would require Americans to overcome their fear of power. The people are the main check on abuse of power in a parliamentary system.

Since adoption of a parliamentary system is not a realistic possibility in the near future, some less radical changes might be helpful. One recently popular solution for problems of congressional responsiveness, the idea of term limits, would actually make the problem worse. While dissatisfaction with politicians is understandable, the term limits idea would cause more problems then it would cure. The power that term limits would give to the executive branch, to interest groups, and to unelected but experienced congressional staffers is dangerous to democracy. In fact, increased power for interest groups and congressional staff would make representatives and senators less responsive to the people and thus would further undermine democracy. The desire for reelection is a powerful motivator which term limits would destroy. Rather than destroying this motivation, there is a way to harness it for the common good.

Self-interest could be used to motivate Congressmen and Senators to be responsible to all the people. Now they serve parochial interests, limited geographic or functional interests, not the interests of the nation. Given American individualism, there will always be some of this, but the system could be changed to give politicians a motive to serve the public good. Since many legislators want to be reelected, one step in the right direction would be federal funding of all congressional and senatorial elections.[20] Just as the capitalist free market relies on the economic profit motive, American democracy depends on the political profit motive, the desire to win reelection. This motivator now works in favor of special interests, but campaign finance reform could make the politician's self-interest a strong support of democracy.

Restoring fair competition to elections requires a thorough overhaul of campaign finances. The electoral playing field is not level. Incumbent advantages, especially in raising funds from Political Action Committees, give interest groups immense power in elections. Legislation which would have provided partial federal funding for congressional elections was vetoed by President Bush. That legislation did not go far enough. Ultimately, federal campaigns should be completely funded by the government. However, using citizens' hard-earned tax dollars to allow unresponsive politicians to run for office seems an affront to common sense. But full funding would actually be a bargain because it would give politicians an incentive to work for all the people; it would make the politicians responsive to the people. After all, they do listen now, to significant contributors to their election campaigns. Remember: he who pays the piper gets to call the tune. Full funding would mean that the political profit motive would favor the people instead of interest groups. Politicians would be responsible to the sovereign citizen because the citizen would be paying the piper. If we are to restore democracy and if democracy means that the people are sovereign, then government must be controlled by the citizens, not by interest groups. There would probably be an important side effect of returning the responsibility to the people: more eligible voters would actually vote because they would see their votes as meaningful.

Short of full federal funding, a constitutional amendment is probably needed so that campaign contributions are not juridically defined as free speech and thus subject to First Amendment protection, a loophole which has emasculated previous campaign finance reform. In addition, William Grieder's suggestion of a $100 or $200 tax credit for political contributions makes sense.[21] This would have the virtue of combining federal financing with freedom of choice of each individual to support his or her own candidate or party or cause. Free postage should be available to all candidates during any election year, not just the incumbents who now have it because of the congressional frank. And, free radio and television air time would level the playing field significantly, to say nothing of the dramatic reduction in campaign expenses that would entail. None of these ideas would deal with the excessive length of American election campaigns, or with negative campaigning, both of which contribute to citizen apathy. But the ideas do suggest that the irresponsibility of the current system, a major cause of citizen apathy, can be attacked.

Neither full federal funding nor any of the other suggestions above would eliminate interest groups, for which there is a very legitimate place in any democracy. But they should not be allowed to lobby for special privileges behind closed doors. It would be better for democracy if they influenced party platforms before the election campaigns, so the people could choose their preferred policies.

It is time that the United States overcame its fear of democracy. I believe that the founders' distrust of the masses is no longer valid. Our long experience with a democratic Constitution, even though that democracy has been limited, has ingrained in our culture the best check on power: the popular will to maintain democracy. If the nascent Russian democracy could be rescued by a citizen uprising, mature American democracy can trust the people as the ultimate check on power.

Another suggestion derives from classical republican tradition: we need to develop a sense of politics as an honorable vocation for all citizens, not just the professional politicians. This is an idea which our founders did not emphasize; "politics as an honorable vocation is a theme missing not only from the work of the founders but from almost all of American intellectual history."[22] To have majority rule, the people must take a more active role in the political system.

It is also time to remember that government can be a positive force in meeting many of our needs as a society. The founders were in basic agreement with the list of government functions John Adams developed in 1772: "Government is nothing more than the combined Force of Society, or the united Power of the Multitude, for the Peace, Order, Safety, Good and Happiness of the People, who compose the Society."[23] Since that address, there has been wide agreement in this country over the peace and order items he listed. Now it is time to pay attention to the safety and "Good and Happiness of the People," as well, because the agreed items are jeopardized by failure to address the other functions. A contemporary analyst puts this point another way. Heilbroner argues that capitalism thrives when the private and public (government) sectors work together symbiotically; one reason for 1980s American economic difficulties, he states, was that government did not provide adequate structure for the economy. By "adequate structure" he means, among other things, transportation networks and education.[24] While the American economy has been strong in the 1990s (in aggregate terms, but with harshly skewed results), in the long run, neglecting community functions will hurt us all.

Pursuit of Happiness

Given the connections between economic power and political power, if government is to contribute to the good and happiness of the people, justice, a crucial virtue for Adams and Smith, must be addressed in broader terms than the impediments to citizen sovereignty discussed above. In what follows, I examine the example of connections between property and the pursuit of happiness, but I am well aware that justice, fair play, as advocated by Adams and Smith, has much broader implications. Equal pay, equal educational opportunity (see preceding section on education), reciprocally fair treatment of employers and employees, in short, the golden rule, could all be discussed.

Jefferson once suggested providing fifty acres to all American males who did not already own any land. What would be the functional equivalent today? How can all citizens (not just white males) be sufficiently free economically to be politically able to defend their own interests within the community, rather than surrendering to a factional view of the community's interest? (In other words, what would have to change for all citizens to be independent and thus capable of democratic citizenship?)

Any solutions must be faithful to the country's founding principles. Morgan presents James Madison's thoughts on three such principles: "Madison believed that prevailing public opinion favored not only popular sovereignty and majority rule moderated by representation, but also responsible, accountable government. 'I believe no principle is more clearly laid down in the Constitution than responsibility.'"[25] These principles might seem like truisms, but when you remember the founders' concerns about faction and about the corrupting influence of wealth, and especially when you combine factions and wealth, you can understand more fully the dilemma the country faces. How are we to have responsible, popular, representative government when interest group money corrupts the process?

Some readers might think that question a bit harsh. But it cuts close to the heart of the matter: moneyed interests undermine our democratic order. This is not just one professor's opinion. Silk, a perspicacious observer of the American economic scene, wrote that political courage would be needed to remove "the corrupting influence on government of the special interests":

> Government must, in the broad public interest, curb those special-interest pressures that distort and waste resources, particularly in multibillion-dollar military programs that not only create inflation but increase the danger of arms races and war itself. The military-industrial-congressional complex is only the most celebrated example of the special interests which capture a huge share of national resources. Other interest groups that have won special benefits and protection from government . . . include the oil industry, the maritime industry, civil aviation, the highway-building industry and its supporters, dairy producers, wheat farmers, cattlemen, steel producers and textile producers. Labor unions fight for a growing share of the national pie.[26]

Silk also argues that we need better ways to harmonize group pressures and to guide the economy to serve social needs,[27] in short to serve the public good.

Given the immense power of interest groups in the United States, how can government control factions without destroying a dynamic economy? Can government regulate commerce so that self-interest is not exploitative but stays creative? Marxists, of course, assume that such is impossible under any capitalist system which, for them, is exploitative by definition. However, given that capitalist systems have been remarkably adaptable in the past, there seems no reason to believe that developing a balanced capitalist system would be impossible. In avoiding the communist position of total government control of the economy, can the United States avoid the dialectical extreme of laissez-faire (which assumes that any government role in the economy is anathema to capitalism)? Can we modify American capitalism so that our society would better support safety, the common good, and the equal opportunity for all people to pursue happiness?

In short, American capitalism needs to adapt if it is to be effective in the twenty-first century. If one's goals are popular sovereignty, responsibility and representative government, the dialectical extremes of laissez-faire capitalism and communism, both fundamentally flawed, must be avoided. Fortunately, such either-or options are not our only choices. We can extend the mixed system we already have. We can have free market capitalism and activist government while improving popular sovereignty, responsibility, and representative government.

Models already exist; our most effective economic competitors (Germany and Japan) have already implemented mixed systems.

Steps could be taken to diffuse property ownership more widely and thus somewhat mitigate the political power of unequal wealth. How could we change the economic organization of society in order to promote democracy? In *A Preface to Economic Democracy,* Dahl argues for worker self-ownership. Barber agrees with Dahl on worker-owned cooperatives and also suggests that shared decision-making, experiments with codetermination (a German practice), profit-sharing and stock-ownership plans all would produce greater economic equity while developing better citizens.[28]

Such ideas have been around for many years. John Stuart Mill advocated "worker-owned competitive enterprises" in the nineteenth century.[29] Kasson writes of the stifling of altruism by an exploitative economic system and notes that "Bellamy, Donnelly, and Howells all strenuously advocated extending the principle of democratic control from government to industry as the essential step in achieving a truly republican order."[30] How else could industry be democratized without worker ownership? Or are you going to try to make the absurd argument that corporations are already democratically controlled by their stockholders?

Worker ownership is not utopian; it has been successful in numerous enterprises in Europe and the United States. Dahl suggests changing from the currently dominant mode of stockholder corporations on an experimental basis, in other words, without a revolutionary restructuring of the entire economy. And he argues that "a complex society cannot protect the rights, needs, and interests of its people with one single, prevailing form of economic organization but requires instead a network of enterprises organized in many different combinations of internal government, external controls, and ownership."[31] It would be foolish to suggest a complete transition to worker ownership in this country. However, government support for different modes of ownership could develop a competitive mixture. To give worker ownership a reasonable chance to succeed, these experiments should not start with failed corporations. However, the successful worker takeover of National Steel Corporation's Weirton Steel Division indicates that some risky businesses are worth trying. (National Steel was planning to close Weirton Steel because it was a money-losing division; under worker ownership, Weirton Steel became highly profitable.)

Government support could include disseminating information on successful experiments, and providing technical advice and loan guarantees. Such actions would not be a radical break from American history. All three have already been done by the American government in the twentieth century, to say nothing of revolutionary era analogs.

Before anyone gets apoplexy at the idea of marginal, experimental changes in forms of property ownership, there are strong arguments for societal determination of the laws governing the specifics of property rights. For the founders, property rights were important but secondary to the pursuit of happiness. Public needs had precedence over private property. Shain argues that Jefferson believed that any laws, especially property laws, could be changed whenever circumstances demanded. For eighteenth-century Americans, the right to property was a social creation valued "to the degree to which it served publicly endorsed social ends."[32] In the twentieth century, Walter Lippmann agreed with the Jeffersonian position, tracing it back to Blackstone. Lippmann argued that "property is the creation of the law for social purposes." He also argued that the "earth is the general property of all mankind" and that private ownership is "assigned by lawmaking authorities to promote the grand ends of civil society." Thus, property rights are determined by government; property rights may be changed when the situation changes, in order to meet the goals of society.[33]

Note also that the father of modern capitalism did not believe that property rights were eternally fixed. Property rights were very important to Adam Smith but he believed that society could define those rights:

> Rights not to be physically harmed, rights to personal liberty, and rights to the preservation of one's reputation are natural rights. They do not depend on conventions, the economy, or society. However, following Hume, Smith contends that 'estate' or property is an acquired right. Property rights, unlike natural rights, are not rights that one possesses simply because one is a human being. Because one possesses or acquires property does not thereby imply that one has a natural right to it, because property, unlike liberty or reputation, is socially defined and can be transferred to and from others.[34]

As one example of the social definition of property rights, Smith states that it would be "the same thing" if a workman who produced two thousand pins in a day received wages or if the artisan "gave five hundred pins to his master for affording him the wire, the tools, and the employment, and kept fifteen hundred to himself, in order to be exchanged for the productions of the other arts which he had occasion for."[35] The complexity of modern production, distribution, and marketing is a good reason for not adopting Smith's hypothetical example. But note its implications. An unquestioned property relationship—the factory owner gets all of the product manufactured in his establishment—is not the natural order of things. Smith's example was every bit as logical as the current model that the businessperson or corporation owns all of the production of the factory. Since society determined the fundamental property relationship which now exists, why not have society decide to encourage increased worker ownership, a yeoman principle for contemporary times?

Our society could, in the spirit of Smith's socially defined property rights, support worker ownership. In the same spirit, and also remembering Jefferson's suggestion of graduated property taxes, we could return to progressive income taxes. The Reagan Revolution massively cut the progressiveness of income taxes; the result was that the rich got richer and everyone else suffered. I am well aware that Americans perceive that they are heavily taxed. The reality is that our tax rates are among the lowest of all the industrialized nations. Progressive taxation could pay for improved services while reducing the federal debt, nice side benefits of a democratizing move.

Community Service

One final suggestion for restoring democracy would have citizens revert, on a community basis, to the tradition of the "bee" for quilting, raising barns, clearing swamps. While those historical uses of common work are less needed today, Barber argues that, whether at the national or local level, common work would be valuable for both the individual participants and for the community. Such work programs "make communities more self-sufficient and thus more self-governing and build a genuine sense of community in the neighborhood."[36] Such work would counteract both the alienation of atomistic individualism, and the crassly material elements of contemporary American life. If community work included an option of a year or two in a community service corps, society would benefit doubly. Building on the experience of successful programs like Americorps and VISTA, high school graduates might be offered reasonable pay for two years of community service work. Since I am not a policy wonk, I do not know what specific services could be performed by these volunteers, nor what services would be most beneficial for the community, nor what rate of pay would be reasonable. The principle I am suggesting would be to supplement the public services already provided by government, not to replace government workers. I define this service broadly; e.g., perhaps some corps members could be aides in day-care centers, so that capacity could be increased and cost reduced, thus easing the financial burdens on single-earner families, and perhaps making it possible for some welfare mothers to work, without fearing for their children's safety.

In return for such service, the volunteer would be guaranteed some equivalent of the GI Bill of Rights education benefit. I am absolutely not equating the service of such a corps of volunteers to the sacrifices of our servicemen and women. I suggest this only as an example of an activist governmental program which worked well both for individuals and the community. The college education benefit of the GI Bill of Rights is a major reason for the economic success of the United States since World War II.[37] Broadly diffused education is not only good for the individual but also adds to the wealth of the nation. There would be short-term benefits in whatever work was done in the community; long-term benefits would include an increasingly competitive American economy. The program would also result in a higher level of citizen education, and thus a stronger democracy.[38] It once was true that a high school education was sufficient to prepare one for a reasonable life in America. That is no longer true, so something like the community service corps education benefit would recognize the higher educational demands of life in a postindustrial economy and would be a modern response consistent with Adams's and Smith's emphasis on education, for both citizenship and economic reasons.

Conclusion

None of the reforms mentioned herein are offered as absolutes; all are suggestions, beginning ruminations on what we might do to apply the principles of Adams and Smith. Just as Adams and Smith based their ideas on the reality they perceived, so also must we be pragmatic and analyze the context of our specific time and place and determine what would really provide political equality and justice for all.

It is time for us to learn from the failures of two great men. Adams failed because he was not reelected president. Smith failed because his major work *(Theory of Moral Sentiments)* was ignored and generations have forgotten what he saw as the imperative moral aspect of economic liberty. But they were magnificent failures. Adams had an enviably successful career, first as a lawyer and then as a statesman who was crucial to American independence and who, as president, kept the United States out of war. And Smith is revered throughout the world, albeit for the wrong reasons. However, their failures were only partially their own; their failures are also ours in that we have misinterpreted and/or ignored them. But, we can do something about our share of the failures; we can all work for a tolerant, just, inclusive, value-based, politically egalitarian government of all the people.

Notes

1.   Daniel J. Boorstin, ed., *An American Primer* (New York: Penguin Books, 1966), xiv.

2.   Andrew Stewart Skinner, *A System of Social Science: Papers Relating to Adam Smith,* 2d ed. (Oxford: Clarendon Press, 1996), 206; Jerry Z. Muller, *Adam Smith: In His Time and Ours* (Princeton: Princeton University Press,1993), 5, writes that Adam Smith was a "brilliant and multifaceted thinker" but that "his work can provide few specific prescriptions for action two centuries after his death."

But, Skinner does provide a list of Smith's principles justifying governmental intervention: "the state should regulate activity to compensate for the imperfect knowledge of individuals"; the state must continually evaluate laws and institutions; the state must "regulate and control the activities of individuals who might otherwise prove damaging to the interest of society at large"; and the state must provide "for public works and services, including education, in cases where the profit motive is likely to prove inadequate" (Skinner, *System of Social Science,* 204).

Barry A. Shain, *The Myth of American Individualism: The Protestant Origins of American Political Thought* (Princeton: Princeton University Press, 1994), 324-25, warns that "it is most unclear how, in this case, the communal vision of a rural,

Protestant, relatively homogeneous slaveholding people can be usefully adapted to the needs of an increasingly urban and ethnically, racially, and religiously diverse people living in a postindustrial world."

3.   Carolyn Curtis, "Rally Convicts Nation of Sins," *Christianity Today* 40 (June 17, 1996): 61ff, reports Jerry Falwell's speech to a Washington for Jesus rally; he said: "'Our children must be told that America is a Christian nation.'" And Governor Kirk Fordice of Mississippi stated on November 17, 1992, that America "'is a Christian nation'" (*New York Times*, November 28, 1992: 7-8).

4.   Note also that India and Pakistan have fought several wars since their 1947 independence. In my view, this does not invalidate the point but reinforces the need for tolerance and moderation.

5.   George Soros, "The Capitalist Threat," *The Atlantic Monthly* (February 1997): 58, argues for such intellectual humility in the pursuit of truth. Richard C. Sinopoli, "Thick-skinned Liberalism: Redefining Civility," *American Political Science Review* 89 (September 1995): 618, discusses tolerance and civility in terms of taking others seriously and recognizing "that they may have something to teach us." Amy Gutmann, "Undemocratic Education," in *Liberalism and the Moral Life,* Nancy L. Rosenblum, ed. (Cambridge: Harvard University Press, 1989), 75, similarly argues for mutual respect, which "requires willingness and ability to accord due intellectual and moral regard to reasonable points of view that we cannot ourselves accept as correct."

6.   John G. West, Jr., *The Politics of Revelation and Reason: Religion and Civic Life in the New Nation* (Lawrence: University Press of Kansas, 1996), 74-75, points out the difficulty of maintaining both freedom of religious belief and of religious action. He argues that, to maintain both these freedoms, reason and revelation "must concur on the moral law."

7.   Stephen Macedo, *Liberal Virtues: Citizenship, Virtue, and Community in Liberal Constitutionalism* (Oxford: Clarendon Press, 1990), 278.

8.   Thomas L. Pangle, *The Ennobling of Democracy: The Challenge of the Postmodern Era* (Baltimore: Johns Hopkins University Press, 1992), 74, states that American religious traditions, the foundation of the American polity, "are regarded with suspicion or contempt in most American universities, journals of opinion, and circles of intellectual sophistication."

Macedo, *Liberal Virtues,* 253, seems perilously close to the vice of arrogance against religion when he states that liberal regimes promote autonomy but "still respect the non-autonomous: people have the right to lead lazy, narrow-minded lives." I am not defending narrow-mindedness, but criticizing an implication that all people of religion are narrow-minded and lacking autonomy.

9.   Joshua Mitchell, *Not by Reason Alone: Religion, History, and Identity in Early Modern Political Thought* (Chicago: University of Chicago Press, 1993), 126-27, argues that Luther, Rousseau, Hobbes, Locke, and even Freud understood this. In addition, he states: "The contemporary tendency to treat early modern political thought entirely under the rubric of reason, to dismiss or ignore portions of texts which try to comprehend the mystery that unassisted reason cannot grasp, evinces

this (worrisome) tendency to dispose of talk about what is beyond the boundary of reason."

10. West, *Politics of Revelation*, 50.

11. Hamilton, *Federalist, #25*, 91.

12. Ralph Lerner, *The Thinking Revolutionary: Principle and Practice in the New Republic* (Ithaca, N.Y.: Cornell University Press, 1979), 22-23.

13. C. Bradley Thompson, *John Adams and the Spirit of Liberty* (Lawrence: University Press of Kansas, 1998), 50. Lorraine Smith Pangle and Thomas L. Pangle, *The Learning of Liberty: The Educational Ideas of the American Founders* (Lawrence: University Press of Kansas, 1993), 1-3 and 139-40, clearly state the importance to Adams of education to enable the new republic to survive, and place his thought within the classic context which argued the importance of education for the maintenance of a republic.

14. Boorstin, ed., *American Primer*, 222.

15. Colleen A. Sheehan and Gary L. McDowell, eds., *Friends of the Constitution; Writings of the "Other" Federalists, 1787-1788* (Indianapolis: Liberty Fund, 1998), 402.

16. Pangle, *Ennobling of Democracy*, 151. James Wilson was a very important leader in the eighteenth century, but he is now virtually forgotten.

17. Robert N. Bellah, et al., *Habits of the Heart: Individualism and Commitment in American Life* (New York: Harper and Row, 1985), 271.

18. Skinner, *System of Social Science*, 191-95 and 205-06, writes of Smith's belief in the public right to compel general education for the population, and even higher education for significant numbers. Such compulsory education was necessary to offset the negative effects of the division of labor and in order to "preserve a capacity for moral judgement" and citizenship. Similarly, Ian Simpson Ross, *The Life of Adam Smith* (Oxford: Oxford University Press,1995), 420, argues that Smith's remedy (education) for the "mental mutilation inflicted on workers by the division of labour" was mocked by Marx but that it did make lives more tolerable while Marxism generally failed. Charles L. Griswold, Jr., *Adam Smith and the Virtues of Enlightenment* (New York: Cambridge University Press, 1999), 210ff, states that "moral education is a continuous theme" in both *Theory of Moral Sentiments* and *Wealth of Nations*, and, along with religion and justice, "one of the bridges between the two books." See also Robert E. Lane, *The Market Experience* (Cambridge: Cambridge University Press, 1991), 324; Stephen Holmes, *Passions and Constraint: On the Theory of Liberal Democracy* (Chicago: University of Chicago Press, 1995), 262-63; and Bellah, *Habits of the Heart*, 214-17.

19. Robert A. Dahl, "On Removing Certain Impediments to Democracy in the United States," in *The Moral Foundations of the American Republic*, 3d ed., Robert H. Horwitz, ed. (Charlottesville: University of Virginia Press, 1986), 235-36.

20. Amitai Etzioni, *The Spirit of Community: The Reinvention of American Society* (New York: Simon and Schuster, 1993), 234-38, lists this reform first in his discussion of several proposals. He also suggests reducing the cost of elections, and he argues for channeling campaign contributions to parties, not candidates.

21. William Greider, *Who Will Tell the People: The Betrayal of American Democracy* (New York: Simon and Schuster, 1992), 52-53.

22. John P. Diggins, *The Lost Soul of American Politics: Virtue, Self-Interest, and the Foundations of Liberalism* (Chicago: University of Chicago Press, 1984), 62-63.

23. John Adams, Notes for an oration at Braintree, Spring 1772, in L. H. Butterfield, ed., *The Adams Papers: Diary and Autobiography of John Adams,* 2 (New York: Atheneum, 1964), 57.

24. Robert Heilbroner, "Realities and Appearances in Capitalism," in *Corporations and the Common Good*, Robert B. Dickie and Leroy S. Rouner, eds. (Notre Dame, Ind.: University of Notre Dame Press, 1986), 36-37.

25. Robert J. Morgan, "Madison's Analysis of the Sources of Political Authority," *American Political Science Review* 75 (September 1981): 618.

26. Leonard Silk, "America in the World Economy," in *America as an Ordinary Country: U. S. Foreign Policy and the Future*, Richard Rosecrance, ed. (Ithaca, N.Y.: Cornell University Press, 1976), 166-67.

27. Silk, "America in the World Economy," in Rosecrance, *America as an Ordinary Country*, 166-167.

28. Benjamin R. Barber, *Strong Democracy: Participatory Politics for a New Age* (Berkeley: University of California Press, 1984), 305.

29. Robert L. Heilbroner, *Visions of the Future: The Distant Past, Yesterday, Today, and Tomorrow* (New York: New York Public Library, Oxford University Press, 1995), 63.

30. John F. Kasson, *Civilizing the Machine: Technology and Republican Values in America, 1776-1900* (New York: Penguin Books, 1976), 232.

31. Dahl, "Impediments to Democracy," in *Moral Foundations*, Horwitz, ed., 248.

32. Shain, *Myth of American Individualism*, 184.

33. Clinton Rossiter and James Lare, eds., *The Essential Lippmann: A Political Philosophy for Liberal Democracy* (Cambridge: Harvard University Press, 1982), 190-91.

34. Patricia H. Werhane, *Adam Smith and His Legacy for Modern Capitalism* (New York: Oxford University Press, 1991), 60.

35. Adam Smith, *Lectures on Jurisprudence*, R. L. Meek, D. D. Raphael, and P. G. Stein, eds. (Oxford: Oxford University Press 1978), 566.

36. Barber, *Strong Democracy*, 210-11.

37. On the educational benefits of the GI Bill of Rights, see Michael J. Bennett, *When Dreams Came True: The GI Bill and the Making of Modern America* (Washington: Brassey's, Inc., 1996), 237ff; on the overall impact of the GI Bill, see 277, 311, and the following quote on 315: "Over the years, the GI Bill subtly has worked to change the face of America."

38. Speaking from over thirty years of experience as an educator, many students would be better prepared for college if they had some experience before entering college. Maturity and motivation make a difference in college performance.

Bibliography

Adams, John Quincy, and Charles Francis Adams. *John Adams*. 2 vols. New York: Chelsea House, 1980 (1871).

Appleby, Joyce. *Capitalism and a New Social Order: The Republican Vision of the 1790s*. New York: New York University Press, 1984.

———. "The Jefferson-Adams Rupture and the First French Translation of John Adams' *Defence*." *American Historical Review* 73 (April 1968): 1084-91.

———. *Liberalism and Republicanism in the Historical Imagination*. Cambridge: Harvard University Press, 1992.

Avineri, Shlomo, and Avner De-Shalit, eds. *Communitarianism and Individualism*. New York: Oxford University Press, 1992.

Bailyn, Bernard. *The Origins of American Politics*. New York: Alfred A. Knopf, 1970.

Ball, Terence. Review of *Virtue Transformed: Political Argument in England, 1688-1740*, by Shelley Burtt. *American Political Science Review* 88 (March 1994): 212.

Barber, Benjamin R. *Strong Democracy: Participatory Politics for a New Age*. Berkeley: University of California Press, 1984.

Barlett, Donald L., and James B. Steele. *America: What Went Wrong?* Kansas City: Andrews and McMeel, 1992.

Barrow, Clyde W. Review of *The Unvarnished Doctrine: Locke, Liberalism, and the American Revolution*, by Steven M. Dworetz, and of *A Union of Interests: Political and Economic Thought in Revolutionary America*, by Cathy D. Matson and Peter S. Onuf. *American Political Science Review* 86 (March 1992): 210-11.

Becker, Carl L. *The Declaration of Independence: A Study in the History of Political Ideas*. New York: Random House, Vintage Books, 1958 (1922).

Bellah, Robert N., Richard Madsen, William M. Sullivan, Ann Swidler, and Steven M. Tipton. *Habits of the Heart: Individualism and Commitment in American Life*. New York: Harper and Row, 1985.

Bennett, Michael J. *When Dreams Came True: The GI Bill and the Making of Modern America.* Washington: Brassey's, Inc., 1996.

Binder, Frederick M. *The Color Problem in Early National America as Viewed by John Adams, Jefferson and Jackson.* The Hague: Mouton, 1968.

Bloch, Ruth. *Visionary Republic: Millennial Themes in American Thought, 1756-1800.* Cambridge: Cambridge University Press, 1985.

Boorstin, Daniel J., ed. *An American Primer.* New York: Penguin Books, Meridian Classic, 1966.

Booth, William James. "On the Idea of the Moral Economy." *American Political Science Review* 88 (September 1994): 653-67.

————. "A Note on the Idea of the Moral Economy." *American Political Science Review* 87 (December 1993): 949-54.

Bourgin, Frank. *The Great Challenge: The Myth of Laissez-Faire in the Early Republic.* New York: George Braziller, 1989.

Bowen, Catherine Drinker. *Miracle at Philadelphia: The Story of the Constitutional Convention, May to September 1787.* Boston: Little Brown and Co., Atlantic Monthly Press Book, 1966.

Bremer, Howard F., ed. *John Adams: 1735-1826, Chronology—Documents—Bibliographical Aids.* Dobbs Ferry, N.Y.: Oceana Publications, 1967.

Brown, Ralph Adams. *The Presidency of John Adams.* Lawrence: University Press of Kansas, 1975.

Budziszewski, J. *The Nearest Coast of Darkness: A Vindication of the Politics of Virtues.* Ithaca, N.Y.: Cornell University Press, 1988.

Burtt, Shelley. "The Politics of Virtue Today: A Critique and a Proposal." *American Political Science Review* 87 (June 1993): 360-68.

Butterfield, L. H., ed. *Adams Family Correspondence.* Vols. 1 and 2. Cambridge: Belknap Press of Harvard University Press, 1963.

————, ed. *The Adams Papers: Diary and Autobiography of John Adams.* 4 vols. New York: Atheneum, 1964. (Originally published by Harvard University Press, 1961.)

Butterfield, L. H., and Marc Friedlaender, eds. *Adams Family Correspondence.* Vols. 3 and 4. Cambridge: Belknap Press of Harvard University Press, 1973.

Cappon, Lester J., ed. *The Adams-Jefferson Letters: The Complete Correspondence between Thomas Jefferson and Abigail and John Adams.* 2 vols. Chapel Hill: University of North Carolina Press, for the Institute of Early American History and Culture, 1959.

Chinard, Gilbert. *Honest John Adams.* Gloucester, Mass.: Peter Smith, 1976 (1933).

Cochran, Thomas C. *Challenges to American Values: Society, Business, and Religion.* New York: Oxford University Press, 1985.

Colbourn, H. Trevor. *The Lamp of Experience: Whig History and the Intellectual Origins of the American Revolution.* Chapel Hill: University of North

Carolina Press, for the Institute of Early American History and Culture, 1965.

Commager, Henry Steele. *Jefferson, Nationalism and the Enlightenment.* New York: George Braziller, 1975.

Conkin, Paul K. *Puritans and Pragmatists: Eight Eminent American Thinkers.* New York: Dodd, Mead and Company, 1968.

Copley, Stephen, and Kathryn Sutherland, eds. *Adam Smith's Wealth of Nations: New Interdisciplinary Essays.* Manchester, U.K.: Manchester University Press, 1995.

Cousins, Norman. *The Republic of Reason: The Personal Philosophies of the Founding Fathers.* San Francisco: Harper and Row, 1988.

Crevecoeur, J. Hector St. John de. *Letters from an American Farmer and Sketches of Eighteenth-Century America.* New York: Penguin Books, 1981.

Croly, Herbert. *The Promise of American Life* (with a new introduction by Scott R. Bowman). New Brunswick, N.J.: Transaction Publishers, 1993 (1909).

Crowley, John E. *The Privileges of Independence: Neomercantilism and the American Revolution.* Baltimore: Johns Hopkins University Press, 1993.

Crozier, Michel. *The Trouble with America: Why the System Is Breaking Down.* Berkeley: University of California Press, 1984.

Curtis, Carolyn. "Rally Convicts Nation of Sins." *Christianity Today* 40 (June 17, 1996): 61ff.

Dagger, Richard. *Civic Virtues: Rights, Citizenship, and Republican Liberalism.* New York: Oxford University Press, 1997.

Dahl, Robert A. *A Preface to Economic Democracy.* Berkeley: University of California Press, 1985.

Dauer, Manning J. *The Adams Federalists.* Baltimore: John Hopkins University Press, 1953.

———. "The Political Economy of John Adams." *Political Science Quarterly* 56 (1941): 545-72.

Dickie, Robert B., and Leroy S. Rouner, eds. *Corporations and the Common Good.* Notre Dame, Ind.: University of Notre Dame Press, 1986.

Diggins, John P. *The Lost Soul of American Politics: Virtue, Self-Interest, and the Foundations of Liberalism.* Chicago: University of Chicago Press, 1984.

Donovan, Frank, editor. *The John Adams Papers.* New York: Dodd, Mead and Co., 1965.

Duncan, Christopher M. "Civic Virtue and Self-Interest: Comment." *American Political Science Review* 89 (March 1995): 147-51.

Ellis, Joseph J. *Passionate Sage: The Character and Legacy of John Adams.* New York: W. W. Norton and Company, 1993.

Elshtain, Jean Bethke. *Democracy on Trial.* New York: Basic Books, 1995.

Estlund, David M., Jeremy Waldron, Bernard Grofman, and Scott Feld. "Democratic Theory and the Public Interest: Condorcet and Rousseau Revisited." *American Political Science Review* 83 (December 1989): 1317-40.

Etzioni, Amitai. *The Moral Dimension, Toward a New Economics.* New York: Free Press, 1988.

————. *The Spirit of Community: The Reinvention of American Society.* New York: Simon and Schuster, 1993.

Farr, James. "Political Science and the Enlightenment of Enthusiasm." *American Political Science Review* 82 (March 1988): 51-69.

Ferling, John. *John Adams: A Life.* Knoxville: University of Tennessee Press, 1992.

Fitzgibbons, Athol. *Adam Smith's System of Liberty, Wealth and Virtue.* Oxford: Clarendon Press, 1995.

Ford, Worthington Chauncey, ed. *Statesman and Friend: Correspondence of John Adams with Benjamin Waterhouse, 1784-1822.* Boston: Little, Brown, and Company, 1927.

Forde, Steven. "Benjamin Franklin's *Autobiography* and the Education of America." *American Political Science Review* 86 (June 1992): 357-68.

Franklin, Benjamin. *The Autobiography and Other Writings.* New York: Penguin Books, 1986.

Fukuyama, Francis. *The End of History and the Last Man.* New York: Avon Books, 1992.

Galston, William A. "Liberal Virtues." *American Political Science Review* 82 (December 1988): 1277-90.

Gebhardt, Jurgen. *Americanism: Revolutionary Order and Societal Self-Interpretation in the American Republic.* Ruth Hein, trans. Baton Rouge: Louisiana State University Press, 1993.

Goodin, Robert E. "Vulnerabilities and Responsibilities: An Ethical Defense of the Welfare State." *American Political Science Review* 79 (September 1985): 775-87.

Gordon, Suzanne. "Herstory in the Making." *Boston Globe Magazine* (January 31, 1993): 22 ff.

Graebner, Norman A., ed. *Traditions and Values: American Diplomacy, 1790-1865.* New York: University Press of America, 1985.

Grafstein, Robert. "Missing the Archimedean Point: Liberalism's Institutional Presuppositions." *American Political Science Review* 84 (March 1990): 177-93.

Grampp, William D. "Adam Smith and the American Revolutionists." *History of Political Economy* 11, (No. 2, 1979): 179-91.

Greider, William. *Who Will Tell the People: The Betrayal of American Democracy.* New York: Simon and Schuster, 1992.

Griswold, Charles L., Jr. *Adam Smith and the Virtues of Enlightenment.* New York: Cambridge University Press, 1999.

Grofman, Bernard, and Scott L. Feld. "Rousseau's General Will: A Condorcetian Perspective." *American Political Science Review* 82 (June 1988): 567-76.

Hamilton, Alexander, John Jay, and James Madison. *The Federalist.* Great Books of the Western World, Vol. 43. Chicago: Encyclopaedia Britannica, Inc., 1952.

Handlin, Oscar, and Mary Flug Handlin. *Commonwealth: A Study of the Role of Government in the American Economy, Massachusetts, 1774-1861.* Rev. ed. Cambridge: Belknap Press of Harvard University Press, 1969.

Haraszti, Zoltan. *John Adams and the Prophets of Progress.* New York: Grosset and Dunlap, Universal Library, 1964 (1952).

Harpham, Edward J. "Liberalism, Civic Humanism, and the Case of Adam Smith." *American Political Science Review* 78 (September 1984): 764-74.

Hartz, Louis. *Economic Policy and Democratic Thought: Pennsylvania, 1776-1860.* Cambridge: Harvard University Press, 1948.

Heilbroner, Robert L. "The Socialization of the Individual in Adam Smith." *History of Political Economy* 14 (No. 3, 1982): 427-39.

———. *Visions of the Future: The Distant Past, Yesterday, Today, and Tomorrow.* New York: New York Public Library, Oxford University Press, 1995.

———. *The Worldly Philosophers.* Rev. ed. New York: Simon and Schuster, Inc., 1961.

Hirschman, Albert O. *The Passions and the Interests: Political Arguments for Capitalism before Its Triumph.* 20th anniversary ed. Princeton: Princeton University Press, 1997.

Hirschmann, Nancy J. "Freedom, Recognition, and Obligation: A Feminist Approach to Political Theory." *American Political Science Review* 83 (December 1989): 1227-44.

Hofstadter, Richard. *Social Darwinism in American Thought.* Boston: Beacon Press, 1983.

Holder, Jean S. "The Sources of Presidential Power: John Adams and the Challenge to Executive Primacy." *Political Science Quarterly* 101 (No. 4, 1986): 601-16.

Hollinger, David A., and Charles Capper, eds. *The American Intellectual Tradition, A Sourcebook.* 2d ed., Vol. 1. New York: Oxford University Press, 1993.

Holmes, Stephen. *Passions and Constraint: On the Theory of Liberal Democracy.* Chicago: University of Chicago Press, 1995.

Horwitz, Robert H., ed. *The Moral Foundations of the American Republic.* 3d ed. Charlottesville: University of Virginia Press, 1986.

Howe, John R., Jr. *The Changing Political Thought of John Adams.* Princeton: Princeton University Press, 1966.

Hutson, James H. ed. *Letters from a Distinguished American: Twelve Essays by John Adams on American Foreign Policy, 1780.* Washington, D.C.: Library of Congress, 1978.

Jameson, J. Franklin. *The American Revolution Considered as a Social Movement.* Boston: Beacon Press, 1956 (1926).

Kammen, Michael. *A Machine That Would Go of Itself: The Constitution in American Culture.* New York: Alfred A. Knopf, 1987.

Kasson, John F. *Civilizing the Machine: Technology and Republican Values in America, 1776-1900.* New York: Penguin Books, 1976.

Kerber, Linda K. *Women of the Republic: Intellect and Ideology in Revolutionary America.* Chapel Hill: University of North Carolina Press, for the Institute of Early American History and Culture, 1980.

Koch, Adrienne, and William Peden, eds. *The Selected Writings of John and John Quincy Adams.* New York: Alfred A. Knopf, 1946.

Kohl, Lawrence Frederick. *The Politics of Individualism: Parties and the American Character in the Jacksonian Era.* New York: Oxford University Press, 1989.

Kolm, Serge-Cristophe. "Altruism and Efficiency." *Ethics* 94 (October 1983): 18-65.

Kramnick, Isaac. "Republican Revisionism Revisited." *American Historical Review* 87 (June 1982): 629-64.

Kraynak, Robert P. "Tocqueville's Constitutionalism." *American Political Science Review* 81 (December 1987): 1175-95.

Kristol, Irving, Martin Diamond, and G. Warren Nutter. *The American Revolution: Three Views.* New York: American Brands, Inc., 1975.

Lane, Robert E. *The Market Experience.* Cambridge: Cambridge University Press, 1991.

———. "Market Justice, Political Justice." *American Political Science Review* 80 (June 1986): 383-402.

Lerner, Ralph. *The Thinking Revolutionary: Principle and Practice in the New Republic.* Ithaca, N.Y.: Cornell University Press, 1979.

Levin-Waldman, Oren M. *Reconceiving Liberalism: Dilemmas of Contemporary Liberal Public Policy.* Pittsburgh: University of Pittsburgh Press, 1996.

Lienesch, Michael. *New Order of the Ages: Time, the Constitution, and the Making of Modern American Political Thought.* Princeton: Princeton University Press, 1988.

Lindblom, Charles E. "Market and Democracy—Obliquely." *PS: Political Science & Politics* (December 1995): 684-88.

Lint, Gregg L., et al., eds. *Papers of John Adams.* Vols. 7-10, September 1778-December 1780. Cambridge: Belknap Press of Harvard University Press, 1989-1996.

Longmore, Paul K. *The Invention of George Washington.* Berkeley: University of California Press, 1988.

Lutz, Donald S. "The Relative Influence of European Writers on Late Eighteenth-Century American Political Thought." *American Political Science Review* 78 (March 1984): 189-97.

McCloskey, Donald N., ed. *Second Thoughts: Myths and Morals of U.S. Economic History.* New York: Oxford University Press, 1993.

McCollough, Thomas E. *The Moral Imagination and Public Life: Raising the Ethical Question.* Chatham, N.J.: Chatham House Publishers, Inc., 1991.

McKibben, Bill. *The Age of Missing Information.* New York: Random House, Inc., 1992.

McNamara, Peter. *Political Economy and Statesmanship: Smith, Hamilton, and the Foundation of the Commercial Republic.* DeKalb: Northern Illinois University Press, 1998.

McPherson, James M. *Abraham Lincoln and the Second American Revolution.* New York: Oxford University Press, 1990.

Macedo, Stephen. *Liberal Virtues: Citizenship, Virtue, and Community in Liberal Constitutionalism.* Oxford: Clarendon Press, 1990.

Maier, Pauline. *From Resistance to Revolution: Colonial Radicals and the Development of American Opposition to Britain, 1765-1776.* New York: Random House, 1972.

———. *The Old Revolutionaries: Political Lives in the Age of Samuel Adams.* New York: Random House, 1980.

Mansbridge, Jane J., ed. *Beyond Self-Interest.* Chicago: University of Chicago Press, 1990.

Marshall, Patrick G. "Transportation: America's 'Quiet Crisis.'" *Editorial Research Reports* 2 (August 11, 1989): 458.

May, Henry F. *The Enlightenment in America.* New York: Oxford University Press, 1976.

Merriam, Charles Edward. *A History of American Political Theories.* New York: Augustus M. Kelley, 1969 (1903).

Merrill, Michael, and Sean Wilentz, eds. *The Key of Liberty: The Life and Democratic Writings of William Manning, "A Laborer," 1747-1814.* Cambridge: Harvard University Press, 1993.

Minowitz, Peter. *Profits, Priests, and Princes: Adam Smith's Emancipation of Economics from Politics and Religion.* Stanford: Stanford University Press, 1993.

Miroff, Bruce. *Icons of Democracy: American Leaders as Heroes, Aristocrats, Dissenters, and Democrats.* New York: Basic Books, 1993.

Mitchell, Joshua. *Not by Reason Alone: Religion, History, and Identity in Early Modern Political Thought.* Chicago: University of Chicago Press, 1993.

Morgan, Robert J. "Madison's Analysis of the Sources of Political Authority." *American Political Science Review* 75 (September 1981): 613-25.

Muller, Jerry Z. *Adam Smith: In His Time and Ours.* Princeton: Princeton University Press, 1993.

Nagel, Paul C. *The Adams Women: Abigail and Louise Adams, Their Sisters and Daughters.* New York: Oxford University Press, 1987.

Nederman, Cary J. "Freedom, Community and Function: Communitarian Lessons of Medieval Political Theory." *American Political Science Review* 86 (December 1992): 977-86.

Nelson, John R., Jr. *Liberty and Property: Political Economy and Policymaking in the New Nation, 1789-1812.* Baltimore: Johns Hopkins University Press, 1987.

Newell, W. R. "Heidegger on Freedom and Community: Some Political Implications of His Early Thought." *American Political Science Review* 78 (September 1984): 775-84.

Norton, David L. *Democracy and Moral Development.* Berkeley: University of California Press, 1991.

Novak, Michael. *Free Persons and the Common Good.* New York: Madison Books, 1989.

Oliver, Andrew. *Portraits of John and Abigail Adams.* Cambridge: Belknap Press of Harvard University Press, 1967.

Pangle, Lorraine Smith and Thomas L. *The Learning of Liberty: The Educational Ideas of the American Founders.* Lawrence: University Press of Kansas, 1993.

Pangle, Thomas L. *The Ennobling of Democracy: The Challenge of the Postmodern Era.* Baltimore: Johns Hopkins University Press, 1992.

————. *The Spirit of Modern Republicanism: The Moral Vision of the American Founders and the Philosophy of Locke.* Chicago: University of Chicago Press, 1988.

Peek, George A., Jr., ed. *The Political Writings of John Adams: Representative Selections.* Indianapolis: Bobbs-Merrill Co., Inc., 1954.

Peterson, Merrill D. *Adams and Jefferson: A Revolutionary Dialogue.* New York: Oxford University Press, 1976.

————, ed. *The Portable Thomas Jefferson.* New York: Penguin Books, 1975.

Picht, Werner. *The Life and Thought of Albert Schweitzer.* New York: Harper and Row, 1964.

Plato. *The Dialogues of Plato.* Benjamin Jowett, trans. Chicago: Encyclopaedia Britannica, Inc., 1952. "Laws," Book V, 726-34.

Plutarch. "Lycurgus." *The Lives of the Noble Grecians and Romans (Dryden Translation).* Chicago: Encyclopaedia Britannica, Inc., 1952: 32-48.

Polanyi, Karl. *The Great Transformation: The Political and Economic Origins of Our Time.* Boston: Beacon Press, 1957.

Potts, Louis W. *Arthur Lee: A Virtuous Revolutionary.* Baton Rouge: Louisiana State University Press, 1981.

Robles, Harold E., ed. *Reverence for Life: The Words of Albert Schweitzer.* New York: HarperSan Francisco, 1993.

Roosevelt, Theodore, *American Ideals and Other Essays, Social and Political.* New York: G. P. Putnam's Sons, 1897.

Rosecrance, Richard, ed. *America as an Ordinary Country: U.S. Foreign Policy and the Future*. Ithaca, N.Y.: Cornell University Press, 1976.

Rosenblum, Nancy L., ed. *Liberalism and the Moral Life*. Cambridge: Harvard University Press, 1989.

Ross, Ian Simpson. *The Life of Adam Smith*. Oxford: Oxford University Press, 1995.

Rossiter, Clinton. "The Legacy of John Adams." *Yale Review* 46 (1957): 528-51.

Rossiter, Clinton, and James Lare, eds. *The Essential Lippmann: A Political Philosophy for Liberal Democracy*. Cambridge: Harvard University Press, 1982.

Ryerson, Richard Alan, et al., eds. *Adams Family Correspondence*. Vols. 5 and 6: October, 1782-December 1785. Cambridge: Belknap Press of Harvard University Press, 1993.

Sabia, Daniel R., Jr. "Political Education and the History of Political Thought." *American Political Science Review* 78 (December 1984): 985-99.

Sandoz, Ellis. *A Government of Laws: Political Theory, Religion, and the American Founding*. Baton Rouge: Louisiana State University Press, 1990.

———, ed. *Political Sermons of the American Founding Era, 1730-1805*. Indianapolis: Liberty Press, 1991.

Sapiro, Virginia. *A Vindication of Political Virtue: The Political Theory of Mary Wollstonecraft*. Chicago: University of Chicago Press, 1992.

Schutz, John A., and Douglass Adair, eds. *The Spur of Fame: Dialogues of John Adams and Benjamin Rush, 1805-1813*. San Marino, Calif.: Huntington Library, 1966.

Shain, Barry A. *The Myth of American Individualism: The Protestant Origins of American Political Thought*. Princeton: Princeton University Press, 1994.

Shapiro, Michael J. *Reading "Adam Smith": Desire, History and Value*. Newbury Park, Calif.: Sage Publications, 1993.

Shaw, Peter. *The Character of John Adams*. Chapel Hill: University of North Carolina Press, for the Institute of Early American History and Culture, 1976.

Sheehan, Colleen A., and Gary L. McDowell eds. *Friends of the Constitution; Writings of the "Other" Federalists, 1787-1788*. Indianapolis: Liberty Fund, 1998.

Sinopoli, Richard C. *The Foundations of American Citizenship: Liberalism, the Constitution, and Civic Virtue*. New York: Oxford University Press, 1992.

———. "Thick-skinned Liberalism: Redefining Civility," *American Political Science Review* 89 (September 1995): 612-20.

Skinner, Andrew Stewart. *A System of Social Science: Papers Relating to Adam Smith*. 2d ed. Oxford: Clarendon Press, 1996.

Smith, Adam. *An Inquiry into the Nature and Causes of the Wealth of Nations.* R. H. Campbell and A. S. Skinner, eds. Oxford: Oxford University Press, 1976 (Liberty *Classics* reprint, 1981).

————. *The Correspondence of Adam Smith.* Ernest Campbell Mossner and Ian Simpson Ross, eds. Oxford, Oxford University Press, 1987 (Liberty *Classics* reprint, 1987).

————. *Essays on Philosophical Subjects.* W. P. D. Wightman and J. C. Bryce, eds. Oxford: Oxford University Press, 1980 (Liberty *Classics* reprint, 1982).

————. *Lectures on Jurisprudence.* R. L. Meek, D. D. Raphael, and P. G. Stein, eds. Oxford: Oxford University Press, 1978 (Liberty *Classics* reprint, 1982).

————. *Lectures on Rhetoric and Belles Lettres.* J. C. Bryce, ed. Oxford: Oxford University Press, 1983 (Liberty *Classics* reprint 1985).

————. *The Theory of Moral Sentiments.* 6th ed. D. D. Raphael and A. L. Macfie, eds. Oxford: Oxford University Press, 1976 (Liberty *Classics* reprint, 1982).

Smith, Rogers M. "Beyond Tocqueville, Myrdal, and Hartz: The Multiple Traditions in America." *American Political Science Review* 87 (September 1993): 549-66.

Smith, Steven B. "Hegel's Critique of Liberalism." *American Political Science Review* 80 (March 1986): 121-39.

Soros, George. "The Capitalist Threat." *The Atlantic Monthly* (February 1997): 45-58.

Springborg, Patricia. "Mary Astell (1666-1731), Critic of Locke." *American Political Science Review* 89 (September 1995): 621-33.

Storing, Herbert J., ed. *The Anti-Federalist: An Abridgment, by Murray Dry, of the Complete Anti-Federalist.* Chicago: University of Chicago Press, 1985.

Takaki, Ronald. *Iron Cages: Race and Culture in 19th-Century America.* New York: Oxford University Press, 1990.

Taylor, Robert J., ed. *Papers of John Adams.* Vols. 1-6. Cambridge: Belknap Press of Harvard University Press, 1977-1983.

Thompson, C. Bradley. *John Adams and the Spirit of Liberty.* Lawrence: University Press of Kansas, 1998.

Tillich, Paul. *The Socialist Decision.* Franklin Sherman, trans. New York: University Press of America, 1977 (reprint; originally published by Harper and Row).

Traxel, David. "Five Fateful Years," Review of *The Last Best Hope of Earth: Abraham Lincoln and the Promise of America,* by Mark E. Neely, Jr. *New York Times Book Review* (June 12, 1994): 17.

Tully, Alan. *William Penn's Legacy: Politics and Social Structure in Provincial Pennsylvania, 1726-1755.* Baltimore: Johns Hopkins University Press, 1977.

U.S. Department of Commerce, Economics and Statistics Administration, Bureau of the Census. *Statistical Abstract of the United States, 1998,* 118th Edition. Washington, D.C.: Government Printing Office, 1998.

Verba, Sidney, and Gary R. Orren. "The Meaning of Equality in America." *Political Science Quarterly* 100 (Fall 1985): 369-87.

Vetterli, Richard, and Gary Bryner. *In Search of the Republic: Public Virtue and the Roots of American Government.* Rev. ed. Lanham, Md.: Rowman and Littlefield Publishers, Inc., 1996.

Webking, Robert H. *The American Revolution and the Politics of Liberty.* Baton Rouge: Louisiana State University Press, 1988.

Werhane, Patricia H. *Adam Smith and His Legacy for Modern Capitalism.* New York: Oxford University Press, 1991.

West, John G., Jr. *The Politics of Revelation and Reason: Religion and Civic Life in the New Nation.* Lawrence: University Press of Kansas, 1996.

Wills, Garry. *Inventing America: Jefferson's Declaration of Independence.* New York: Random House, 1978.

Wilson, James Q. "The Moral Sense." *American Political Science Review* 87 (March 1993): 1-11.

Withey, Lynne. *Dearest Friend: A Life of Abigail Adams.* New York: Free Press, 1981.

Withington, Ann Fairfax. *Toward a More Perfect Union: Virtue and the Formation of American Republics.* New York: Oxford University Press, 1991.

Wood, Gordon S. *The Creation of the American Republic 1776-1787.* Chapel Hill: University of North Carolina Press, for the Institute of Early American History and Culture, 1969.

———. *The Radicalism of the American Revolution.* New York: Alfred A. Knopf, 1992.

Young, Alfred F., and Terry J. Fife, with Mary E. Janzen. *We the People: Voices and Images of the New Nation.* Philadelphia: Temple University Press, 1993.

Zinn, Howard. *A People's History of the United States.* New York: Harper and Row, 1980.

———. *Declarations of Independence: Cross-Examining American Ideology.* New York: HarperCollins, 1990.

Index

About the Author

John E. Hill is professor of politics and history at Curry College in Milton, Massachusetts, where he has taught for more than thirty years. Among other offices, he has served in the elective positions of chairperson of the faculty and president of the Curry Chapter of the AAUP. He founded and was for many years director of Curry's Academic Advising Team; in addition, he initiated the College's Essential Skills Center. He has published in various journals.